The Knights Templar
in Popular Culture

The Knights Templar in Popular Culture

Films, Video Games and Fan Tourism

PATRICK MASTERS

McFarland & Company, Inc., Publishers
Jefferson, North Carolina

This book has undergone peer review.

Frontispiece: Latin cross worn by *Ironclad*'s Templar Knight (2011, Mythic International Entertainment).

ISBN (print) 978-1-4766-8197-9
ISBN (ebook) 978-1-4766-4571-1

LIBRARY OF CONGRESS AND BRITISH LIBRARY
CATALOGUING DATA ARE AVAILABLE

Library of Congress Control Number 2022001638

Front cover image © 2022 Vuk Kostic/Shutterstock

Printed in the United States of America

*McFarland & Company, Inc., Publishers
Box 611, Jefferson, North Carolina 28640
www.mcfarlandpub.com*

For my wife
and daughter

Table of Contents

Acknowledgments

I would like to express my deepest gratitude to my first supervisor, Professor Geraghty, for his expert guidance, encouragement and for giving so much of his time throughout the process of researching and writing this book. I would also like to thank my supervisors Professor Shaw and Dr. Austin for their valuable input and constructive criticism. I am particularly grateful to Celia for proofreading my work for me and to Sarah, who was incredibly supportive and flexible by allowing me time off work to focus on my research at various stages throughout the years. I also wish to thank Joseph for his valuable insight into the history of Philadelphia and a brilliant tour of the city. When gaining my primary fan tourism evidence, I did not want to travel alone, so I would like to thank my friend Ben for coming to Philadelphia with me and visiting the Old Pine Church in the rain. Thank you also to my friends Helen and Ivan for coming along with me to visit Rosslyn Chapel and for allowing me to stay with you during my trip.

Finally, I would like to thank my family: firstly, my parents Brian and Nicky and sister Felicity who supported me throughout the entire project. I would like to offer a special thank-you to my wife, Charlotte, and my daughter, Violet, who continue to be my inspiration, and without their support, this book would not be possible.

Publications

Part of the introduction was published as "Knights Templar: Still Loved by Conspiracy Theorists 900 Years Later," *The Conversation* (December 23, 2019). Retrieved from https://theconversation.com/knights-templar-still-loved-by-conspiracy-theorists-900-years-on-128582.

Part of the introduction and Chapter 1 were published as "Alt-Right Claims to Match in Step with Knights Templar—This Is Fake History," *The Conversation* (December 5, 2017). Retrieved from https://theconversation.

com/alt-right-claims-to-march-in-step-with-the-knights-templar-this-is-fake-history-88103.

Part of Chapter 1 was published as "Historical Movies: Why a Good Story Is More Important than the Facts," *The Conversation* (August 1, 2018). Retrieved from https://theconversation.com/historical-movies-why-a-good-story-is-more-important-than-the-facts-99892.

Preface

The Order of the Knights Templar has appeared in popular fiction dating back to the 13th century. The Templars first appeared in Arthurian literature as guardians of the Holy Grail before emerging in the 19th-century novels of Sir Walter Scott, this time as the evil extremist knights. Scott's books did not include the Templars as guardians of the grail but reintroduced the Order to popular culture as antagonists to the chivalric hero. This story theme has been repurposed for other fictional works such as the Hollywood film *Kingdom of Heaven* (Scott, 2005) and the computer game *Assassin's Creed* (Ubisoft, 2007). The Templars' role within popular fiction would become more contradictory as the Knights Templar became the subject of medieval conspiracies in novels such as Dan Brown's *The Da Vinci Code* (2003) and as the chivalric multicultural hero in Jan Guillou's book, *The Road to Jerusalem* (1998). The Order of the Knights Templar continues to be a popular theme for directors and producers to draw upon, with the multifaceted Templar knight being recycled to produce new Templar texts. These new texts have further embedded popular perceptions of the historical order and created different Templar representations within popular culture.

The 21st-century legacy of the Knights Templar is not only confined to recycling and expanding Templar aspects for fiction but has a new association with extreme right-wing groups. The most horrific and infamous of these associations are the claims made by the mass murderer, Anders Behring Breivik, who carried out two terrorist attacks in 2011. After the attacks, a manifesto appeared in which Breivik claimed to be "ordinated as the 8th Justiciar Knight for the PCCTS, Knights Templar Europe" (BBC News, 2011). Breivik's identification with the order of warrior monks is not the only instance of extremist propaganda. Groups such as The Knights Templar–UK ignore "the monastic lifestyle of the order and [use] it as a platform for the right-wing views" (Masters, 2017). Although significant, the Templars' right-wing appropriation is not the object of this study; instead, the book examines the Knights Templar as a multifaceted, thematic narrative recycled within popular culture. The Templar phenomenon as depicted in film, television and computer games is based on contradictory historical perceptions through the emergence of four defining thematic aspects: the good Templar, the bad Templar, the quest of the knight and the quest to follow in the Templars' footsteps. This study consists of two narrative parts: the narrative of the knight and the narrative of the quest. This book addresses the gap of understanding in Templar scholarship by linking the historical Knights Templar to their depiction in popular culture. How the historical Templar influences the myth has been well documented, but this study argues how that myth influences the popular culture depiction. This book establishes the key Templar archetypes in fiction and investigates how this narrative has evolved over the centuries within popular culture, thus addressing the gap of understanding of the Knights Templar phenomenon.

Introduction

The Knights Templar—Rise and Fall

To understand the significance of the contradictory popular perceptions of the Templars it is vital to establish the Order's origin, the organization's role and their untimely demise as this will inform how far the depictions of the Templars have evolved through the centuries. The Order of the Knights Templar was a revolutionary form of knighthood: noblemen who would live their lives as monks, dedicated to protecting civilians traveling the dangerous roads of the newly conquered Kingdom of Jerusalem. In the early 12th century a group of French knights led by Hugh de Payns arrived in Jerusalem wishing to live a monastic lifestyle but were persuaded by the King of Jerusalem, Baldwin II, "alive to the urgent dangers confronting travellers in his kingdom … to save their souls by protecting pilgrims on the roads, or as one chronicler put it, they were to take vows of poverty, chastity and obedience but were also 'to defend pilgrims against brigands and rapists'" (Haag, 2009, pp. 95–96).

This new order was formed on Christmas Day 1119 and was named The Poor Fellow-Soldiers of Christ, and due to their vows of poverty, the Order's original symbol emphasized two knights riding a single horse. From these humble beginnings, the Order would grow to become one of the premier Christian military forces of the Crusades. Because this new order was impoverished, Baldwin II gave the new knighthood quarters in his palace at Jerusalem, a section that was believed to be built upon the foundations of the Temple of Solomon. The site of the Order's headquarters holds great significance as the Order became known as The Poor Fellow-Soldiers of Christ and of the Temple of Solomon, from which the Order eventually became known by the infamous name the Order of the Knights Templar.

The Templars' first grand master, Hugh de Payns, and Templar Knight Godfrey de St Omer traveled to Europe as part of a delegation sent by Baldwin II, where this new concept of knighthood could find validation among the European elite. This revolutionary notion of monk and knight was well received in Europe as "Hugh and Godfrey reminded people of the purpose of the crusades. The Templar knights were not looking for individual wealth or land or political power" (Newman, 2007, p. 21). The Templars returned to Outremer with papal approval, donated wealth and increased the workforce. Newman proposes that the success of the Templars' reception was, "Europe saw men of good birth who had abandoned their lands and families in order to defend the places where Christ had lived and died for all people. The example of the Templars was a shaming reminder to those who had stayed behind" (2007, p. 21).

Bernard of Clairvaux's early 12th-century work *In Praise of the New Knighthood* demonstrates the well-received virtuous perceptions of the Order, writing, "The knight of Christ may strike with honor and perish with honor. For when he strikes he serves Christ, and when he perishes in Christ he serves himself. He does not carry a sword without just cause, for he is a minister of God, and he punishes malicious men for the praise of the truth" (Wasserman, 2001, p. 280). Concerning the Templars' monastic culture, Bernard wrote, "They live like monks in delightful and sober community, without wife and without children. And indeed that evangelical perfection is not lacking, for they live apart from the world in one family. Anxious to guard the sole unity of spirit in the bonds of peace" (Wasserman, 2001, p. 282). Bernard's writing is not only significant as a critical source to identify the virtuous perception of the new knighthood but also played a "central role in popularising the Templar movement across Latin Europe" (Asbridge, 2012, p. 169).

This new type of knighthood's financial success prompted an older charitable organization to take on military aspects. In Jerusalem, the Hospital of St John provided hospital care for pilgrims and grew in stature following the city's conquest in the First Crusade and would emerge as the second military order in the middle 12th century. These military orders provided the wealthy Christian nobility with a financial option for serving Christ in the Holy Land by donating land and funds to the Christian cause. Crusades historian Thomas Asbridge explains, "the Templars and Hospitallers brought a desperately needed influx of manpower and martial expertise to crusader states starved of military resources. Crucially, they also possessed the wealth to maintain, and in time extend, Outremer's network of forts and castles" (2012, p. 170). The significance of the military orders was "they were the only authority in the Christian East to hold a standing army always in readiness" (Mayer, 1972, p. 82).

The Knights Templar were one of the premier fighting forces of the Christian factions during the Crusades period. They played a significant role in the majority of the Crusade campaigns, such as in the Second

Crusade (1147–1150), where they demonstrated their invaluable military prowess when 300 Templars escorted the remainder of the Christian army across Asia Minor. The Crusade would have ended before reaching the Holy Land were it not for the Templars' leadership, which Jonathan Phillips asserts shows "just how soon after their foundation the Templars had become a highly respected fighting unit" (2010, p. 202). The Templars played a similar role during the successful long march from Acre to Jaffa during the Third Crusade (1189–1192). The Crusaders, led by King Richard I of England, were vulnerable to harassing strikes from Saladin's forces, drawing a similarity to the journey across Asia Minor in the Second Crusade. Once again, the Templars, along with the Hospitallers, played a critical role in the Christians' Holy Land military campaigns' successes by repelling their attackers and keeping the Crusaders' columns' shape intact (Haag, 2014, p. 297).

The Templars as a force were vital to Crusader victories; however, they were involved in their many defeats as the majority of the Crusaders' military campaigns in the Holy Land would ultimately fail. The Knights Templar were involved in the Fifth Crusade's (1217–1221) strategic disaster, influencing the decision to reject a treaty from the Sultan of Egypt, al-Kamil, for the Crusaders to return the newly conquered, fortified port city of Damietta in exchange for control of Jerusalem. The Crusaders' goal was to conquer Egypt, so they marched south in search of greater victory, where their campaign collapsed. The Sultan ordered the Nile sluice gates to be opened, which left the terrain so waterlogged it was almost impossible to traverse. The humiliated Crusaders had no choice but to surrender and relinquish Damietta in exchange for their lives and leave empty-handed. The Seventh Crusade (1248–1254), led by French King Louis IX, would also capture Damietta but fail to conquer Egypt, not learning from the Fifth Crusade's failings. The Templars were involved in the disastrous Battle of Mansurah (1250), where hundreds of Templar knights followed the king's brother, Count Robert of Artois, on his ill-judged charge into the town chasing the routed Egyptian forces, only for themselves to be trapped and slaughtered by regrouped forces under the command of infamous Mamluk general and future Sultan, Baibars. The battle resulted in a stalemate and left Louis in a weakened position due to heavy losses, so failing to agree to a treaty for his troops' lives, the Crusaders attempted to retreat to Damietta. However, the remnants of his army were slaughtered and Louis himself captured.

The Templars' military reputation among their enemies was notorious, which is demonstrated by the mass execution of the captured Templars after the Battle of Hattin in 1187. Ibn Al-thīr was an eyewitness to the aftermath of Saladin's total victory at Hattin, and he recounted that Saladin "had these particular men killed because they were the fiercest of all the Frankish warriors, and in this he rid the Muslim people of them" (1969, p. 124). The desire to execute the Templar prisoners was not due to their mistreatment of Muslims but their effectiveness in battle. Syrian contemporary writer Usama provides an example of how the Templars were respectful of the Islamic faith and protected the Muslim citizens of Jerusalem's right to practice their religion. He recounts an incident where he was harassed at the Masjid al-Aqsa by a Christian, saying that the man "threw himself on me from behind, lifted me up and turned me so that I was facing east. 'That is the way to pray!' He said" (Usama, 1969, p. 80). Usama then describes how the Templars, who he says, "were friends of mine … intervened, seized the man and took him out of my way, while I resumed my prayer" (Usama, 1969, p. 80). Although the account by Ibn Al-thīr highlighted the desire for the execution of Templars, Usama's anecdote coincides with Ibn Al-thīr's explanation that they were killed due to their abilities and not because of oppression or violent crime.

The Christian ventures in the Holy Land ended in 1291 after Acre (the Christian capital) fell to the Mamluk forces. Following this, the Templars abandoned their final strongholds of Sidon and Tortosa with the surviving Templars taking refuge on the island of Cyprus. The island was a Frankish Kingdom Richard I seized from Byzantines in 1191 and sold to the Templars. Michael Haag argues, "The entire future of the Templars might have been different had they devoted more resources to the island, but they placed only twenty knights on Cyprus and another hundred men at arms, insufficient to secure it, and so they gave it back to Richard" (2009, p. 183). The second military order, The Hospitallers, secured their independent state on the island of Rhodes in 1309, and, without the war for Outremer, the Order fell back on its original operation of providing humane treatment. The Templars found themselves in a redundant position, as despite their wealth and European holdings their reason for existence was to wage war in defense of the Holy Land, which they could not, due to the recent loss of all Christian lands in what was once Outremer.

The French King Philip IV capitalized on the Templars' vulnerability, to whom he was in financial debt, as he knew they possessed a significantly large amount of liquid wealth due to their banking services. Philip IV had inherited huge debts and accumulated higher still from his wars with Flanders and England. Phillip had already stolen from and exiled the Italian bankers and resident Jews and viewed the Templars as the next means to an end. The Templars were arrested in France on Friday, October 13, 1307, in a dawn raid on the Paris Temple and residences. Haag proposes: "the efficiency of the operation probably benefited from previous raids against the Italian bankers" in 1291 and "Jews in 1306" (2009, p. 217). This attack on the once-powerful Templars was possible due to a 1230 law created by Pope Honorius III to suppress the Cathari heresy. In keeping with that 77-year-old law, the Templars could be arrested by the French king if they were accused of heresy, "so heresy it had to be" (Haag, 2009, p. 219). Peter Partner notes, "around the year 1307, magical charges became one of the standard methods of aggression among the jealous and competitive servants of King Phillip the Fair" (1982, p. 54).

The Catholic Church exonerated the Templars as documented by the Chinon Parchment, discovered in the Vatican archives in 2001. Despite this, due to the defamation, the Templar Order was abolished in 1312 by papal decree, and the Templars' property was then redistributed to the Knights Hospitaller. Now, without papal protection, the former Templar prisoners were at the mercy of royal sentencing, and in 1314 the French king had the last grand master, Jacques de Molay, and three other Templars burned at the stake in Paris. With the Order abolished, the surviving former members joined other orders or monasteries. Although, due to the prominent role of Templars in creating the kingdom of Portugal in 1319 with papal permission, King Diniz reconstituted the Order as Ordem dos Cavaleiros de Nosso Senhor Jesus Cristo/The Order of the Knights of Jesus Christ. The new knighthood moved into the Templars' former headquarters at Tomar. For Haag, this new order "was the Templars under another name, the main difference being that, in addition to their vows of poverty and chastity, the knights pledged obedience to the king" (2009, p. 246). The essence of the Order of the Knights of Jesus Christ exists today in 21st-century Portugal as an order of merit for outstanding service.

Legacy in Popular Culture

Although the Templars survived in the form of the Portuguese military order, the Templars' legacy seen in popular culture is far removed from its historical roots. The Order's seemingly unexplained sudden fall created a vacuum in public perception of the Order, and it became filled with associations of the occult and secret treasures. Many of the Templar myths trace back to the French king's accusations of heresy, as the king extracted confessions under torture where some Templars confessed to worshiping an idol dubbed Baphomet (Newman, 2007, p. 338). Modern literature draws upon the myth that the Templars discovered secret knowledge within their headquarters upon the Temple of Solomon and therefore had to be repressed by the church. The myth also ties into the Templars' medieval literature role as guardians of the Holy Grail.

The Templars' total suppression meant that there remained no authority or safeguarding over the Templars' legacy. The destruction resulted in the appearance of false associations that went unchallenged and became myths that continue to be fashionable without authorization over the narrative. Without an influence over the Templars' legacy, the infamous Order has been appropriated by other organizations, most notably as ancestors to the Masonic order in the 18th century and more recently by right-wing extremist groups such as the Knights Templar–UK. However, medieval romantic notions and the Templars' infamy provided a rich tapestry for artists and producers to draw upon with the Templars' presence in fiction stretching from the 13th century into the 21st century. I have identified that the Templar phenomenon in popular culture is encapsulated into four story themes listed here in order of appearance in fiction: the Holy Grail, the villainous knight, the Templar conspiracy, and the heroic knight. This book examines these four types to define the thematic Templar narrative and then articulate how the Templar narrative has evolved through centuries of popular representations, across emerging media platforms that expand the multifaceted perceptions of the Knights Templar in popular culture.

The Templars have been referred to by many names throughout history since their 12th-century debut, with the most recent being commonly known as the Knights Templar in popular culture. This book follows the scholarship trend and refers to them as a collective as Knights Templar or the Templars. When mentioning a single knight of the Order, this book addresses them as a Templar knight, as they are a knight of the Temple, or simply as a Templar.

Templar Archetypes and the Urtext

The popular perceptions of the Knights Templar are built upon two archetypal pillars that date back to the 12th and 13th centuries: the archetype of the Templar warrior monk and the Templar grail guardian. The warrior monk archetype depicts the Templar as a crusading knight in medieval warfare. The grail guardian archetype features the Templar as the guardian of a powerful treasure. Both of these archetypes feature the infamous Templar iconography of a red cross on a white background. It is these two medieval archetypes that provide the foundation for what this book defines as the Templar narrative. It is not just the historical Templars but also the Templar story that is recycled. These reoccurring archetypes include the thematic aspects of the bad/good knight as well as the quest of the knight/ quest to follow in the Templars' footsteps, which appear across multiple genres and media platforms, further evolving the depiction of the Knights

Templar. The four thematic Templar aspects I have identified will be used to analyze their continual evolvement into and throughout the 21st century.

The two Templar archetypes can be seen as major components of the Templar story, the urtext. The historical Templars receded into memory in the 14th century; after that came multiple stories of Templar villainy and violence which became part of their urtext. Conspiracy theories, narrative archetypes and stereotyped imagery further added to the original story of the Templars. Sarah Cardwell argues that an urtext "stands outside and before retelling of the story, and which contains the most fundamental parts of the tale" (2002, p. 26). Cardwell uses Shakespeare's play *Macbeth* as an example of how various productions draw from the Macbeth urtext and further develop the story through retelling and adaption, which means that every version changes the original through expanding and altering reader perceptions. It is in this way that the Templars' presence in popular culture can be understood and analyzed because the story of the Templars includes (or chooses not to include) key aspects of the Templar urtext such as archetypes and iconography. The continual recycling of these aspects further expands the representation of the Knights Templar in popular culture and therefore expands and alters the urtext. Cardwell explains that the urtext "does not exist as a separate, concrete entity outside these texts" (2002, p. 26), meaning that the Macbeth urtext is not separate from its various adaptations. The Templar narrative is also not separate from the Templar urtext, as it consists of the central thematic aspects identified in this study, the two Templar archetypes of the warrior monk and of the grail guardian that are the foundation of the popular depictions of the Knights Templar. The two archetypes will be used as a thematic structure to examine the Templar narrative by constructing the book into two parts: first what I call the narrative of the knight and the second part called the narrative of the quest.

Templar Scholarship

The historical significance of the Order of the Knights Templar is addressed in numerous accounts detailing the Order's existence from the 12th–14th centuries and their impact on medieval Europe and the Middle East. However, the Templar legacy continued after the Order's abolishment with myths attributed to their untimely demise. These myths have been addressed by historians such as Peter Partner in his book *The Murdered Magicians: The Templars and Their Myth* (1981), as well as authors of quasi-historical works such as Steven Sora's *The Lost Treasure of the Knights Templar: Solving the Oak Island Mystery* (1999). However numerous the amount of academic and popular historical works addressing the historical

Templars and examining the Templars in fiction, there is minimal exploration by academics of the Templar phenomenon in popular culture.

Historian Michael Haag provides a useful study that examines the Templar history alongside the mythical legacy and offers a brief overview of consumable Templar fiction in his book *The Templars: History and Myth* (2009). The majority of this book addresses the historical Templar and the myths and falsehoods following their abolition, with Haag highlighting the primary Templar texts within popular culture. Haag attributes the Order's resurgence in popular culture to Steven Spielberg's third Indiana Jones film, *Indiana Jones and the Last Crusade* (1989), stating that after its release, "an order that had officially died out seven hundred years ago suddenly came to feel like part of the zeitgeist" (2009, p. 331). However, for each of the Templar texts listed, Haag provides only a brief synopsis of the text and informs us of what role the Templars played in the story. Haag's overview ends with addressing the Templars' appearance in the computer games *Assassin's Creed* (Ubisoft, 2007) and *Medieval: Total War* (Creative Assembly, 2002) concluding, "There is clearly pop culture life in the order yet" (2009, p. 346).

Historian Sharan Newman briefly mentions the appearance of the Knights Templar in popular culture in her book *The Real History Behind the Templars* (2007), where she concludes the brief chapter with the observation, "The last part of the twentieth century saw an explosion of myths and theories about the Templars, most of which can be categorized with Bigfoot and UFOs. These unhistorical theories yielded a gold mine of plot ideas that are still being refined into fun and exciting stories" (2007, p. 356). The Templars' significance within popular culture is not addressed in any detail in these works as their focus is how the Templar myth is related to history. This focus, Newman states, is to "make it easier for people who are reading the latest Templar book, either fiction or history, to separate fact from fiction and give them a base from which to evaluate the ideas presented" (2007, p. xv). This study addresses the latter part of these works, building on the evaluations of how Templar history influences Templar myth. However, this study adds new depth to that knowledge by addressing in particular why that myth has been adapted to forge the Templars' prominence within popular culture. The book will examine the Templars' place in popular culture via a close analysis of how they evolved over the centuries from popular perceptions to create a multifaceted Templar narrative in popular culture. This book complements Newman's work by addressing specific fictional Templar tropes within popular culture and mapping out how these popular depictions have evolved through the centuries.

Although not focusing on the Templars or entirely on the Crusades, John Aberth examines depictions of the medieval period on film in his 2003 book, *A Knight at the Movies: Medieval History on Film*. Aberth examines the representations of the Crusades in cinema but also provides a concise overview of the Crusades' 200-year history as the first part of his chapter. As well as providing a historical context, Aberth examines the major Crusade film productions, starting with Cecil B. DeMille's *The Crusades* (1935) as the first case study. Aberth carries out a detailed textual analysis of the film and articulates how the film promotes a message of peace, noting, "the word 'peace' is mentioned on no less than eleven occasions" in one scene (2003, p. 91). Aberth's final crusade film case study is *El Cid* (1961), for which he analyzes the film's production alongside the political climate, arguing, "*El Cid* itself can be viewed as among Bronston's propaganda 'presents' to Franco, a movie designed to put Spain's best face forward on the international stage" (2003, p. 136). Although Aberth does not cover *Kingdom of Heaven* (as it came out in 2005), his work demonstrates the significance of analyzing medieval films concerning the political climate at the time of production, which is an approach that this book uses to ascertain the influences behind differing Templar depictions in the media.

Although the Templars' presence in popular culture has not been addressed with significant detail in the works by Haag and Newman, *Kingdom of Heaven*, which features the Templars in a major way, has been critically examined alongside the post 9–11 political climate. Matthew Richard Schlimm examined "how *Kingdom of Heaven* participated in a discourse that convinced many of the necessity of invading Iraq, upholding fanciful visions of the invasion's aftermath that blinded viewers to the potential difficulties that lie ahead" (2010, p. 132). In his argument of the film's justification for the invasion, Schlimm asserts, "the movie presents two types of colonizers/Crusaders, each with clear parallels to American culture, so that the viewers clearly identify themselves with one type but not the other" (2010, p. 135). Schlimm explains that the unpalatable type is Scott's depiction of the Order of the Knights Templar, who epitomizes the notion of the "malevolent Crusader" (2010, p. 135). In an article for *Conspiracy Theories in the United States and the Middle East*, Brian Johnsrud examines how the cultural relationship with the Crusades supersedes fiction and that it was senior political figures making such comparisons between the Iraq War and the Crusades. He asserts, "there have been a number of events that have aided in stirring the conspiratorial coals suggesting that the U.S.-led wars in Iraq and Afghanistan were religious wars continuing the medieval Crusading legacy" (2014, p. 101). Johnsrud gives examples including figures such as President George W. Bush and Lt Gen William G. Boykin (2014, p. 101), directly comparing themselves to Crusaders.

Nickolas Haydock addresses the political connotations of *Kingdom of Heaven* in the book, *Movie Medievalism: The Imaginary Middle Ages*

(2008), explaining the film's controversy by citing Professor of Islamic Law Khaled Abou El Fadl, who stated: "I believe this movie teaches people to hate Muslims." He also highlights the British Crusades historian Jonathan Riley-Smith, who asserted that the film was the result of Scott's "misunderstanding of the Crusades" which was "an invention of nineteenth-century medievalism, exemplified in the works of Sir Walter Scott and Joseph François Michaud" (2008, p. 137). Although Haydock mentions the influence of Sir Walter Scott, like Schlimm the analysis is focused on the film's relationship with the Iraq War and not the Order of the Knights Templar as a reoccurring story theme or medieval archetype.

The analysis of Templar texts depicting current political zeitgeists and policies has been addressed concerning Richard Thorpe's 1952 adaptation of Sir Walter Scott's *Ivanhoe*. In an article for *Film & History* (1999) Walter Srebnick explores the film's significance, stating, "the film is a product of the culture of early Cold War period in America, a culture that included McCarthyism, the Hollywood ten, and blacklists, as well as the problem of intolerance and of anti–Semitism in particular" (1999, p. 47). However, most significantly for this study, Srebnick's notion of Thorpe's intention for Rebecca's trial to "reflect the 1950s witch hunts and the contemporary paranoia about the spread of Communism" (1999, p. 51) suggests why the role of the Templars was reduced for Thorpe's adaptation. Jonathan Stubbs addresses the conflation of the corrupt court of Prince John with the House Un-American Activities Committee in an overview of the production history in *Exemplaria*. He argues, "the court's spurious and politically motivated identification of Rebecca as a witch neatly echoes the popular disparagement of the HUAC's activities as a 'witch hunt,' a term popularly applied to HAUC activities since the committee's inception in 1938" (2009, p. 408).

Andrew Elliott's recent publication revisited the Templars' perception with the political climate in *Medievalism, Politics and Mass Media: Appropriating the Middle Ages in the Twenty-First Century* (2017). This publication highlights the current associations of the Templars with far-right extremism such as Anders Breivik and the English Defence League. Elliott's work examines the politicization of medievalism, and he highlights Breivik's perception of the medieval citing from Ravndal to inform "while seemingly much of his 'research' into the Middle Ages came from medieval games such as World of Warcraft, Age of Conan or Lord of the Rings Online" (2017, pp. 149–150) and not actual medieval history. However, Elliott's study of Templar medievalism focuses predominately on the politicization of the Order while not concentrating on specific Templar fictional case studies. Elliott draws upon examples of Templar memes that are used to promote extremist ideology. He asserts that these demonstrate "a movement rooted around English identity as Templar Knights fighting in the Holy Land, online copy-and-paste culture has embedded the Middle Ages at the very heart of the English Defence League" (2017, p. 167). Distinct from this focus, my study examines the use of the Templars to create the reoccurring thematic narrative. Although radical fringe movements have politicized aspects of the Templar narrative, the overtly political activism is not my emphasis. It is how the Templar narrative has evolved to become embedded within sociopolitical and popular culture.

To analyze the depiction of the fictional Templar, this project will first build on Elliott's work examining representations of the medieval knight in film. Elliott's book *Remaking the Middle Ages: The Methods of Cinema and History in Portraying the Medieval World* (2011) offers a way for studying the Templars' unique role as both warrior and monk. Elliott examines the archetype of the fictional knight in his chapter, "When Knights Were Bold: Those Who Fight" and the archetype of the fictional priest in the chapter, "Clergy and Saints: Those Who Pray." Elliott's examination of the depiction of knighthood provides a useful approach to address the different aspects of the heroic and villainous portrayal of the medieval Knights Templar. Elliott proposes that it is how the knight wields their knightly abilities noting, "harnessing the shocking power of raw, unrestrained violence, these qualities are transferred to the villains who as a result come to embody its negative elements" (2011, p. 60). Elliott's assertions that the level of violence is a major defining part of the evil knight provide a fundamental approach to analyzing the villainous Knights Templar archetype. However, Elliott's notion of the depiction of violence also enables us to examine the heroic Knights Templar archetype. Elliott argues, "codes of chivalry were added to later medieval imaginations of knights to play down their violence and emphasize their servitude, even when attempting to 'faithfully' render the medieval knight, a modern film must try to convey the same values in order to align the knight with a modern understanding of a hero" (2011, p. 60). This book uses this model of analyzing depictions of medieval knights but uses it to provide a more specific analysis of Templar depictions when defining my original concept of the Templar thematic narrative.

Lesley A. Coote addresses the thematic use of violence in medieval fiction in the chapter, "Remembering Dismembering: Reading the Violated Body Medievally" in the edited book *Neomedievalism in the Media: Essays on Film, Television, and Electronic Games* (Robinson & Clements, 2012). She addresses the prominence of the thematic use of violence in medieval literature. Coote explains the significance of analyzing violence as a theme, writing, "In epic, both medieval and modern, literary and cinematic, the hero is validated, redeemed, saved, or all of these, by violence against the person of others. Chivalric honour is gained by the dishonouring of others,

and masculinity is displayed, maintained and enhanced by their emasculation" (2012, p. 23). The thematic analysis of violence in medieval fiction
showcased by Elliott and Coote provides a framework to approach the contrasting hero and villainous Templar archetypes in fiction.

Analyzing violence as a theme provides an approach to examine
the different Templar knight archetypes, but this is only half of the Templar's role, as the Templar also lived as a monk. To address the depiction of the secondary temperament of this unique form of knighthood
this study draws from Elliott's analysis of the representation of medieval
clergy. Elliott's chapter identifies key traits for the archetypes of the good
and bad religious characters, which will apply to define the heroic and villainous Templar archetypes. For the villainous religious figure, Elliott summarizes the archetype as "linked to all types of consumption, such as an
insatiable appetite, monetary greed, and unchecked concupiscence board-
ing [sic] on lechery, as he remorselessly 'consumes' the poor man's goods—
his wife included" (2011, p. 117). However, there is not the same clarity
when pinpointing the archetype of the good priest, as Elliott asserts that
the priest depicts authority. This is encapsulated in what he defines as "the
two dominant forms of priesthood" (2011, p. 118) and explains that these
two forms of "high earthly status and 'feudal' leadership, risk becoming
two critical extremes of the same function when intended to continue this
anti-clericalism, giving away two symbols which the cinema has favoured:
the rich priest and the powerful priest" (2011, p. 118). This further enables an
original approach for identifying the archetypal depictions of the Templar
knight, which has not been established in academic study and is essential to
examine how Templar depictions have evolved through the centuries.

While Elliott's two forms of priesthood coincide with aspects of villainy, an approach to the religious aspects of the archetype of the good
Templar knight is provided by Christopher Roman's chapter, "The Use of
Nature: Repressing Religion in Medieval Film" in the edited book by Robinson & Clements (2012). Roman proposes that in the Western medieval
film, "the Catholic Church is portrayed as a totalitarian institution and
medieval religiosity as reactionary; the only way for the hero of the film
to practise an authentic spirituality is to reject the trappings of the church
for a greater freedom found in nature" (2012, p. 56). Roman's research indicates an approach to address the religiosity of the hero Templar knight and
how the hero relates to the authority of the church. Roman proposes that
the religious hero must be an outcast from the church and that the heroes
are "Othered by the institution of the church, although they are rebels with
whom the directors want the audience to empathize" (2012, p. 77). The relationship of the archetypical Templar character with the church provides a
framework to define further the conflicting traits of the good and villainous

Templar in medieval fiction. To identify the Templar knight character, this study draws from Elliott's and Coote's thematic analysis of violence and Elliott's and Roman's overview of medieval religiosity in medieval films to illustrate the multifaceted narrative of the fictional Templar knight character. In examining the fictional Templar knight using this approach, it enables the study to pinpoint the key tropes of the archetypal Templar, thus allowing the analysis of medieval set films and literature to trace how the thematic narrative archetypes have evolved through popular culture. These studies have focused on case studies of individual films and games; however, this book cuts across centuries of Templar adaptations, and to define my Templar urtext concept, the approach needs to be more historically grounded and address the historiography of the Templar myth.

The next part of the book is structured to examine the second half of the Templar narrative, which focuses on the use of the Templar myth, including the Templar conspiracy story and Holy Grail associations. The Templar myth incorporates aspects of the Arthurian grail legends, and though Arthurian literature has had much scholarly attention to address how the modern grail legend includes the Templar narrative, this project will draw from academic works that examine how the grail myth is retold and featured in contemporary media. In the book, *The Use of Arthurian Legend in Hollywood Film: From Connecticut Yankees to Fisher Kings* (1996), Rebecca A. Umland and Samuel J. Umland provide an overview of the grail legend adaptations by Hollywood. They claim, "Hollywood has rarely attempted, or even wished to create an actual 'Arthurian film,'" and "[t]hey have very different purposes and use the legend—or, more accurately, activate only certain features of it—to achieve their particular ends" (1996, p. 4). Although Umland and Umland's work does not address the Templars' role in the Arthurian legend, it does examine how the grail story has been repackaged over the 20th century, which bears a resemblance to how producers have drawn upon the Templar myth to create new media texts. This study builds on the analysis of the 20th-century grail stories in articulating how the Templars' role has further evolved popular perception of the Templar into a new type of grail story set in the modern day, with the Templar conspiracy replacing the physical grail concept with a symbolic one in the form of a forgotten Templar secret. This transition of the Templar myth into the 21st century completes the last significant aspect of the Templar narrative that this book not only identifies but also analyzes in culturally relevant texts dating from the 13th century to the 21st century to map its continual evolution.

The inclusion of the pseudohistorical Templar myth within fiction was examined by Susan Aronstein and Robert Torry in their chapter, "Chivalric Conspiracies: Templar Romance and the Redemption of History in *National Treasure* and *The Da Vinci Code*," in Haydock's and Risden's edited book *Hollywood in the Holy Land: Essays in Film Depictions of the Crusades and Christian-Muslim Clashes* (2009). In it, they explain, "Templar history was almost immediately identified with American history, this legend of the Templars' hidden truth merged with the myth of America's privileged destiny" (2009, p. 226). Aronstein and Torry argued that the protagonists' discovery of the Templar myth would "restore faith—whether in a miraculous divine or in America's privileged destiny" (2009, p. 226). Aronstein and Torry compare the Templar myth with the concept of typology to explain the Templars' pseudohistorical relationship with American history, explaining, "Templar romance that relocate both the Templars and treasure to the New World identify America as the end of history, the repository of truth and revelation" (2009, p. 229).

Aronstein and Torry propose that the Templar conspiracy has a beneficial revelation that restores faith in the Western foundations and is empowering, which is the polar opposite of the conspiracy concept of powerlessness addressed by Timothy Melley in his 2000 book *Empire of Conspiracy: The Culture of Paranoia in Postwar America*. However, according to Melley, the popularity of dark conspiracy is due to "an odd sort of comfort in an uncertain age" (2000, p. 8) for feelings of powerlessness. However, Aronstein and Torry propose that the Templar conspiracy is empowering as it provides historical legitimacy and a direct link for America to the Knights Templar. Although not a negative conspiracy, the Templar conspiracy Aronstein and Torry propose coincides with Melley's concept that conspiracy themes provide a sense of ease. The relationship of the Templar myth with popular perceptions proposed by Aronstein and Torry will be incorporated as a model to address how the Templar narrative has evolved in the modern day and used as a reoccurring theme within popular fiction such as *The Da Vinci Code*. The Templar typology provides a link between Western values and the West's historical heritage, which this book identifies as the quest narrative. The study of the Templars' relationship with heritage tourism will determine how fan participation with the Templar text creates tensions between the mythical and the reality of the heritage site by using the tourist experience of Rosslyn Chapel and Independence landmarks of Philadelphia as case studies.

In terms of examining the depiction of the Templar in participatory media, the Order's appearance in computer games is discussed in greater detail than their role within feature films. In the chapter, "Medievalism and The Epic in *Assassin's Creed*: The Hero's Quest," in the edited book *The Middle Ages in Popular Culture: Medievalism and Genre* (Young, 2015) Elisabeth Herbst Buzay and Emmanuel Buzay examined the computer game *Assassin's Creed* as a contemporary take on the hero's quest story function. Buzay and Buzay draw a comparison between the hero's quest of game protagonist Desmond Miles and Balian of Ibelin in *Kingdom of Heaven*. Although the chapter does not specifically address the significance of the Templar knight's role nor provide a definition of how digital games utilize the Templar, it does include interviews with the game's producer. These interviews will enable this book to argue for the reason behind the game's inclusion and changes to Templar depiction, which previous academic *Assassin's Creed* studies have not examined.

The chapter, "The Consolation of Paranoia: Conspiracy, Epistemology, and the Templars in Assassin's Creed, Deus Ex, and Dragon," in the edited book *Digital Gaming Re-imagines the Middle Ages* (Kline, 2014) by Harry J. Brown examines the re-emergence of the Templar conspiracy theme with the computer games listed in the chapter title. Brown provides a brief overview of the historical Templars, drawing from the contentious recordings of William of Tyre, and then highlights the events of the Order's demise before introducing how they became associated with conspiracy, mentioning the appropriation of the Masons and theories of Baigent, Leigh and Lincoln in *Holy Blood, Holy Grail* (1982). While Brown provides context for the emergence of the Templar conspiracy theme, Brown does not provide the historical context for the Templars' emergence in popular culture nor focus upon the changes *Assassin's Creed* made to the established fictional depiction of the Knights Templar as villains. This is an evolution of the Templar archetype that my book addresses.

Accounting for the continued popularity of digital media alongside traditional entertainment will provide a complete evaluation of the Templar phenomenon within popular culture. This book examines how fans of these texts engage with the thematic Templar narrative by acts of tourism, digital gaming, fan-generated content to ascertain how these interactions further embed and evolve the fictional narrative of the Templar. To provide an analysis of the immersive interaction and fan-generated texts produced during Templar participation, this project draws from Kurt Lancaster's book *Interacting with Babylon 5: Fan Performance in a Media Universe* (2001), which addresses the immersive experience generated from fan performance. Lancaster asserts that for fans of *Babylon 5*, "the only way they can get out into space is through immersive simulations. The role-playing game allows players to enact, through surrogation, unfulfilled romantic dreams of space colonization" (2001, pp. 41–42). Although Lancaster does not use fan tourism or fan film as examples, his theories around the transformative nature of performance will help to address the performance aspects of immersion within the Templar fan film and Templar fan tourism. This creates a transmedia coverage of the Knights Templar and gives the phenomenon an original level of analysis. This study is also useful

to help examine how the Templar narrative expands through fan participation with texts such as video games like *Assassin's Creed* and the massive
multiple-player online game *Secret Worlds*. Lancaster explains that taking
on an immersive role-playing experience enables fans to "create and perform in their own stories—enacting plots and character behaviours similar
to those found on the television series" (2001, p. 37). This notion of performance helps to understand the immersive experience for fans of these
Templar texts and how the Templar narrative has further evolved within
popular culture through character emulation and creation of new stories
through digital and user-generated content.

For fan participation, this study focuses on fan tourism, as the Templar enthusiast can recreate the thematic quest journey, venturing on their
quest to interact with the myth and history. Modern-day films set the quest
narrative focus on a search for Templar truth, which is emulated by the fans
who venture to associated heritage sites to discover the truth behind the
Templar myth. This activity of Templar text tourism coincides with heritage tourism, as the sites featured in the films such as *The Da Vinci Code* are
significant heritage sites. Although not a Templar tourism article, David
Martin Jones examines the relationship between film tourism and heritage
tourism in "Film tourism as heritage tourism: Scotland diaspora and The
Da Vinci Code" (2006). In the article, Jones analyzes the Scottish Tourist
Board's use of the release of Howard's *The Da Vinci Code* to promote the
heritage site of Rosslyn Chapel. Although not examining the sites focused
on in this study, Jennifer Laing and Warwick Frost examine tourism and
historical reimagining in their chapter, "Imagining the Medieval in the
Modern World: Film, Fantasy and heritage," in the edited book *The Routledge Handbook of Popular Culture and Tourism* (Lundberg & Ziakas, 2018).
Laing and Frost's chapter examines the tourism around the iconic fables
of *King Arthur* and *Robin Hood*, which provides an interesting parallel to
this Knights Templar study, as Laing and Frost highlight how tourist sites
cater the experience to popular perceptions of the Arthurian and Robin
Hood stories. To examine how these sites are perceived as sites of history
and popular culture, this study draws upon Foucault's concept of heterotopia incorporated for a study of fan tourism in Lincoln Geraghty's chapter,
"'I've a feeling we're not in Kansas anymore': Examining Smallville's Canadian Cult Geography" in the edited book *The Smallville Chronicles: Critical
Essays on the Television Series* (Geraghty, 2011). It provides a method to analyze the significance of coexisting realities within a site, which for the Templar tourist is the conflicting reality of the myth and history come together.

Fan tourism provides a particularly immersive experience for fans,
and this experience Will Brooker discusses in his chapter, "The Blade Runner Experience: Pilgrimage and Liminal Space" in the edited book *The*

Blade Runner Experience: The Legacy of a Science Fiction Classic (Brooker, 2005). This chapter examines the immersive experience for fans, drawing from the concept of liminality to explain how fans attempt to gain a more profound sense of immersion. The methods to gain a deeper sense of immersion are addressed by Matt Hills in his book *Fan Cultures* (2002), which examines practices of *The X-Files* fan tourist and the use of scene recreation to feel closer to the text. Stijn Reijinders's article "On the trail of 007: media pilgrimages into the world of James Bond" (2010), examines the use of fan performance to achieve that more profound sense of immersion within the world of James Bond. Although not addressing the Templar case studies or heritage tourism, these works provide useful ways to address the experience sought out by fans of Templar narratives featured in film texts.

The literature addressing the Templars as a widespread cultural phenomenon is therefore scarce, aside from the brief overviews of Haag and Newman. The academic literature available on the Templars in popular culture is featured around the major Templar-themed films like Haydock and Schlimm's work on *Kingdom of Heaven*, which focuses on the depiction's relationship with the political climate but is useful when analyzing the text's use of the Templar knight archetype. However, these studies mentioned above provide little cover regarding the scope of the Templars' appearance in popular culture. Even though Buzay and Buzay and Brown provide an analysis of *Assassin's Creed*, it is not Templar focused but rather compares the game's protagonist to Balian from *Kingdom of Heaven*. From examining the literature, it is clear that by providing a transmedia analysis of Templar-themed texts, this book provides an original contribution and addresses a missing part of knowledge around the Knights Templar. Academia has addressed the history of the Templar and how history has influenced the myth but not how the myth has influenced popular culture texts. The Templar thematic narrative addresses the gap in knowledge of the Templar phenomenon, as it analyzes how the popular perception of the Templar has expanded and evolved within popular culture through the centuries.

The Structure of This Book

To analyze the Templar narrative of the knight this book selects four major films as case studies to firstly identify the aspect of the good Templar knight and the aspect of the bad Templar knight. This will be done by using textual analysis to determine how the level of violence used by the fictional knight highlights the separation of the two aspects of the Templar urtext warrior monk archetype. To define how the depiction of the thematic narrative has evolved in popular culture, the book examines production sources as well as interviews with directors to ascertain the creative impetus behind the inclusion of the Templars as a story tool. In Chapter 1, the case studies to examine the villainous Templar archetype are Ridley Scott's 2005 film *Kingdom of Heaven* and Richard Thorpe's critically acclaimed 1952 film adaptation of *Ivanhoe*. *Kingdom of Heaven* was the last major Hollywood Crusades film and featured the Templars prominently as an antagonist, depicting the Templars as a violent extremist order. Thorpe's adaptation of Sir Walter Scott's 19th-century novel was the last major production of *Ivanhoe* and featured the bad Templar aspect, albeit removing the Templar iconography, playing down the Order's role within Scott's original novel. To address the aspect of the good Templar this book examines the Swedish film series *Arn: The Knight Templar* and the British film *Ironclad*. *Arn: The Knight Templar* is an adaptation of Jan Guillou's novel series *The Crusades Trilogy* (1998–2000), as well as being the most expensive Scandinavian film production at release, and features a Templar knight as the protagonist, who is a multicultural national hero. The significance in using the Arn series as a case study is that the high profile of this Scandinavian production demonstrates how widely the thematic Templar narrative has spread through popular culture. It also demonstrates that the Templar narrative is not only confined to majority English-speaking countries such as the United States and the United Kingdom. The final film case study for the narrative of the Templar knight is the relatively low-budget British film *Ironclad*. Although the film failed financially at the box office, it has an inclusive national Templar hero, a character that is perceived as unofficially referenced with other later Templar texts.

To critically engage with these case studies, the chapter uses the methods outlined from medievalist works such as Haydock's *Movie Medievalism* (2008) and Aberth's *Knight at the Movies* (2003) that examine the medieval film concerning the political climate during production. The methodology of these works incorporates a textual analysis examined against the historical context depicted in the film case studies, which is then supported by primary sources such as interviews and reviews and provides an ideal approach to emulate in this book. This study will draw upon these additional sources to support the textual analysis as the book endeavors to examine the cultural context alongside the textual analysis in the form of interviews, reviews, and social media posts.

To examine the role of the Templar knight as both hero and villain, this study draws from the knight archetypes defined in Elliott's *Remaking the Middle Ages* (2011) and the use of violence as a story tool in Coote's chapter, "Remembering Dismembering: Reading the Violated Body Medievally" (2008). Examining the critical distinctions of the knight archetypes that are distinguished by the use of violence will enable the chapter to define the two polar aspects of the Templar narrative of the knight. This study will draw from interviews with the directors and writers, production sources and critical reviews to provide academic clarity to these close readings and ascertain the artistic intentions behind the inclusion of the thematic narrative of the Templar knight.

To map out the Templar narrative from its point of origin in popular culture, Chapter 3 addresses the Templar urtext grail guardian archetype and examines medieval Arthurian grail literature and the prevalence of the Templar narrative of the quest in the 20th century using two iconic grail films as case studies. Wolfram von Eschenbach's 13th-century Arthurian poem *Parzival* will provide an ideal source to define and analyze the thematic narrative's evolution within popular culture by comparing the origin to the case studies *Monty Python and the Holy Grail* (Gilliam & Jones, 1975) and *Indiana Jones and the Last Crusade* (Spielberg, 1989). The choice for these case studies is not down to only their popularity and grail associations in popular culture but because these films are examples of how the Templar quest narrative incorporates within popular culture through these unorthodox grail adaptations. To address the further evolution of the narrative of the quest into the 21st century, the case studies analyzed are the hugely popular *The Da Vinci Code* (Brown, 2003) and the film *National Treasure* (Turteltaub, 2004), which both feature the Templars as part of a conspiracy the protagonist must solve.

Given the interactive nature of media and the prominence of user-generated content, to fully evaluate the prevalence and evolution of the Templar narrative within popular culture this study examines in Chapters 2 and 4 case studies that enable participation with the Templar urtext through an immersive experience. This study addresses two types of immersive experiences looking at digital immersion such as computer games and fan-generated videos to physical immersion sought by fan tourists. This study uses this approach to ascertain how individual immersive participations further embed aspects of the Templar myth within popular culture. The case studies for digital immersion and physical immersion are analyzed to confirm how the Templar narratives of the knight and the quest have been incorporated to market and provide a Templar-themed experience.

Chapter 2 further examines the warrior monk archetype through digital participation with computer games and fan films to define how the narrative of the Templar knight influences the participatory experience for players and fan filmmakers. This analysis is carried out by examining the immersive experience and narratives of the computer games *Assassin's Creed, The First Templar* (Kalypso Media, 2011) and *The Secret World* (Funcom, 2012) and the fan film *Predator: Dark Ages* (Bushe, 2015). The game

Assassin's Creed was the first title in what would be a globally recognized franchise and took the Templar narrative to the medium of gaming by making the Templars the franchise's villains. Although not commercially successful, the game *The First Templar* was released years after *Assassin's Creed* and included a Templar knight as the hero playable protagonist but also sets the game within the Crusades. The massively multiplayer online game (MMO) *The Secret World* is themed around infamous global and secret conspiracies, which, due to the Templars' notoriety with shadowy conspiracies, places them as a crucial part of this game as players can join a modern Knights Templar guild. The significance of this case study is that it enables a higher level of character customization, which through textual analysis of the gaming experience demonstrates how the Templar iconography as a type of digital cosplay depicts the role of the Templar in the thematic narrative. The final case study *Predator: Dark Ages* was chosen due to the project's popularity on social media with Templar enthusiasts. The film was a unique case study in that it was crowdfunded using Kickstarter to make a low-budget short that pitches the alien from the *Predator* franchise against a group of Templar knights. To ascertain the filmmaker's creative intentions, I will analyze the film's Kickstarter campaign and interviews with the director/writer James Bushe. The fan film was well received online with well over 1,000,000 views on YouTube and is an interesting example for how the Templar phenomenon is expanded by user-generated content focusing on the recycled, established Templar traits to produce a new Templar text, which further evolves the narrative.

To examine the player experience from these games, I played these games in 2017 and took notes of my play experience as well as carried out a textual analysis of the case studies. I also drew upon interviews with producers and game reviewers to support my analysis and articulate the producer's influences and intentions. To support my analysis of the play experience, I used a web ethnography study of YouTube message boards to provide primary evidence of how *Assassin's Creed* players' experience has further expanded the Templar urtext. As this book is in many ways a transmedia Templar study, it incorporates methods used by other transmedia studies on paratexts such as Henry Jenkins's study of *The Matrix* franchise in *Convergence Culture: Where Old and New Media Collide* (2006). The chapter also draws from Jonathan Gray's book *Show Sold Separately: Promos, Spoilers, and Other Media Paratexts* (2010) to support the analysis of the computer game as a paratext. To understand how significant the concept of play is for analysis of the case studies the chapter uses Paul Booth's book *Game Play: Paratextuality in Contemporary Board Games* (2015) as a conceptional method to help analyze how the Templar narrative is adapted for a playable experience. Booth examines the concept of play alongside the adaptation of franchises to a board games format, explaining that for play to be possible, the player must conform to the rules of the franchise and the board game. This approach provides a vehicle to address how the Templar narrative influences the play experience of the computer game's users and how the adaptation expands the perception of the Templars in a virtual environment.

Chapter 4 further examines the grail guardian archetype through case studies which depict the Templar-themed narrative of the quest as related to geographical locations associated with the Templar history via fan tourism. This chapter will examine the fans' immersive personal experience by citing uploaded reviews and examining photos posted on social media to determine how fan tourism continues the Templar narrative in contemporary popular culture. This analysis is carried out by utilizing the immersive experience of visiting heritage sites associated with Templars and Templar media texts like *National Treasure and The Da Vinci Code*. The sites visited were Rosslyn Chapel in Scotland and the Independence landmarks in Philadelphia, the United States, as these heritage sites prominently feature in the films mentioned. As it is about the visiting of the sites themselves and the immersive experience offered at them, the chapter will not focus on quantifying tourist numbers. However, the chapter will be based on my own examination of the physical sites themselves, mirroring an approach taken by Rebecca Williams in her chapter, "Replacing Maelstrom: Theme Park Fandom, Place, and the Disney Brand." Her focus was to analyze "the places of the Disney theme parks themselves that are of particular interest and, in some cases, particular theme park attractions" as case studies (2018, p. 170), physically experiencing them herself and drawing conclusions from those experiences.

I traveled to both sites in 2018 and collected data on my own experiences. I traveled to Philadelphia in January of that year, staying several days to visit the Independence landmarks featured in *National Treasure*. While there I spent several hours at the city's Independence landmarks including Independence Hall, the Liberty Bell and the Old Pine Street churchyard. While at the sites, I used data-gathering techniques such as taking photographs, taking notes and speaking to officials such as park rangers and tour guides. I took photos of the film's filming locations and attended a four-hour walking tour of the city's historical and cultural landmarks. In April, I traveled to Scotland to visit the Rosslyn Chapel for the day and collect data of the tourist experience. To collect data, I attended the visitor talk provided by the Chapel trust and took photographs of items for sale in the gift shop and outside the chapel, as photography is not allowed inside the chapel. I also took notes to record the information signs provided for the most significant parts of the chapel's architecture and the sign that indicates where *The Da Vinci Code* was filmed. These are data collection methods used by Hills (2002), Brooker (2005) and Geraghty (2011) in their fan tourism studies and therefore are an ideal approach to uncover how these sites create an immersive experience for fans seeking a greater understanding of the media text. This chapter also uses autoethnographic methods by drawing upon tourist reviews, social media posts and photos to analyze how participation strengthens the Templar urtext through the thematic narrative of the quest. I am using this approach to examine the immersive experience and how fans recreate the quest carried out by the films' protagonists to gain a greater understanding of the urtext and the Templar story that the films promote. Incorporating fan theory and autographic methods will help me unpack the Templar urtext as shown in different media that have their own distinct fan communities.

In using this thematic structure, the book can examine not only fundamental case studies such as major motion pictures and early influential literature but also interactive and user-generated media. In dedicating two chapters to the engagement with the narrative digitally or physically, the study can determine how a religious order of knights abolished in the 14th century became widespread in popular culture. The scope of the Templar narrative has grown through the centuries, expanding the Templar urtext as the thematic narrative ventures into different mediums such as literature, film and digital games. This expansion has created a multifaceted theme that has several contradicting aspects which originate from the archetypes of the warrior monk and the grail guardian that have stood the test of time and will undoubtedly influence stories to come.

CHAPTER 1

The Templar Knight in Medieval Film

Archetypal Hero and Villain

The part of the Templar urtext that this chapter is examining is the warrior monk archetype which is adapted and reused as part of the reoccurring Templar narrative. The chapter aims to identify how my concept of the thematic Templar narrative has evolved over the centuries to include two aspects: the earlier aspect of the bad Templar knight from the 19th century and the second aspect of the good Templar knight originating in the 20th century. This chapter examines how the narrative has become fictionalized and how the Templar narrative emphasizes myth over historical fact. The case studies selected are the medieval epics *Ivanhoe* (Thorpe, 1952), a major Hollywood film and *Kingdom of Heaven* (Scott, 2005), a major American production with a budget of $130,000,000 (Box Office Mojo). *Ironclad* (English, 2010) is a smaller British production with a budget of $25,000,000 (IMDb). The multicountry-funded film series, *Arn: The Knight Templar* (Flinth, 2007) and *Arn: The Kingdom at the End of the Road* (Flinth, 2008), is defined by Film International as a "Scandinavian-German-British co-production" (Hedling, 2008, p. 63). With a combined budget for both films at "22 million euros" (Hedling, 2008, p. 63), the films were the most expensive Scandinavian film production at release.

I have chosen these case studies because they demonstrate my concept of the Templar urtext. This chapter aims to understand why these notable films still incorporate and adapt the main warrior monk archetype. In examining the first pillar of the warrior monk, this chapter can explore how these different depictions of the Templar adapt the urtext and expand the popular perceptions of the Knights Templar in broader popular culture. The methodology will include a textual analysis of the case studies but also an analysis of the producer's influences and intentions, including the political climate at the time of the film's production. The chapter will draw on production sources, interviews, directors' commentary, film critiques to understand the creative decisions and will use academic sources to highlight how the Templar narrative is being evolved. This approach will provide evidence for the filmmakers' intentions and help us to understand how the film text has evolved the Templar narrative.

This chapter will firstly draw from Andrew Elliott's work, which explores the archetype of the medieval knight as both hero and villain. Of course, the Templars were not just knights but also monks, so to address this, Chapter 1 also draws from Christopher Roman's work on religion in film to frame the archetypes of religious characters and to analyze the portrayal of the Templar's religion in these films. Once the archetypes are established, the chapter will then analyze the influence of the political climate in the films' depiction of the Knights Templar. The case studies will be compared to the political climate at release, using analysis from Nickolas Haydock and Matthew Richard Schlimm in their comparisons with the post 9/11 climate and Jonathan Stubbs and Walter Srebnick's critique of McCarthyism. This comparison is needed as looking at how historiography is interpreted and what function historical sources have in the medieval film will further enable a clearer understanding of the artistic choices behind the Templar depictions.

Pierre Sorlin demonstrates the importance of highlighting the significance of addressing the political climate at the time of production as he argues that the use of a fictional past in film "is no more than a useful device to speak of the present time" (Hughes-Warrington, 2007, p. 58). Hughes-Warrington clarifies the role of historical events in a film by stating it "as a signifier of issues contemporary with filming, ranging from ethical beliefs to political aspirations" (2007, p. 58). If a historical film is assessed from that perspective, then the Templar narrative of the knight must be examined alongside the political climate during production. This approach will assist in ascertaining how the Templar urtext has expanded through the evolution of visual depictions in the Templar narrative.

Heroes and Villains—Separated by Violence

To understand the archetype of the medieval knight and to define the narrative of the knight's separation into two aspects, this chapter must critique the depiction of violence in contrast to notions of chivalry. The hero and villainous knight are both defined by their actions; both are killers, and this chapter will first explore how the good and bad archetypes are separated. The Templars were both knights as well as monks, men of chastity and prayer, but first we will explore these men from their knightly perspectives (i.e., their warrior actions). However, violence has always been part of war, and it is no different for its depiction in the heroes' narrative. In a chapter on violence in medieval fiction, Lesley A. Coote writes, "graphic violence is powerful because it seizes, and holds, the audience's attention" (2012, p. 15). It is true that medieval epics climax in a battle to the death, such as with *Ironclad's* desperate attempt to defend the keep, and both installments of *Arn: The Knight Templar* and *Arn: The Kingdom at the End of the Road* end with a full-scale field battle. Therefore, violence is a crucial audience expectation, and the predominant narratives are constructed around this theme.

Coote's notion is, "The physical wound forms a *punctum* within the text, visual or literary" (2012, pp. 15–16). Coote defines punctum by citing Roland Barthes and writing, "Puncta … are particular points on a photographic image that add meaning to the image as a whole" (2012, p. 16). Coote uses this term in the argument: "The filmmaker needs the *punctum's* specificity and dynamic to engage his/her audience with the medieval, at the same time opening up the possibility of other, related, meanings" (2012, p. 16). Coote's notion that violence is a way of engaging the audience with the medieval world is reflected in the opening acts of *Kingdom of Heaven*. In the first act Balian murders his own brother (a priest played by Michael Sheen), and when a group of men come to arrest him, he and his father's men (including Godfrey) brutally kill them. Even Godfrey's nephew (Nikolaj Coster-Waldau) and a knight who surrendered meet the same violent end. This encounter could be an introduction to the violence that will underpin the rest of the film; using Coote's notion this scene is a "welcome to Middle Ages" greeting from the director.

Coote references the significance of violence within the Arthurian legends. On the story of *Sir Gawain and the Green Knight,* she writes, "The poet emphasizes the physicality of the wound, in order to fix attention on what the wounding signifies. This wound is punishment for Gawain's deceit over his keeping of the green girdle," (2012, p. 19). It is not what the wound represents that is of interest in this study; it is using violence as a story narrative in the chivalric tale. Coote highlights the importance of violence in the Arthurian romances, commenting on the aftermath of Sir Gawain decapitating the Green Knight: "Instead of continuing with the story, the poet describes how the bloodied head begins to roll around the room" (2012, p. 26). William F. Woods argues that violence is prevalent in the medieval film because "the pain in medieval movies is physical and bloody, and that is because our senses of the real is fundamentally visual; we tend to believe what we see" (2004, p. 45). Essentially, using violence as a narrative tool cements verisimilitude with the audience as physical pain is all too real.

However, if these chivalrous knights commit acts of violence, such as beheadings or like Balian and his father executing unarmed men, then they are no better than the villainous knights and warriors, the supposed chivalrous knights set out to defeat. Elliott informs us that:

> codes of chivalry were added to later medieval imaginations of knights to play down their violence and emphasize their servitude, even while attempting to "faithfully" render the medieval knight, a modern film must try to convey these same values in order to align the knight with a modern understanding of a hero [2011, p. 60].

Elliott suggests that the film must align the knight with the guise of a modern hero to make the traditional Hollywood narrative work, one that the film *Braveheart* (Gibson, 1995) encapsulates. The peace-loving William Wallace (Mel Gibson) must inspire his country to take up arms and fight for freedom from the oppression of the cruel English. Elliott notes that medieval films create a relatable hero knight, still keeping with the spirit of the medieval tale by "Harnessing the shocking power of raw, unrestrained violence, these qualities are transferred to the villains who as a result come to embody its negative elements" (2011, p. 60). Elliott offers a strong example of this notion with his example of the protagonist and antagonist in Jerry Zucker's *First Knight* (1995), which stars Sean Connery as the iconic King Arthur. Elliott writes, "by polarizing the pacifist Arthur ... with the distinctly unhinged, and one-dimensional Malagant," it paints "Arthur as the ideal, pacifist hero" (2011, p. 60). This depiction, of course, would justify any violence that Arthur or his knights commit as an act of self-defense against dangerous Malagant.

However, as King Arthur has been featured in stories since the Middle Ages, perhaps he may not need his role to be as established, unlike newer characters. Elliott offers an example from the Rob Cohen film *Dragonheart* (1996) which stars Dennis Quaid as Bowen the dragon slayer and David Thewlis as the villainous King Einon. Elliott writes, "the henchmen of the villainous Prince Einon are constructed as evil because of their aggression towards 'the weak villagers' ..., which includes not only unarmed men but also women, children and the elderly" (2011, p. 60). Elliott then summarizes his point by simply stating, "[b]y constructing the 'evil' knights as an oppressive and brutal force, therefore, *Dragonheart* simply needs to place its hero, Bowen, into the opposite role of Redeemer/Deliverer for him to represent all of the positive values which the anti-hero lacks" (2011, p. 61). Coote states, "Scenes of violence to the body, on whatever type of screen..., make a very effective way for the writer/director to create meaning" (2012, p. 30), and this approach by writers and directors can be used to justify their heroes' actions. The story uses violence to not only set the medieval scene but also to highlight the ideological differences of two warring factions, which inserts them into the traditional roles of hero and villain.

In medieval fiction, violence is used to introduce to the viewer what type of knight the Templar will be, either as the heroic Templar knight encapsulated within the later good Templar or the villainous Knights Templar as depicted in the 19th-century works of Sir Walter Scott. Violence is a key indicator to depict the moral compass of the character as perceptions of knighthood are contrasted in the oppressive force and romantic notions. This contrast is highlighted by Elliott who references T.H. White, writing, "knighthood is based on a fundamental paradox: as one who fights for right, the knight is both lover and a fighter, responsible for both protection and aggression, peace and violence, honour and villainy" (2011, p. 53). Comparisons for these positive ideals are found in the second aspect of the Templar knight narrative, the good Templar. The protagonist in the film *Ironclad* is the English Templar knight Marshall (James Purefoy); introduced through immediate violent acts that tell the audience what kind of knight he is and what aspect of the Templar narrative the film is including. In one of the film's opening scenes, King John (Paul Giamatti) and his army of German mercenaries arrive at the Darnay Castle, where Marshall, two of his Templar brothers and an abbot (who is a white-haired elderly man) are taking shelter from the previous day's storm. King John hangs the castle's rebellious lord, and then when the abbot tries to intervene, King John has his German mercenary leader, Captain Tiberius (Vladimir Kulich), brutally saw off the monk's tongue with a dagger. This horrific image will justify to the audience the violent actions that Marshall then takes by rushing to the abbot's rescue and slashing one of King John's soldiers across the face with an axe. Marshall, King John and his soldiers committed acts of violence, but Marshall's actions were for a just cause and "heroic" in comparison to the actions of King John.

Arn: The Knight Templar shows a similar example when Arn must kill a man to save a woman from a forced marriage. Direct comparisons can be made to the stereotypical trope of the damsel in distress, but it is a cliché that quickly establishes Arn as adhering to the good Templar aspect. Arn Magnusson (Joakim Nätterqvist) is a young monk trained by Broder Guilbert (Vincent Perez), who was once a Templar knight, but despite being indoctrinated into the warrior ideology, it was not until Arn grew to manhood that he had to put his abilities into use. By chance, Arn stumbles across a terrified woman who is being pursued by a group of armed men with dogs. The group's leader accuses Arn of trying to steal his bride, despite the apparent fact that Arn is dressed as a monk. The group throw the young monk a weapon, and then the leader attacks Arn, forcing the young monk to kill his attackers in self-defense. With the attackers dead,

Arn stares at his blood-covered hands, a clear depiction of the guilt for his arguably heroic actions.

Both the scenes from *Ironclad* and *Arn: The Knight Templar* described are clear examples of how the depiction of violence is used in the medieval epic to depict the morality of the character. Arn was acting entirely in self-defense against a group of brutish aggressors. Elliott explains, "the notion of unchecked violence is largely repugnant, and our modern heroes must walk a very fine line between cowardice and aggression" (2011, p. 59). This notion is evident in the scene described as Arn could have fled and left the girl to her fate, but he defended himself and repelled the attackers. If it was not any clearer to the audience that Arn's actions were that of a hero, when he confesses his sins back at the monastery, the priest tells him, "You killed those men in self-defence. They were sinners; trying to force that poor young girl to marry against her will" (Flinth, 2007). It is how Arn uses his violent skills that define him as a medieval hero or as a good knight. Such as the necessity of Marshall's actions to save the helpless old abbot, Arn's heroics, with the inclusion of the damsel in distress, justify the violence as chivalrous. The actions described above demonstrate the critical defining factor in the good knight aspect of the Templar narrative as warrior violence is a key theme. However, it is how the Templar's actions are perceived by the audience that establishes the Templar as the good Templar knight. At its essence, to be part of the good Templar aspect, the Templar's violent actions must be justified, and in that they are protective and not oppressive.

In comparison to the good Templar knight, *Kingdom of Heaven* provides an example of how violence can also distinguish a Templar knight as an outright villain. *Kingdom of Heaven* first lets the audience glimpse the kind of characters these Templar knights are, when a large group of Templar horsemen commanded by Guy of Lusignan (Marton Csokas), Raynald of Châtillon (Brendan Gleeson) and the Grand Master Gerard de Ridefort (Ulrich Thomsen) brutally attack a convoy of Muslim merchants. Before charging down the hill towards the convoy, Guy comments, "This caravan is armed, Rainald," then, Raynald replies, "Aye, no sport otherwise." The Templars then roar, "God wills it!" (Scott, 2005), before they charge down the hill to slaughter the merchants. Scott uses close-ups on Guy to show his ecstasy as blood splatters across his face, while he and the Templars slaughter the almost defenseless merchants. Compare this to Arn and Marshall's introduction to violence, which was defensive and justifiable. Guy and the Templars act without any justification, only that they enjoy plundering and killing Muslims. These Templars adhere to the bad Templar aspect of the knight narrative due to their excessive use of force that is not justifiable to the audience due to its purely oppressive nature.

Balian (Orlando Bloom) is the hero of *Kingdom of Heaven*; he is not a Templar, but his introduction to violence is the murder of his half-brother. On the surface, this sounds like the making of a villain, but it is the reason for his half-brother's murder that the audience will find justifiable. At the beginning, Balian is a blacksmith and a tragic character; his first child was a stillbirth, and his wife took her own life as a result of the tragedy. Balian's half-brother is a priest who attempts to gain Balian's property for himself by trying to persuade Balian to leave for the Holy Land with Balian's father, Godfrey of Ibelin. In a frustrated attempt to persuade him he tells Balian, "If you take the crusade you may relieve your wife's position in Hell. I put it delicately; she was a suicide; she is in Hell." When that fails to change Balian's mind, he taunts that he had his wife's head cut off before burial; he says, "For what she does there without a head?" (Scott, 2005). Balian realizes that the priest stole his wife's golden cross necklace from her grave. In a fit of rage, Balian grabs the sword he is working on and stabs the priest in the chest, pushing him back onto the lit forge. Elliott explains "that the raw aggression which may well have brought knighthood into existence had to be pared down for the big screen, by the use of vengeance themes to justify them, and by increasing the delay between action and retaliation" (2011, p. 81). The vengeance of Balian's actions justifies his violence, while in direct contrast to this Guy and the Templars portray raw aggression that an audience would find repulsive.

Elliott argues that even the knight's choice of weapon singles him out as a disciplined noble warrior, writing, "The sword itself, then, acts as a device used to distance the knight from his opponent, and thereby to tame the raw aggression" (2011, p. 63). If the sword represents discipline, then how can the audience differentiate between the hero and villain if they are both using swords? In *Kingdom of Heaven*, Balian used a sword to slay his half-brother, while the Templars also used swords to slaughter merchants, but it is due to the level of bloodshed in the deeds that the audience can differentiate between the hero and villain. Balian's killing of his half-brother, although brutal, had minimal bloodshed, while the Templars opening violence is a bloodbath. Elliott writes, "On a purely thematic level, therefore, the absence of blood serves to hint that the violence … is disciplined and pure, and that the knight was not transported by pure rage or fury, but— as is appropriate when the violence is suitably motivated—was enacted 'humanely,' and only to a degree which is justifiable and sufficient" (2011, p. 63). The emphasis on the Templars' bloodshed depicts the horrors of the Templars' wild and unchecked cruelty, which implies that Balian's violence is more controlled and was justified in its reasoning. *Kingdom of Heaven* is about the clash of two cultures and the war that follows, so, of course, there will be an amount of blood spilling within the war, so the amount of blood spilled during the Templars' murders of Muslim merchants underlines the unacceptable level of violence used by the Templars.

The Templar hero of the good Templar aspect carries an iconic weapon that stands the hero out from the other warriors in a similar way to King Arthur's sword, Excalibur. When informed that Arn will be leaving the monastery, Broder Guilbert presents him with the sword he carried when he served as a Knights Templar. The sword has a cross carved into the pommel, and the guard has the Latin inscription translated to "In this sign thou shall conquer," and Broder Guilbert tells Arn, "with this sword, no one has ever defeated me. But you may never draw it in anger or use it for your own gain (Flinth, 2007)." Marshall's great two-handed sword is not introduced in such a way, but the significance of the weapon is shown as it cuts through his enemies with ease; again this sword has a Templar cross on the sword's pommel. Carl James Grindley describes the role of the hero's weapon as "In its purest form, the weapon's tale is an encomium that sings the praises of arms and armour that, for the most part, contribute little to the overall narrative structure of a text but contain a concentrated symbolic functionality" (2004, p. 151). Although Arn and Marshall's weapons provide little narrative propulsion, they are symbols for the knight's martial ability and for marketing the film. For example, both films' DVD covers prominently feature the Templar hero's sword.

From looking at how the Templars can fit into the archetype of the fictional knight it is clear that the two distinct aspects of the Templar narrative of the knight run parallel with the use of violence to distinguish between these archetypes. The narrative of the knight includes both the good Templar knight and bad Templar aspects as these coincide with the obverse notions of violence and chivalry established in medieval romance. However, in reality, the Templars are more than warriors, and to understand how this Templar narrative of the knight has evolved in popular culture it is essential to explore the depiction of the Templar's role as a monk in these films. In the same way of comparing the Knights Templar to good and bad knight archetypes, Templar knights should be examined as depictions of medieval religious acolytes to ascertain what aspects of their religious lifestyle the Templar knight narrative features in popular culture.

Warrior Monks

Despite the significance of the monastic lifestyle within the Order of the Knights Templar, it features minimally in the three films described previously. The most we see of a religious lifestyle for the Templars is the character of Arn, and that is him growing up in the monastery, engaging in prayer, studying literacy and learning martial skills; all of this was long before he became a Templar. Although, as a Templar knight, Arn prays after every victory by kneeling on the ground and bowing his head to his sword, turned upside down, symbolizing a cross. Prayer before or after a battle is a recurring physical representation of the religious devotion of the Knights Templar in the Templar film texts. The Knights Templar in *Kingdom of Heaven* scream "God wills it" (Scott, 2005) before they charge down the hill to murder the Saracen merchants. Of course, this is not pious like the silent prayers of Arn, but these Templars are polar opposites of the good Templar aspect, and their prayers would be just as villainous as their actions. However, the Templars in *Kingdom of Heaven* show utter contempt for the Christian ideology; for example, when arguing with Guy, Tiberius says to him, "I would rather live with men than kill them," to which Guy replies sarcastically, "That sort of Christianity has its uses, I suppose," followed by his Templar brothers laughing at his remark. In *Kingdom of Heaven*'s depiction of the bad Templar knight, we see them mock their own religion and only use it to justify war and violence. Later in that same scene Godfrey, the grand master of the Templars, calls for Jerusalem to go to war by declaring, "There must be war. God wills it," and then the Templars all cry, "God wills it!" (Scott, 2005), despite openly mocking their own faith moments before. For the bad Templar, Christian faith is little more than a justification to go to war, which is the polar opposite to the pious Arn of the good Templar aspect.

The distancing of religious association in film is found in depictions of other medieval characters. For example, Christopher Roman addresses this by citing Gwendolyn Morgan's work on the depiction of Joan of Arc. He writes, "in our efforts to explain away the religious experience so believable to her contemporaries and so unbelievable to the scientific rationalist impulse of the twentieth century, we have left the real Joan behind and rendered her an icon defining our own concept of human identity" (2012, p. 57). Roman explains, "icons have become stand-ins; rather than the depth of human experience that was relevant to the Middle Ages" (2012, p. 57). If we look at the lack of religious devotion to the Templar role in film, it does suggest that Morgan's notions of the medieval reality are ignored in favor of the preference of a modern audience. This disparity towards Christianity is apparent in both aspects of the Templar knight narrative, as with all three Templar texts the heroes are outsiders from the religious institutions. In *Arn: The Knight Templar*, Arn is forced to serve as a Templar by the injustice of the church, while distraught Marshall in *Ironclad* is desperate to leave the service of the Templars. In *Kingdom of Heaven* the hero, Balian, is an agnostic who is the enemy of the fanatical religious Order of the Knights Templar (who ridicule their faith). Roman explores similar themes in his critique of the films *The Seventh Seal* (1957), *Brother Sun, Sister Moon* (1972) and *Anchoress* (1993); he writes, "the Catholic church is portrayed as a totalitarian institution and medieval religiosity as reactionary; the only way for the hero of the film to practise an authentic spirituality is to reject the trappings of the church for greater freedom" (2012, p. 56). All three of the Templar texts portray the Catholic Church in a negative light. Arn experiences a repressive, tyrannical church that harasses him and his lover while also finding little acceptance in the Order of the Knights Templar. It is even more so in *Kingdom of Heaven* in that Balian's half-brother, the priest, steals from his wife's grave, and bloodthirsty Templars overshadow Jerusalem.

When discussing his chosen texts, Roman writes, "The films problematize religion for the hero of the film by representing the religious other as caught between institutional conformity and a primal relation to nature that represents freedom" (2012, p. 56). The heroes' unwillingness to be part of the religious institution is apparent in all three Templar texts: the agnostic hero (Balian), the reluctant Templar (Arn) and the traumatized Templar (Marshall). With the exception of Balian (as he is not a Templar), the Knights Templar led an extraordinarily pious and monastic lifestyle, and the writer's decision to distance Arn and Marshall from that medieval institution tends to suggest that Morgan's notion of appeasing the modern audience is evident in these themes. The Templar knights of the good knight aspect are more akin to modern action heroes in terms of their faith than the devoutly Christian knights of medieval literature.

The amount of time the story focuses on religion in the film version of *Arn* is different from the original novel. Jan Guillou's *The Road to Jerusalem* (1998) focuses a lot more on monastic lifestyle; a great deal of the first novel of the trilogy focuses on Arn growing up in the monastery where he would debate Christian philosophy with Father Henri. Arn's mother, Sigrid, even has a vision from the Holy Spirit of her fully grown son dressed as a Templar. Sigrid's vision is the introduction of God's plan for Arn, similar to that of actual canonized saints and Mary, mother of Jesus, as Sigrid was only pregnant with Arn when she received the vision. "She knew the young man and yet did not. He carried a shield but wore no helmet. She didn't recognize the coat of arms from any of her own kinsmen or her husband's; the shield was completely white with a large blood-red cross, nothing more" (Guillou, 1998, pp. 7–8). The book is written more like a fictional hagiography, while the film is more akin to a Roman-Christian epic. Pamela Grace details the differences between the two:

> Most of the epics are based on novels whose narratives involve historical figures but whose central may be fictional. The protagonists in the epics are ordinary mortals, not saints: they are not chosen by God for reasons unknown to human

beings; they do not have contact with heavenly beings; and they do not work miracles during their lifetime or after their death [2009, p. 36].

As the character Arn is an invention of Guillou and not a saint, the Arn films are not a hagiopic, but the novels do have elements of a hagiography. For example, Sigrid's vision from the Holy Spirit shows the connection to God, which is not featured in the films, and depicts Arn's impossible martial feats and tragic punishments as amazing soldiery or coincidences. The novel describes Arn's brilliance as miracles or God's guidance and the tragic misfortunes as God's will. In *The Road to Jerusalem*, when Arn killed two men as he protected a young woman, Father Henri explained:

> When God saw this He grew angry and set you in the path of the sinners in order to punish them as severely as only He can. That cathedral Dean Torkel was thus not entirely wrong when he spoke of how he saw an angel guiding your hand [Guillou, 1998, p. 211].

It is by having Sigrid contacted by the Holy Spirit that Arn's deeds show him to be more than an ordinary mortal, and perhaps his deeds are miracles. So, in this way, the novel is more akin to hagiography, unlike the film version, which stays shy of those themes, planting itself firmly in what is Grace's definition of the epic genre. These differences would suggest that the low levels of detail around Arn's monk lifestyle are due to the running time limitations of film, whereas with the Arn novel, religious piety is a vital staple of the medieval literature good knight.

In Andrew Elliott's chapter, "Clergy and Saints: Those Who Pray," he explains that religious figures are represented in one of two ways. He highlights them as "high earthly status and 'feudal' leadership, risks becoming two critical extremes of the same function when intended to continue this anti-clericalism, giving way to two symbols which the cinema has favoured: the rich priest and the powerful priest, each of which comes replete with his own iconography" (2011, p. 118). Although in the film, the Templars do not engage in monastic practices associated with the order, the Templar film does conform to these anticlerical clichés. On the first type, Elliott writes, "the wealthy priest, whose material wealth is frequently used as a symbol for his power within society, although it is just as often meant to be a slight on the perceived avarice of the medieval Catholic Church" (2011, p. 118). In the Templar text, the wealth and privilege of the Templars are represented in the form of the bad Templar knight character. For example, in *Kingdom of Heaven* the physical wealth of the Order is not literally depicted. However, the elitist status of the Templars is depicted in the superior behaviors of the villainous Templars towards what they perceive as people of lower status.

Arn: The Knight Templar showcases the difference between the humility of Arn and his Templar brothers, with the attitude toward wealth shown by Arn's Templar nemesis, Gerard de Ridefort. Gerard shows his pomposity when he arrives at a Templar meeting before a battle with Saladin, marching into the room and presenting the true cross. The true cross is a small piece of wood from Christ's cross encased in a giant golden cross. The extravagance of the true cross is superseded by the tiny carved wooden cross that Arn wears. Arn does not need a giant golden cross to inspire him but a sentimental piece of wood, unlike the rest of his Templar brothers who are in awe of the golden cross.

The thematic Templar narrative of the knight incorporates archetypes from religious figures such as monks and priests, but unlike the archetype of the knight, which is incorporated in both the Templar knight narrative aspect and can be both good and bad, the Templar knight narrative focuses on the negative traits depicted in the fiction of medieval Christianity. The Templar knight either portrays these negative traits such as in *Kingdom of Heaven*, or he rejects them and is an outsider from the organization he has supposedly dedicated his life to serving. The Templar narrative of the knight benefits from its malleability, which enables it to absorb other preconceived archetypes such as the knight or the priest. This flexibility has allowed the Templar narrative to evolve in popular culture as a result of the lack of official authority over the Templar phenomenon due to the Order's extinction in the 14th century. Therefore, this flexibility has enabled the knight narrative to diverge into two Templar knight aspects that both conform to the expected knight archetypes in that his character is shown not just through his actions but by his use of his martial abilities. For both aspects of the knight narrative, the relationship between warrior and monk is somewhat diminished in film as the narrative has been adapted to fit within anticlerical notions. This depiction can be part of both aspects of the knight narrative, the good Templar knight and the bad Templar knight.

Historical Accuracy

After examining how the Templar narrative of the knight is an extension of the archetypes of the chivalrous and villainous knight and priest archetypes, this chapter turns its attention to examining the role that the Templar narrative plays in popular culture, focusing on major film productions *Ivanhoe, Kingdom of Heaven, Arn: The Knight Templar* and *Ironclad*. Film texts will often play with history, leave out parts that do not work with the constructed narrative or invent happenings to enable them to tell the story they want to tell. This section will analyze the attractiveness of including the Templar narrative of the knight in fiction and how this further imbeds the Templar narrative in popular culture.

The ethics of historical accuracy in film has been fervently debated by historians and film scholars on whether accuracy underlines a historical film's legitimacy and quality of the product. For example, A. Kelly argues, "Any attempt to render the distant past in any form other than intellectual understanding (if even that is exempt) is to create a certain fiction. But this crafted fiction does not detract from the value of the film" (2004, p. 9). Martha Driver comments that authenticity is only authentic as long as the illusion is hidden from the audience; she writes, "As film critic Jonathan Rosenbaum commented to me some years ago, 'It doesn't matter if the historical details of the film are authentic. They just have to look authentic to the audience'" (2004, p. 20). She adds, "Film provides an imaginative immediacy and reality, a luminous world we physically enter by watching and listening" (2004, p. 21). When the writer William Monahan discusses the historiography of *Kingdom of Heaven* in the DVD audio commentary, he states, "What you use as a dramatist is what plays. It's all an eye for the things you can use, incident, colour, ideas … that resonate with you personally. You use what plays, or can be made to play, and you don't use what doesn't." This comment implies that it was the story and visuals and not historical accuracy that was important to the project. Monahan's statement coincides with Kelly's above argument: "crafted fiction" does not diminish the quality of the film.

Elliott explores historiography in film, writing, "On one extreme we find the conservative viewpoint of critics such as Hughes, whose underlying argument seems to reject films as inevitably inaccurate, suggesting that their usefulness only demonstrates how mankind leaves his mark on history with each rewriting of it" (2011, p. 11). He then compares this to Ferro's argument: "even while committing factual errors, historical films may usefully be seen as a kind of document chronicling the way that man understands his own history" (2011, p. 11). Elliott theorizes, "we are forced to accept that there is no real, single truth about the Middle Ages" (2011, p. 34). He concludes, "What emerges from such historical inquiry, therefore, is not a single, absolute version of the Middle Ages, but a concatenation of beliefs and known facts, from which we extrapolate an imaginary version of the period" (2011, p. 34). If historical accuracy is not the focus of the historical film, then analyzing the differences between fiction and reality enables the film to be interpreted at a deeper level. The role of the historical film genre is explained by Driver and Ray citing Kevin J. Harty, who hypothesize that:

> The genre itself is like a crystal ball or magical mirror, Harty adds, "in which the present and the future can be studied in light of the past and the past can be reimagined in light of the present and the future" [Driver & Ray, 2004, p. 7].

Chapman, Glancy, and Harper suggest that the reflectionist model suggested above offers "too simplistic an understanding of the relationship between film and its social content" (2007, p. 4). Harty's notion that the present is depicted in the past coincides with Arthur Lindley's idea that the present day can be studied in the guise of the historical. In using the film, *The Seventh Seal* (Bergman, 1957), as an example Lindley explains that:

> Not to labour an obvious point for too long, we are looking at a version of the Middle Ages that has been carefully lifted out of historical sequence in order to serve as a mirror and an alienating device for viewing the mid-century present and/or the timeless present of parable [Lindley, 1998].

The idea of film acting as a mirror to society is further challenged by Chapman, Glancy, and Harper. They cite Graeme Turner, writing, "Film does not reflect or even record reality; like any other medium of representation it constructs and 're-presents' its pictures of reality by the way of codes, conventions, myths and ideologies of its culture as well as by way of the specific signifying practices of the medium" (2007, p. 4). This, though, is an argument for all film and not just any particular genre.

Regarding the medieval genre representing contemporary issues coincides with Rick Altman's theories on the role of genre. He writes, "from Lévi-Strauss and other structural anthropologists, genre critics learnt that narrative can serve as a form of societal self-expression, directly addressing the society's constructive contradictions" (1999, p. 26). Elliott argues that it is not just the medieval film that represents present values but the whole knightly character type. Elliott cites Martha Driver and Sid Ray, writing:

> in order to appeal to a contemporary audience, film must reinvent the Middle Ages and create the medieval hero a hodge-podge of traits derived from a mixed understanding of what is medieval and of traits we value in the heroes of post-millennial Western culture [2011, p. 54].

The narrative may construct society's self-expression, but it is not as simple as the criticized reflectionist model; Chapman, Glancy, and Harper explain, "The more common metaphor now, rather than reflection, is mediation" (2007, p. 4). They cite from John Belton, writing, "They do, nevertheless, 'reveal something about the cultural conditions that produced them and attracted audiences to them ... they reflect what audiences want to see rather than what is really there'" (2007, p. 4). When dealing with the relationship between the political climate at the time of the case studies release and the Templar narrative in popular culture, this chapter explores what the director is potentially using the constructed fictional historical setting to comment upon. This analysis is done by examining interviews and production information, which avoids the problematic practice of interpreting the texts in line with the political climate of the time.

This next section will look at the Templar texts *Ivanhoe, Kingdom of Heaven, Ironclad* and *Arn: The Knight Templar.* The case studies will be analyzed from the perspective outlined above to understand what does including the thematic Templar narrative bring to the text's narrative and how this repetition of the malleable Templar narrative further evolves representations of the Templar in popular culture. Historiography is essential in examining these texts because, if the history has been reworked to benefit the writer, then this chapter will examine why the change was made and what the Templars' inclusion brings to the story. The first film addressed is the 1952 release of *Ivanhoe* (Thorpe), and despite its release over 50 years before the other chosen texts, Thorpe's version was the last major production of the Sir Walter Scott classic and also chose to play down the Templar's role within the story. This text will be addressed from the perspective of how the lessening of the Templar's role impacts the 19th-century novel's story. This section will begin with Thorpe's adaptation of *Ivanhoe* and how the exclusion of the Templar iconography affects the adaptation of the 19th-century novel.

The Bad Templar Knight

The original and most prestigious instance of the Templar narrative of the knight appearing in popular culture as a capital consumable was the bad Templar knight, and it came in Sir Walter Scott's Crusade novels, the first being *Ivanhoe* in 1820. Phillips explains the popularity of Scott's Crusade literature, writing, "Scott's works were translated into numerous languages and in France alone he had sold over two million books by 1840. *Ivanhoe* alone inspired almost 300 dramas: within a year of its publication, 16 versions of the story were staged across England" (2009, p. 13). Phillips notes the political climate during the early 19th-century, writing:

> … the 19th century saw a dramatic expansion of European political power into the Muslim near east, largely at the expense of the declining Ottoman Empire. France invaded Algeria in 1830 and soon afterwards Spain and Italy, too, embarked upon North African adventures. Some looked to the crusades as a forerunner, especially after France took control of Syria in 1920 [2009, p. 13].

From examining Phillips's summary of the European political climate in the 19th century, we see how Scott's Crusade novels became so popular in Western Europe and why King Richard and his man, Sir Ivanhoe, were the heroes of this 19th-century blockbuster. However, as Phillips suggests, "As a

Calvinist, Scott's view of 'intolerant zeal' was restrained, but overall he gave a positive impression of the Crusades" (2009, pp. 12–13). This perspective could explain the origin of the bad Templar narrative in fiction in that the Templars were the outright villains of *Ivanhoe* because the Templars were a relic of the Catholic Church, who answered only to the Pope.

Although *Ivanhoe* returned to mainstream fiction once again in 1913 in two silent films, the American production directed by Herbert Brenon and the British *Ivanhoe* directed by Leedham Bantock, it is Richard Thorpe's 1952 release of *Ivanhoe* that this chapter now focuses on due to its success at the box office and the director's creative choices with the adaptation. In Thorpe's version of the story, the grand master of the Templars was completely removed from the film and his role in the trial of Rebecca given to Prince John. Also, Richard the Lionheart's role was reduced to having him and his soldiers arrive at the end of the film after the dual between Ivanhoe and de Bois-Guilbert. Before analyzing the film text, the context of the environment that the production arose from needs to be established as Thorpe's *Ivanhoe* was many years in the making and rewritten many times.

The most notable development in the project was "Between April 1946 and June 1947 a series of drafts were written by screenwriter Aeneas MacKenzie…. Mackenzie's script emphasized the destiny of England as an emerging nation" (Stubbs, 2009, p. 405). Stubbs explains Mackenzie's changes to the story "According to MacKenzie, 'the touch of a Jew's finger' 'fuses' Norman and Saxon. The character of Isaac assumes a greater stature than in Scott's original conception, and it is he who provides Ivanhoe with the ransom for King Richard" (2009, p. 406). His most significant change though would have to be his idea to "revise the love plot between Ivanhoe and Rebecca, Isaac's daughter… [He] eliminates Ivanhoe's romance with Rowena by making her his half-sister, allowing his relationship with Rebecca to develop in its place" (Stubbs, 2009, p. 406). With regard to MacKenzie's influences for the story's new angle, Stubbs states, "It seems very likely that MacKenzie's particular interest in these Jewish characters was motivated, at least in part, by the aftermath of the Nazi Holocaust and the campaign for the creation of the Jewish State" (2009, p. 407). Stubbs's notion is, "MacKenzie's depiction of utopian racial harmony in a newly formed English nation, as experienced by a character returning from war, was presumably intended to inspire change in postwar American society" (2009, p. 407).

Unfortunately MacKenzie's version "appears to have been too controversial for Paramount and in June 1947 they sold it to RKO for $110,000" (Stubbs, 2009, p. 407). Stubbs believes that Paramount's decision to move away from the project was due to the formation of the HUAC (House Committee on Un-American Activities). Stubbs cites from Buhle and Wagner,

"The committee informally associated antiracist messages, such as those proposed in the *Ivanhoe* screenplay, with communist subversion, and regarded Communism and Judaism as intricately bound" (2009, p. 407). Jeffrey Richards informs, "Waldo Salt was next assigned to the project and he, writing in 1948 as the HUAC hearings got underway, turned Rebecca's trial into a parody of the HUAC hearings. Salt was later named as one of the 19 unfriendly witnesses and blacklisted" (2007, p. 131). *Ivanhoe* was then passed back to MGM as "Howard Hughes (RKO owner) declared he had no interest in producing it" (2007, p. 131). *Ivanhoe* had two more writers before filming, Marguerite Roberts and Noel Langley; Roberts, however, was "called before the HUAC, refused to name names and was blacklisted in 1951" (2007, p. 131). Stubbs cites John H. Lenihan writing,

> Lenihan argues that changes devised by Salt and reinforced by both Roberts and Langley made Ivanhoe a reflection of the anger and anxieties felt by Hollywood personnel ... he notes that the trial of Rebecca for witchcraft is transformed from a case of religious prejudice into "a political red-herring orchestrated by the wicked Prince John to cast suspicions on and thereby smear his Saxon enemies, particularly Ivanhoe and King Richard" [2009, p. 408].

Srebnick shares this interpretation of Rebecca's trial by emphasizing Prince John's line from her trial, writing, "Prince John declares that she must be destroyed because the 'scourge of witchcraft [is spreading] across [the] land.' This sequence in the narrative and John's words reflect the 1950s witch hunts and the contemporary paranoia about the spread of Communism" (1999, p. 51).

In Thorpe's film, the Templars role in the story was significantly reduced, and this is most likely done to highlight the film's criticism of McCarthyism and the HUAC. Thorpe's production may appear as less significant than the other three case studies in this chapter due to the Templars' downplaying, but it is how the film underuses the Templar narrative of the knight in this version that is of interest. Sir Walter Scott used the Templars as the outright villains of his novel, which suggests that in deliberately reducing their presence, Thorpe is using the bad Templar aspect in their reduced role to comment on separate issues. Richards explains the significance of the narrative change, devising that Rebecca "is put on trial not, as in the book, by the Grandmaster of the Templars but by Prince John. It is made clear that this is a political trial. John's advisor, Waldemar FitzUrse, says that he does not believe in sorcery and witchcraft, but adds, 'But your people will.' Prince John makes a speech claiming that witchcraft (i.e., Communism in contemporary context) is spreading through the land and must be stamped out" (2007, p. 130). Richards notes regarding the film's attack on the HUAC, "No one, however, seems to have noticed at the time that that is what it is" (2007, p. 131). Another change to the bad Templar aspect was the playing down of de Bois-Guilbert's Templar iconography; instead of having him dressed in the Templar uniform of the white mantle and red cross, he has blue stripes across his white mantle. Although he still stands out from the Norman knights, the choice to change from the traditional Templar iconography is most likely due to the film's desire to show England as a state in disarray. Also, excluding the Templar mantle prevents confusion as it resembles the more modern cross of St George on the English flag. When King Richard returns to England, he and his troops are draped in white mantles with the red cross of St George, with the perceived intention of representing that a unified England will be created now that he has returned. The image of Richard's troops dressed in homage to the English flag would have been confusing had de Bois-Guilbert been dressed in his traditional Templar mantle.

Ivanhoe became the first in a cycle of Hollywood medieval epics for which Richards lists the cycle running up to 1967 (2007, p. 125). Scott's work returned during the cycle in an adaptation of the *Talisman, King Richard and the Crusaders* (Butler, 1954), but it did not share the same box office success as *Ivanhoe*, taking only $2,100,000 in America (The Numbers) compared to *Ivanhoe*'s $13,643,440 (Sackett, 1990). It would take nearly three decades before the Templar villain would return to the big screen in the Spanish horror film, *Tombs of the Blind Dead* (de Ossorio, 1972), but the Templars would not return to Jerusalem until 2005 in *Kingdom of Heaven*.

The negative traits of the bad Templar aspect featured in *Ivanhoe* are also depicted in Ridley Scott's *Kingdom of Heaven*, which depicts Saladin's conquest of Jerusalem from the perspective of Balian of Ibelin. Ridley Scott paints his Templars in the same light as Sir Walter Scott's de Bois-Guilbert; Haag supports this notion, believing that Ridley Scott's "war-crazed Templars are partly descended from the Templar baddie in *Ivanhoe*" (2009, p. 344). However, de Bois-Guilbert is not made to be the scapegoat for the film's ideology, unlike the irredeemable Templars in *Kingdom of Heaven*. Whereas *Ivanhoe* is set in a fictional medieval period, *Kingdom of Heaven* depicts historical events, but Scott changed these events in order to suit his vision. He made powerful Outremer lords into Templar knights when they were not. Michael Haag reviews *Kingdom of Heaven* and comments on its historical accuracy; he writes:

> Both Guy of Lusignan, the King of Jerusalem, and Rainald of Chatillion, who are presented as unmitigated villains, are also presented as Templars, which in reality they were not. The real Templar in the film, the Grand Master Gerard of Ridefort, is presented in the worst possible terms, exceeding the most hostile accounts given of him in the more biased chronicles of the time [2009, p. 344].

The changes to these historical characters by including them within the Templar trope is a deliberate choice by the production. However, this analysis of Scott's depiction of the Templars is not focused on historical accuracy. Recreating historical accuracy is an impossible task, and a film needs to compromise accuracy for narrative to understand what the film's inclusion of the Templar narrative of the knight enables the film to comment on. Writer William Monahan explains, "You use what plays, or can be made to play, and you don't use what doesn't. So, we know all about the missing bits" (*Kingdom of Heaven Definitive Edition commentary*). In Charlotte Edwardes's article, Ridley Scott's new Crusades film "panders to Osama Bin Laden"; in *The Telegraph* online she cites Professor Riley-Smith, "who said the plot was 'complete and utter nonsense.' He said that it relied on the romanticised view of the Crusades propagated by Sir Walter Scott in his book, *The Talisman*, published in 1825 and now discredited by academics" (2004). Although Monahan does not mention the Templars directly, this could benefit the flow of the story and the visuals by grouping all the villains in a single uniform. Scott made it clear in an article on the Guardian website, "He [Tiberius] was under pressure from his people, and on the other side there was the radical faction of the Templars and other knights— what we might call the right-wing or Christian fundamentalists of their day" (2005). This interview would suggest that by extending the bad Templar aspect to Guy and Raynald, he could represent this faction without having to explain it.

The racist hatred from *Kingdom of Heaven's* Templars is reminiscent of de Bois-Guilbert's treatment of the Jewish characters in *Ivanhoe*. Walter Srebnick explains, "The theme of anti–Semitism emerges in the film as soon as Cedric, in the presence of Norman 'guests,' is informed that a Jew and his daughter have asked for lodging for the night. The Normans protest, refusing to share the same quarters with the 'infidels'" (1999, p. 50). De Bois-Guilbert, the leader of these Norman knights, organizes an attack on Isaac while he sleeps in the barn, only to be saved by Ivanhoe and his squire, Wamba. Like the Templars' attack on the Muslim merchants, this attack appears to be motivated by racial hatred. When the Normans voice their racism to Isaac, it is Wamba "who articulates the film's ideology of justice and toleration" (Srebnick, 1999, p. 51) with the line, "For every Jew you show me who is not a Christian, I will show you a Christian who is not a Christian" (Thorpe, 1952). There is a similar articulation of the film's ideology in *Kingdom of Heaven*; Schlimm notes that when Balian "learns the words of Muslim prayers, he says, 'Sounds like our prayers,' reinforcing the popular purist conviction that all religions are not really all that different" (2010, p. 138). In both films, there is a desire not to depict two religions as outsiders, and it is the villains of the films that see them as such, de

Bois-Guilbert and the Normans in *Ivanhoe* and Lusignan and the Templars in *Kingdom of Heaven*. Both of these factions openly talk of their hatred and launch violent attacks due to their warped ideology; de Bois-Guilbert's attack on Isaac is significantly less brutal than Lusignan's on the merchants, possibly due to different levels in technology available to Scott's production more than 50 years later.

When Monahan discussed his view on the ideology of the Crusader in the DVD commentary, it is clear that he is influenced by a historical perspective discredited by Riley-Smith. Monahan states, "Anyone who thinks the Crusades were all about religion is definitely crazy. It was an excuse … the Holy Land was the only place that a European could go before 1492. It was the only safety valve; it was the only place for dispossessed" (*Kingdom of Heaven Definitive Edition*). Haydock challenges this perspective, writing:

> The older view, most authoritatively represented by Sir Steven Runciman's three-volume *A History of the Crusades* (1951–54), broadly characterized crusading as a frenzied, greedy dash for plunder fuelled by revenge and religious hatred. For Riley-Smith this misunderstanding of the Crusades is an invention of nineteenth-century medievalism, exemplified in the works of Sir Walter Scott and Joseph François Michaud [2008, p. 137].

Monahan's comments demonstrate the perspective of the "greedy dash for plunder," which is evident in his comparison with the American colonizers: "It was, in many ways, a land of opportunity" (*Kingdom of Heaven Definitive Edition*). The film also carries forth traits of the bad Templar aspect created with Sir Walter Scott's novel and depicted in Thorpe's *Ivanhoe*.

Kingdom of Heaven was a worldwide box office success, taking $211,652,051 worldwide (Box Office Mojo). The film was not just successful in the West, taking $14,535,907 in the United Kingdom, $16,415,805 in Germany and $9,533,590 in France—countries where this medieval epic has a healthy return. *Kingdom of Heaven* also had success in its reception in the Middle East and Egyptian box office, taking $2,209,991 in the Middle East and $437,374 in Egypt (Box Office Mojo). Although slightly less than the takings for *Robin Hood* (2010), Scott's return to the genre, the film took $1,802,373 in the UAE alone; however, *Robin Hood* was more successful at the box office worldwide, taking $321,669,741. Despite the greater success of *Robin Hood*, it is surprising that *Kingdom of Heaven* took that much money in the Middle East given the amount of controversy surrounding it before the film was even released. Schlimm highlights the strains of the political climate at release, writing: "Given the Iraq War, the Israeli-Palestinian conflict, and other post–9/11 realities, many wondered if the timing was right for a movie that featured Christians and Muslims killing one another on an epic scale. Though Hollywood had not made a major film about the Crusades in 70 years, many doubted that this was the time" (2010, pp. 129–130).

Haydock, though, offers a more specific reference to the hysteria surrounding a film depicting the Crusades in a post 9–11 climate by referencing the concerns of a leading Islamic academic, as well as a Western Crusades historian. Haydock describes the two most prominent critiques of the project, writing:

> Jonathan Riley-Smith, the reigning dean of British Crusade historians, who thought the film a politically correct and dangerous distortion of history that would feed the flames of radical Islam; Khaled Abou el-Fadl [*sic*], professor of Islamic Law at the University of California, who judged its portrayal of Muslims stereotypically and likely to provoke hate crimes against Arabs [2008, p. 136].

Riley-Smith claimed that the film was "fatally ignorant of the new orthodox among Crusade historians, which takes the religious inspirations of the Crusaders and tries to respect the differences between their worldview and that of post–Enlightened cultures" (Haydock, 2008, p. 137). Riley-Smith was concerned for the Crusader's depiction as one-sided monsters, and from exploring the archetype of knighthood in fiction, the tropes described above (i.e., religious hatred and greed) are not tropes of the heroic knight and imply the Crusaders would be the outright villains of the text. Haydock summarizes his concerns as the film "presents a very real and present danger in the propaganda wars surrounding the recent clash of civilizations" (2008, p. 138).

Riley-Smith was not alone in his concerns about historical events from hundreds of years earlier being propaganda; this view was shared by senior leaders from both the West and Middle East. In his article in *Conspiracy Theories in the United States and the Middle East* (2014) Brian Johnsrud notes several references to the Crusades made by senior American officials. Johnsrud writes:

> President George W. Bush called the war on terror "Crusade" in 2001; Donald Rumsfeld's classified World Wide Intelligence updates to President Bush in 2003 with biblical verses and images on the title pages were leaked to GQ magazine in 2009; Lt Gen. William G. Boykin spoke to church congregations in 2003 in his military uniform, explaining that the U.S. was engaged in a holy war against Satan in Iraq and Afghanistan [2014, p. 101].

Osama Bin Laden and Saddam Hussein mirrored these self-made comparisons from American leaders with the Crusades. Schlimm cites these comparisons by referencing Cline, writing, "Bin Laden, similarly, not only referred to Americans as Crusaders but also cast himself as a second Saladin. Saddam Hussein did the same, which is quite remarkable given that Saladin was a Kurd" (2010, p. 136). The Bush administration was not the first from the West to compare a Middle Eastern campaign to the Crusades. Comparisons to the Third Crusade were made praising the achievement after the capture of Jerusalem in 1917. Jonathan Phillips details the Crusading references in an article for *History Today*, writing, "The Symbolism of a British commander entering the Holy City was apparent to all and *Punch* magazine published a cartoon of Richard the Lionheart gazing at Jerusalem saying: 'At last my dreams come true,' a reference to his failure to take the city during the Third Crusade" (2009, p. 13). When addressing George W. Bush's comparison to the Crusades, Phillips highlights the severity of those comparisons, writing, "When President Bush so disastrously used the word 'crusade' in his unscripted response to the 9/11 atrocities he simply fulfilled the claims Bin Laden had been making for years" (2009, p. 16). Riley-Smith's concerns that *Kingdom of Heaven's* negative portrayal of Crusaders is a dangerous piece of propaganda are underlined by senior American leaders, having decided to cast themselves in these roles.

When asked about these comparisons in Brett's interview, Scott claimed that he was in preproduction when 9/11 happened. "We were concerned whether or not the film would happen.... Bill came back and suggested I do something in the period of the Crusades when there was an uneasy truce, because then we could discuss the idea of tolerance. That's it in its simple form" (BBC online, 2014). Lindsey Irvine comes to a different conclusion from her interview with Scott, writing:

> Although the parallels toll pretty insistently throughout the film, Scott denies it was a deliberate attempt to address the problems of the contemporary Middle East. "I develop all my own material, and you always have a wish list on your shelf, you know. One of them has always been about this period—although I love period full stop. Any period is fascinating, the more ancient the better" [Irvine, 2005].

Irvine's interview does contrast with Scott's other thoughts on the comparisons; when he wrote an article in *The Guardian* earlier that year. Scott stated:

> We set out to tell a terrific story from a dramatic age—not to make a documentary or a piece that aims to moralise or propagandise. But since our subject is the clash of these two civilisations, and we are now living in the post–9/11 world, *Kingdom of Heaven* will be looked at from that perspective. We did make some choices about the values expressed through the story, beginning with the central situation of two leaders trying to serve their own people and their sense of mission, while exercising a degree of tolerance of the "other" [2005].

These comments would suggest that the comparisons made by Schlimm and Haydock to the current political climate are very apt. However, Riley-Smith's concerns of an anti–Western Crusader theme are not shared by Khaled Abou El Fadl; he believed that the movie would be anti–Islamic. Haydock cites an interview Khaled Abou El Fadl gave in March 2005 to the *Herald*; he writes, "UCLA professor of Islamic Law Khaled Abou el-Fadl [*sic*] opined more or less the opposite of Riley-Smith, 'I believe this movie teaches people to hate Muslims.' The incendiary nature of this rhetoric about a movie he too had not seen is comparable to that of Riley-Smith" (2008, p. 142). Haydock cites in greater detail the professor's criticism of the film, writing:

> I'm willing to risk my reputation on this—that after this movie is released there will be hate crimes committed directly because of it. People will go to see it on a weekend and decide to teach some turbanhead a lesson [...]. There is a single (Muslim) character who is human-like—Saladin, he has a conscious and awareness. There's another character who is a mad, ranting, raving, bloodthirsty lunatic, screaming "jihad, jihad, jihad." The rest of the Muslim characters are willing to die without any emotion [2008, p. 142].

Khaled Abou El Fadl's fears of a negative representation are similar to their portrayal in the opening scenes of DeMille's 1935 film *The Crusades*, which begins in the aftermath of the fall of Jerusalem. John Aberth describes the one-sided depiction in that opening, writing:

> One of the first images we see is of Saracens pulling down a giant crucifix on top of the church of the Holy Sepulchre in Jerusalem, while others gleefully cast Christian icons, holy books, and the wood of the True Cross into a raging bonfire. Next we cut to a scene showing captive Christians being led away in chains as slaves, followed by a bevy of Christian women being sold at a Muslim slave auction [2003, p. 87].

DeMille's depiction of the fall of Jerusalem was the opposite of Scott's telling; in *Kingdom of Heaven* Saladin and Balian reach an agreement where all the Christians inside the city can leave unmolested, meaning no Christian woman would have been chained and sold into slavery. Saladin's treatment of Christian symbols is different as well; in Scott's film, Saladin enters the Holy Sepulchre and picks up a discarded cross from the floor and places it carefully upon the altar. DeMille's film depicts a Saladin with far less compassion towards the defeated Christians. Aberth describes Saladin's introduction and says, "When confronted by Peter the Hermit, Saladin acknowledges that it is he who is behind all the atrocities we have just been witnessing" (2003, p. 88). Aberth cites Saladin's opening line, writing, "Go, hermit. Carry your thunder across the sea. Tell your Christian kings what you have seen: your woman sold as slaves, your knights trampled under our horses, your gospels cast into the flames, the power of your cross broken, forever!" (2003, p. 88). This villainous portrayal of Saladin and his forces is similar to what Khaled Abou El Fadl feared would be depicted in Scott's film when he "was responding to an advance copy of the original screen-play sent to him by the *New York Times*" (2008, 142). However, the theatrical release for Scott's *Kingdom of Heaven* did not support Khaled Abou El Fadl's criticisms and "the version privately screened in late April 2005 for the Council on American-Islamic Relations (CAIR) in Los Angeles was lacking many of the elements el-Fadl [*sic*] had found so offensive and it received the organisation's unqualified approval" (Haydock, 2008, p. 143). In an interview in *The Guardian* Scott stated, "I've had so many letters from Islamic groups and societies thanking me for a very understanding film about Muslims. So everything [the studio] was afraid of is in reverse–180 degrees in reverse" (Irvine, 2015). Scott's comment suggests that the film received more positive reviews for its depiction of Islam than negative critiques, such as El Fadl's concerns.

In analyzing an early draft of the script both from the DVD special features and the website dailyscript.com, the vague examples described by El Fadl do not appear, which suggests that the early script available is not that criticized by El Fadl. However, the specific examples taken from the script's portrayal of Muslim soldiers are still part of the early draft sourced for this project. According to the online article, "The script reads: 'As the Muslim army of thousands advances at a run, ready to kill the Christians at a single rush, Balian looks to his left in the shield wall. The Saracen knights fire a sky-blackening volley of arrows and charge, screaming "Allah." This is their chance; they will take Jerusalem at this rush and are not afraid of martyrdom.'" (Waxman, *New York Times*, 2004). Although not written exactly as described in the article, the early draft does reflect the references described. For example, the script says "The SARACEN ARCHERS fire a volley of arrows and the INFANTRY charges. This is their chance: they will take Jerusalem at this rush and are not afraid of martyrdom." (dailyscript.com). Although the description is slightly different, with one describing "Saracen knights" firing arrows and the other describing them as "SARACEN ARCHERS," which suggests a misquote from the script or the available script is a later draft. If this early copy critiqued in this article is not the early draft released on the *Kingdom of Heaven Definitive Edition*, then it would appear that only the description of the action has slightly changed.

Khaled Abou El Fadl's criticisms of the film do not materialize in the early draft of the script. It is doubtful that an even earlier version would address Islam in such a negative way, as Scott has said in an interview with Brett before the film's release "People forget that the crusaders were the bad guys" (BBC online, 2014). From looking at the story notes from the special features of the *Kingdom of Heaven Definitive Edition* it is clear whom he wants to vilify by story card number 6, which says, "Guy + Knights Take Over Palace.... Templars All the Bad Guys." Story card number 6 suggests that there was not a huge refocus away from depicting Islam in a negative light and that the early draft of the script available more or less reflects the tone of the draft reviewed by El Fadl.

Scott did not want the villains of the film to be either the Saracens or Christians but a third party, the villainous Knights Templar. This can be seen by his story notes and by the description of Guy's introduction in the script, which says, "GUY DE LUSIGNAN, a splendid knight in the red cross we will associate with extremists in Jerusalem" (*Kingdom of Heaven Definitive Edition*). Scott wanted the film to depict the Knights Templar as an extreme faction within the Christian Kingdom of Jerusalem, who are entirely to blame for starting the war with Saladin. Depicting the Templars as an oppositional faction was simple due to the Templars' unique white mantle with a red cross, in contrast to the Kingdom of Jerusalem's forces' light blue uniform. The first courtroom scene highlights the difference between the two polar opposite factions, which has the Kingdom of Jerusalem's forces seated on the right and the Templars seated on the left of King Baldwin. When the Templar grand master Gerard de Rideforte (who incidentally is Arn Magnusson's rival in the Arn films) declares his intentions for war, crying aloud, "There must be war! God wills it!" (Scott, 2005), Guy de Lusignan joins his cry for war and the camera shifts its perspective, placing Guy on the right-hand side of the King and thus right of the camera shot. This change in perspective suggests a representation of Guy's and the Templars' right-wing ideology and seems similar to El Fadl's criticisms of the film. However, instead of "a mad, ranting, raving, bloodthirsty lunatic, screaming 'jihad, jihad, jihad,'" as he claims from reading an advance copy of the script, Scott depicts the Templars as mad, ranting, bloodthirsty lunatics, screaming, "God wills it!" as they charge down the hill to slaughter Muslim merchants. The early draft script gives an excellent example of how Scott planned to depict the Templars as bloodthirsty; the script describes this scene as:

> The KNIGHTS charge. Reverse it. The CAMELS and people are running. Men grabbing weapons of every kind. The heavy knights smash through the defenders, killing everyone they come near. People trying to surrender are killed. We see the TEMPLARS killing with particular savagery. Leave the fight in the dust, the knights murdering, the camels running, silks and silver spilling.... It's over almost at once [Monahan, *Kingdom of Heaven Definitive Edition*].

According to Schlimm, "A *USA Today* review observed that 'the medieval holy wars known as the Crusades don't usually bring to mind merciful Muslim warriors or faith-doubting Christians or happy scenes of religious diversity in the Holy Land'" (2010, p. 130). In incorporating the bad Templar aspect Scott could use the Templars as scapegoats, meaning

Kingdom of Heaven can visit the hot topic of holy war and achieve favorable reviews. Schlimm cites the *New York Times,* writing that the "review called the film 'an ostensibly fair-minded, even-handed account of one of the least fair-minded, even-handed chapters in human history'" (2010, p. 130). It is worth noting that historian Hagg's critique regards the historical accuracy of the film as, "Apart from some generalities-there was such a place as Jerusalem and it fell to Saladin—there is nothing that bears much relation to historical fact" (2009, p. 344). Schlimm argues that by making the Templars the outright villains of the film, they feel safe in recognizing Balian as the good knight. In regard to Balian, Schlimm writes, "Balian is, in short, the polar opposite of Guy, Reynold.... Audiences identify with him, cheer for him, and see his cause as their cause. With him, they are able to admire a crusader who occupied Arab lands and killed Muslims but without a tinge of guilt" (2010, p. 138). Balian "is a kind and benevolent man who earns the respect even of Muslims" (Schlimm, 2010, p. 137). In contrast to Balian's goodness, Scott depicts the Templars as extremists who launch hate crimes against Muslims and plunder innocent merchants for personal gratification.

The bad Templar aspect of the Templar narrative of the knight has been used in *Kingdom of Heaven* by Scott as shorthand to demonstrate a theme of extremism. Scott grouped the film's villains with the Templars and dressing them with the iconic red cross, the audience can associate the Order with extremism and a hateful ideology that is rejected by all the film's heroes, both Christian and Muslim. Scott depicted traits found with the villainous Templar from Sir Walter Scott's fiction and imbued characters with the iconic Templar cross to group together a faction of right-wing fanatics. The use of the Templars in *Kingdom of Heaven* demonstrates the malleability of the Templar narrative in that it can be molded to work within the desired project outcome. The historical fiction can use the flexibility to draw from the Templar narrative the aspects that work for their story themes and ignore the aspects of the Templar urtext that do not work.

The Good Templar

The British film *Ironclad* and Swedish collaboration film, *Arn: The Knight Templar*, portray the Knights Templar in a different light to that of *Ivanhoe* and *Kingdom of Heaven's* Templars; it depicts the Templar knight as a hero. The essence of the good Templar appears in fiction as early as the late 16th century. Edmund Spenser's epic poem, *The Faerie Queene* (1596), featured the hero The Redcrosse Knight, a virtuous knight who wears a red cross upon his chest. Elizabeth Heale describes his attire, writing, "The 'bloudie cross' on armour and shield suggests that Redcrosse wears the spiritual armour which St Paul tells us God provides for his children" (1999, p. 33). Redcrosse does indeed bear the red cross of the Templars upon his armor, but that cross has also become associated with St George, becoming the patron saint of England during the Reformation. Of course, Redcrosse is later revealed to be St George, but it is not merely the cross that is reminiscent of the infamous Knights Templar (the order having been abolished in 1312), the Redcrosse Arthurian character is mixed with Templar characteristics. Maurice Evans describes Redcrosse as "the hero of faith, and his actions demonstrate its nature and the factors which help or hinder its achievement" (1970, pp. 14–15). Despite being a holy warrior, Redcrosse is susceptible to lust, which is his undoing. Heale explains, "Redcrosse's human frailty is evident from the episode: his faith wavers, his power to tell the true from the false is uncertain, and his fleshly lusts are easily stirred up" (1999, p. 35). The Templar hero in both *Arn: The Knight Templar* and *Ironclad* are privy to the same weakness as Redcrosse. Arn is seduced by a temptress, leading to his banishment. While in *Ironclad*, the Templar Knight is distracted from his duty by sleeping with a young noblewoman, enabling the enemy to storm the castle. Both the Templar knight and Redcrosse gain their strength from their Christian faith, but they also share the weakness of succumbing to the charms of women, a reoccurring theme within Arthurian literature. Redcrosse is also used as a device to comment upon the political climate at the time, particularly his most famous deed of slaying the dragon and rescuing his lady Una. Heale notes that:

> With Redcrosse's assumption of the name St George, we are reminded, too, of the historical dimension of the English Knight's long effort, and the national significance of his imminent restoration of Una to her Kingdom, suggesting as they do the restoration of a pure Reformed Church of England after the nation's long error in or servitude to, Roman Catholicism [1999, p. 42].

The traits introduced with The Redcrosse Knight are apparent within the late 2000s good Templar narrative. They are dressed the same, have similar strengths and weaknesses, address contemporary issues through reference to the past or, in *The Faerie Queene's* case, to myth. It seems as if Arthurian chivalry and the Templar mythos have been mixed together, much in the same way that the good Templar protagonist is fashioned as a national hero in *Arn: The Knight Templar* and *Ironclad*. Heale claims that Redcrosse comments on the political climate, addressing the Reformation in the text. This section will explore if the Templar narrative aspect of the good Templar in *Ironclad* and *Arn: The Knight Templar* also serves this purpose. Critiquing the historical accuracy can be a useful tool for interpreting the story that the filmmaker wishes to tell. As the writer of *Kingdom of Heaven*, Monahan explains "You use what plays" (*Kingdom of Heaven Definitive Edition*) and by examining what the film has included or left out will offer indications of the filmmaker's intentions.

Ironclad was a complicated collaboration, with producer Andrew Curtis saying, "*Ironclad* was among the largest British indie films shot in 2009. Made without a U.S. or U.K. distributor, its financial structure was 'more complex than a London Underground map,' according to producer Andrew Curtis. The fact that the film has 18 exec producers tells its own story" (Dawtrey, 2010). The film's modest budget was $25 million (IMDb), and according to an article in *Variety*, "the credit crunch also knocked away some pre-sales, and the cast wobbled as the producers juggled their financing options and shaved their budget" (Dawtrey, 2010). The production's multi-funded budget would explain the large number of executive producers and production companies attached to *Ironclad*. The film's protagonist is similar to the 16th-century Redcrosse in that he is a quasi St George, with his Templar garb connoting the cross of St George as he leads the defense of Rochester Castle and ultimately that of England. The film had a short, unsuccessful release at the box office, taking only $175,440 in the UK, (Box Office Mojo) but had more success at the European box office. In Spain *Ironclad* took $2,550,097, in France it took $931,122 (Box Office Mojo), as well $794,809 in Russia (Box Office Mojo), all considerably more than in the UK.

The events of *Ironclad* take place during the First Barons' War against King John in 1215, during the siege of Rochester. The film opens with a montage explaining the wickedness of King John and origins of Magna Carta; the montage ends with the voice-over, "The Magna Carta was sealed at Runnymede on the 15th of June in the year of our Lord, 1215. It will be remembered throughout history. What is not remembered is what King John did next" (2011, English). The film then begins its narrative of King John's campaign to reassert dominance over his subjects, which leads to King John's siege of Rochester Castle. The siege defense is led by William d'Aubigny (Brian Cox), who was believed to have led the defenses of the historical event. What is interesting is that William d'Aubigny is not the film's main protagonist, as the actual leader of the defense is sidelined by a fictional Templar knight called Marshall. Of course, there was a major player in the First Barons' War who was called William Marshall, and perhaps this is where the film took its inspiration for the character. The historical William Marshall and Earl of Pembroke was a lifelong supporter of the Plantagenet family, who once fought alongside Richard the Lionheart and during the barons' revolt led royal forces against the French prince and rebel barons in the Second Battle of Lincoln 1217, which secured the reign of the infant King Henry III. Dan Jones explains the significance of the victory, writing, "The future of Henry's Reign was decided at Lincoln. It was the last and perhaps the greatest military engagement of William Marshall's long and distinguished life" (2012, p. 221). Richard Brooks details the career of Marshall in his book *The Knight Who Saved England: William Marshall and the French Invasion, 1217* (2014); he summarizes the excellence of Marshall's career, writing:

> William's charge at Lincoln elevates him from the status of an international sporting champion, or another self-seeking magnate, to that of saviour of his country. If his early career made him a super-star in his own time, its dramatic conclusion, with its long-term significance for England and the World, should make him a national hero today [2014, p. 22].

If William Marshall was a great sever of the crown, then is it possible that *Ironclad*'s Marshall is inspired by this historical person? Although the historical William Marshall was in his seventies by the time of the First Barons' revolt. What further makes a comparison compelling is that *Ironclad*'s Marshall is a Templar and William Marshall became one. According to Jones "In the days before he died Marshall dealt with many things, not least his children's futures, and his wish to be invested as a Knight Templar in fulfilment of his crusader vow" (2012, p. 224). The similarity suggests that the makers of *Ironclad* were so keen to feature the Knights Templar in the story, that they reinvented William Marshall, had him change sides and made him a middle-aged Templar knight. The notion that *Ironclad*'s Marshall is inspired by the historical person William Marshall is shared by a review from Medievalists.net which states, "Thomas is loosely based on medieval knight extraordinaire, William Marshall" (Peter Konieczny, 2013). Unfortunately, Jonathan English has not commented on whether William Marshall was the inspiration for his Templar hero, but in an interview on comingsoon.net, English did state, "A lot of the other characters, the heroes like James Purefoy and Jason Flemyng and Mackenzie Crook, those were fictional characters" (Edward Douglas, 2011). This statement from English, who also wrote the story, means that these comparisons can only be considered speculative, despite the comparison of similarities between the fictional and historical character.

The film even goes as far as to invent that the Templars were involved with Barons' War, stating that they fought against the king. Charles Dance narrates the opening, saying,:

> England, in the year 1215, had been under the reign of King John for 16 years. The most villainous of England's monarchs, John was renowned for losing wars with France, leveeing punitive taxes and sleeping with the wives of barons. The barons finally rebelled against their king and became locked in a bloody civil war, lasting for over three years and decimating both armies. In time the

Knights Templar were drawn into this conflict; with the help of these highly trained warrior monks King John and his royal army were eventually defeated [English, 2011].

Apart from this voice-over, there is no mention of the Templars supporting either side in this war, as they remained neutral and provided manor houses to be used for negotiations between the two factions. In an article for *The Guardian online,* "*Ironclad*'s historical credentials are made of mulch" (2012), Alex Von Tunzelmann writes:

> The real John awarded the Templars special privileges, including exemption from all taxation and extraordinary protection of their property. In 1215, when this movie is set, the Templars let John use their headquarters, the New Temple in London, as a treasury. He stayed there often and stored the crown jewels and his top-secret documents there. Ironclad has this entirely wrong. Perhaps you can't have a medieval movie these days without a badass Templar.

Charles Dance's character Archbishop Langton, stating that the Templars helped in the creation of Magna Carta, shows a clear statement of the producer's wish to include the Knights Templar in this story. This begs the question, why did they want the Templars included as a symbol in rebellion against the established order?

At the end of the film, the quasi St George was only able to stop the tyrannical old establishment by teaming up with a European superpower, the French. Of course, the historical William Marshall was the one who won the victory that expelled the French forces from England, which suggests that by twisting the historical events to team the English hero with the French, the film has an underlying theme of a pro–European enterprise. Although as English has never commented upon any nationalist themes within his film, it is more than likely that the Templar hero's inclusion was true to Tunzelmann's implication that including a Templar in a medieval film helps with the marketing in the wake of the success of *The Da Vinci Code* and *Kingdom of Heaven*. The Knights Templar provides storytellers with a historical property ideal for remolding to fit the story's theme due to the suppression of a Templar authority in the early 14th century. The Templar popular culture phenomenon has further expanded and evolved due to its malleability, which is demonstrated by the ease in which *Ironclad* can absorb the Templar narrative within its film, offering a sense of historical authenticity to the viewer.

The final case study of the good Templar is *Arn: The Knight Templar* and *Arn: The Kingdom at the End of the Road.* The Arn series of films was, at the time, the most expensive Swedish production ever and according to *Variety*, "achieved the biggest opening ever for a Swedish pic," and in its first two days it took "160,310 admissions and a gross of 14,336,235 kroner

($2,240,000) from 207 prints, delivering a $10,821 screen average" (Reh-lin, 2007). The financial backing and success of a film depicting a national hero as a white Christian knight do not conform to Sweden's desire for a multicultural image. Erik Hedling explains the breakdown of funding in thirds; he states that the first third came from "Sweden's largest morning paper, Svensk Filmindustri…. Another third came from the commercial television channel TV4 … production company Film i Vast, and German film distributor Telepool. The last third came from Danmarks Radio (pub-lic Danish television), YLE (public Finnish television), ESP (Europa Sound Production), Norwegian TV 2, the Swedish Film Institute and the produc-tion company Dagsljus" (2008, p. 63). Hedling describes this production as a "Scandinavian-German-British co-production," noting the involvement of smaller co-production companies "British Molinare Studios and Arion Communications" (2008, p. 63). Such a collaboration indicates a pro–Euro-pean film using a traditionally nationalist trope of the knight.

It seems unusual that a pro-national medieval epic would have such a considerable investment let alone take $15,599,053 at the Swedish box office (Boxofficemojo.com). A.J Heinö describes the Swedish political climate as, "Comparative global value studies identify Sweden as one of the most individualist societies, while at the same time the Swedish political elite for several decades have been strongly anti-nationalist, embracing multicul-tural ideals instead" (2009, p. 298). Alternatively, *Arn: The Knight Templar* took significantly less in Denmark, the outright villains of the film; the box office takings were $1,971,834, which was a fraction of the money taken in Sweden.

Danish literary critic Bo Tao Michaëlis states that the author's aim for the novels was "to show that Sweden and the rest of Scandinavia is a prod-uct of the encounter with others and higher cultures, particularly Islam and Judaism" (forfatterweb, 2001). He describes author Guillou as a "left-ist" but is critical of the trilogy's themes, claiming, "the idea of a singular Norse development, the flower of the 'blond' Viking culture, is a danger-ous and romantic myth that can taste of Nazi theories of a Teutonic mas-ter race" (forfatterweb, 2001). This comparison with Nazism and the Order of the Teutonic Knights is almost parallel to Gwladys Fouché's criticisms of the film adaptations. In *The Guardian Online*, she writes, "Arn is try-ing to make a hero out of someone who wasn't…. Arn is a tolerant and multicultural-friendly crusader. He speaks fluent Arabic and quotes the Koran as he would the Bible. His first reflex upon seeing a Saracen is to defend him rather than slaughter him, and he becomes buddies with Sal-adin" (2008). Hedling explains that author Jan Guillou is "well known in Sweden for his strong pro–Palestinian and generally pro–Arabic senti-ments" (2008, p. 62). This would suggest that any comparisons drawn from the story's theme of forging a multicultural nation and perceived Teutonic Nazism connotations are unintentional by the author. Hedling cites from the 2007 edition's epilogue, writing, "already by the mid–1990s one could see that the big war—what we now label as the 'War on Terror'—was approaching…. Everywhere, Arabs and Muslims were depicted as demons. In precisely that way, the first Holy War, the medieval crusade to Palestine was initiated" (2008, p. 62). Guillou's desire for a positive portrayal of Arabic culture is evident in his hero's friendship with Saladin and his fluency in Arabic. Guillou expresses his aim to represent the Middle Eastern conflict in that epilogue. Hedling cites him, writing, "on our way towards the third millennium, the Holy War was to start again, as if we had learnt nothing from history. Thus, I have to write the story about how this war appeared when it was first fought" (2008, p. 62). Guillou's style of portraying the modern world through the past is transferred to the movie adaptation; in an interview for *Arn: The Complete Series* (2010) *DVD Feature 2*, when asked, "Don't you feel honoured when people say they love your work?" He replied, "They understand that the story is about the world today, our conflicts; but taking place 800 years back in time." With Guillou stating, "the story is about the world today" and his stated desire to address the current conflicts in the Middle East, then his creation of a multicultural national hero reflects his perception of a modern-day multicultural Sweden.

At the time of production, nationalism was a self-conscious issue in Sweden. Carly Elizabeth Schall cites Löfgren's article, writing, "The Swedish flag is enthusiastically waved at sporting events, but has come to be seen by many as a racist symbol in other contexts (Löfgren, 2007). Likewise, some have come to see singing the national anthem as a provocation to Sweden's non-ethnically Swedish population" (2014, p. 356). Given the film's comparisons between the Iraq War and the Crusades, it seems the opposite subject for a country that is "embracing multiculturalist ideals" (Heinö, 2009, p. 298) to have a national Crusader hero. Schall references the Larsmo article from Sweden's largest newspaper, *Dagens Nyheter* (2008), writing: "Swedes are a little ambivalent when it comes to nationalism. A study presented on the radio today revealed that only about a third of respondents wanted to celebrate a national day (in some way other than having the day off). Many see it as 'un–Swedish' to be a nationalist—a paradox worth considering" (2014, p. 363). Sweden's National Holiday is a relatively recent creation; Schall states, "Sweden's National Day is remarkably young, dating back only to 2005" (2014, p. 355). This new holiday was not about promoting an old Swedish order that would discriminate against the new multicultural Sweden; in fact; it was "an attempt to bring the state into the cultural processes of integration" (2014, p. 357). Schall describes the official narrative from the media coverage, writing: "This official meaning crystallized around (1) an affirmation of the need to have a national anchor in a global-izing world, and (2) a promotion of a progressive, diverse and multicultural Sweden" (2014, p. 362). If diversity and multiculturalism are what the Swed-ish elite wished to promote, then perhaps the Arn series were the ideal films to promote both "a national anchor" and a "diverse and multicultural Swe-den." As a result, Arn is only able to return to defend his homeland because of help from his friend Saladin. Arn's respect for Islam and his friendship with an Islamic hero would coincide with the two major aims of the Swed-ish national agenda, which is supported by Guillou's outspoken pro–Ara-bic sentiments and his desire to address the Middle Eastern conflict in his work. In an online article, "Templars Occupies Avenue," for Swedish news-paper Göteborgs-Posten, Swedish journalist Jonas Eek drew comparisons from the film to multiculturalism; he asked, "How to change our society? And how we respect the faith of others? Saladin and Arn were opponents on the battlefield, but they could still be met with respect for each other in conversation. How do we manage it today?" (Heyman, 2007). The film's positive depiction of Islam would be deemed welcome due to a supposed negative public opinion to the religion. Heinö writes, "Surveys on which religion Swedes 'like the most' places Islam in the bottom, distanced not only by Christianity but also by very peripheral religions in Sweden such as Judaism and Buddhism" (2009, p. 304). In *Arn: The Knight Templar* depict-ing a popular symbol of the Crusades working in friendship with an Islamic hero, the film meets both aims of Sweden's National Day.

Sweden's preference of individualism is also promoted by having Arn returning to his homeland to lead the defense against the Sverker clan, individualized by his white with a red cross Templar mantle. In hav-ing Arn individual to others in his homeland, this highlights the impor-tance an individual can make, and the Templar uniform is not to conform but to stand out. Heinö writes, "An individualist society is accordingly one which highly values the individual human being's free choice of identity" (2009, p. 301). In this way, having Arn, a Templar knight who is a friend to Saladin, can represent the celebration of multiculturalism associated with its National Day. Schall says the meanings of "National Day tend toward a definition of multiculturalism that is uniting, rather than dividing, setting the difference in the center of a Swedish national identity" (2014, p. 370). Although Guillou is known for his pro–Arabic sentiments, he "got the idea for the story of the Templar Arn Magnusson in 1995. The purpose of the books was to provide a balanced view of Islam" (Dagens Nyheter, 2007), which was ten years before Sweden's National Day was first celebrated. Although the themes of Arn do conform to the values of this national holi-day, this was not the original intent of Guillou's depiction for the multicul-tural Knights Templar hero. However, this use of the good Templar aspect of the narrative of the knight does conform to Sweden's modern-day multicultural identity. In the Arn series, the thematic Templar narrative has been used to create a multicultural hero in Arn. He is the opposite of the prejudiced extremist Templars depicted in *Ivanhoe* and *Kingdom of Heaven*.

The good Templar aspect is not entirely a new heroic character, despite only making his appearance on screen in 2007. He shares traits with medieval chivalry and shares the same look and character as his forebear The Redcrosse Knight. However, he is unique in that he is an individual, and as we have seen from the texts described, the Templar hero can stand for a positive message such as the value of inclusivity. The characteristics of the Templar hero are that he can be used as an agent to explore current issues from the safe distance of the past, and the hero represents the positive attributes of those current ideologies. Arn's friendship with Saladin promotes Sweden's multicultural ideology, and having Arn lead the defense of his homeland, standing out from the others dressed in his Templar garb, also underlines Sweden's emphasis on the importance of individualism. Arn is a symbol of Sweden's inclusive, multicultural nationalism, and by having a Templar hero, Arn can stand out from the rest to represent these ideals. *Ironclad* uses the lone figure of the Templar, dressed in white with a red cross to portray a quasi St George who fights to defend the rights of the English people. Like Arn, Marshall is able to stand for this theme of inclusion due to his symbolism as the lone hero, standing out from the rest by his Templar/St George outfit. The good Templar aspect of the Templar narrative of the knight is defined as a hero through the deployment of his martial skills, using them to defend himself or others, and stands as a symbol of tolerance and inclusion. Due to his iconic appearance, the good Templar knight stands apart and is easily recognizable from the other knights on screen.

Conclusion

The narrative of the knight is rooted in the warrior monk archetype of the Templar urtext and is the first part of the reoccurring Templar narrative in popular culture. This chapter has defined this narrative from the perspective of its two aspects: the bad Templar and the good Templar. Although the medieval historical genre typically personifies this part of the narrative, the requirement to split the narrative of the knight into two aspects shows the malleability of the Templar narrative. The emergence of the good knight aspect demonstrates how this phenomenon has evolved to create a polar opposite of characteristics despite mirroring Templar iconography exemplified in the case studies *Kingdom of Heaven* and *Arn: The*

Knight Templar. The first case draws on the villainous Templar established in the 19th-century works of Sir Walter Scott, depicting the Templar as a prejudiced extremist. However, the latter depicts the Templar protagonist as a paragon of virtue and multiculturalism that incorporates the characteristics of the 16th-century literary hero, The Redcrosse Knight.

With the fictional Templar stories set in a medieval historical setting, the Templars are depicted with a modicum of historical authenticity in that the depiction revolves around expectations from the Templar phenomenon in popular culture. The knightly prowess of the Templar is exemplified, while their monastic lifestyle is minimized in favor of highlighted acts of chivalric or unkept violence. The use of violence is one of the critical distinguishers between the good knight and the bad knight. This use of violence is exemplified in Ridley Scott's *Kingdom of Heaven*, where the Templars' violence is unjustifiable underlined by the amount of blood they spill in their acts compared to the recognition Balian's deeds receive from Saladin.

The iconic imagery of the Templars enables filmmakers to distinguish the Templars from other factions within the story. Ridley Scott uses the Templars to represent the negative associations of Western colonialism by imbuing his historical antagonists with the distinct Templar iconography. Therefore, they are the characters with all the criticisms and accusations labeled against the Western occupation. The Templars are in contrast to Balian, who has been distanced from those ideals and can stand as the undisputed hero knight of *Kingdom of Heaven*. In grouping the film's villains with the Knights Templar and dressing them with the iconic red cross, the audience can associate the Order as representing an extremist and a hateful ideology. This ideology is rejected by all the film's heroes, both Christian and Muslim.

Ridley Scott draws inspiration from Sir Walter Scott's villainous Templar de Bois-Guilbert, who like Guy, launches an unjustifiable attack on a member of another religion, whom Ivanhoe must protect. Sir Walter Scott's original version of the bad knight personified a negative incarnation of the Catholic Church. However, in Thorpe's picture, de Bois-Guilbert represents the oppression of the establishment and the perversion of justice represented in postwar America. These examples demonstrate the malleability of the Templar narrative. As the bad Templar knight can be used to represent society's negative traits and is a stand-in for the ugly side of history in current times, due to their iconic imagery and infamy they can be depicted as a nation unto themselves. *Kingdom of Heaven* and *Ivanhoe* both use this group to distance and demonstrate the worst parts of contemporary society, protecting the films' heroes and the filmmakers from being associated with such unfavorable circumstances.

Knights from the good Templar aspect champion inclusion and

tolerance, while Templars from the bad Templar aspect promote hatred and prejudice. Their actions distinguish the two aspects. They are defined by their use of martial skills and political influence; one will use the position to oppress the weak, while the good Templar knight uses his fighting prowess defensively and to protect the weak. *Ironclad* introduces the fictional Templar in the film by using his martial skills to protect an unarmed elderly priest. While the bad Templar knight shows extremist and prejudiced views, the good Templar introduced in Jan Guillou's 1998 novel *The Road to Jerusalem* has respect for other cultures and is depicted as a multicultural knight for a multicultural Sweden. The film adaptation of the novel introduces the good Templar knight using his martial skills to protect historic Islamic hero, Saladin. The Templar narrative of the knight must be analyzed using the two aspects as they are polar opposites that run parallel alongside each other but in contrasting directions. One is a symbol for the very worst in men through his oppressive force and represents the unattractiveness of single-minded extremism. These values are the opposite of the character of the good Templar knight, who stands in contrast to Sir Walter Scott's villainous Templar archetype; he still has nationalist connotations but for the benefit of an inclusive, wider society.

The narrative of the knight is the first part of my original concept of the thematic Templar narrative, and it is split into two aspects: highlighting how the Templar urtext has expanded and evolved with contrasting connotations. Presenting a singular Templar narrative would be an arduous task due to the varied manifestations of the infamous warrior monks; the lack of a singular representation extends from a lack of Templar authority following the Order's extinction in 1312. This malleability of the Templar phenomenon enables storytellers to present the Templar knight as both villain and hero as both become established archetypes, with each aspect serving a function in the story. The popularity and evolution of this narrative have resulted in the extension of the Templar urtext, as new texts include new traits for that character which can be incorporated by future texts that desire to depict the Templar narrative. This notion of malleability has resulted in the thematic Templar narrative reoccurring and evolving to expand further within popular culture. This malleability has expanded the Templar warrior monk archetype to create a series of contrasting Templar tropes. These new aspects of the narrative of the knight influence new texts, which reimagine and reinterpret to expand the Templar phenomenon in popular culture.

CHAPTER 2

Playing the Templar

Evolution Through Participatory Media

Chapter 1 defined the two aspects of the Templar narrative of the knight in popular culture using case studies from film and literature. This chapter will continue the analysis of the warrior monk archetype by examining how this part of the Templar urtext has expanded and evolved across transmedia platforms such as games and online fan films. These fan practices will be analyzed using the bad Templar and the good Templar aspects explored in Chapter 1 to ascertain how the Templar narrative has reoccurred and evolved, infusing narrative with participatory media. The chapter's case studies will be the first game of the *Assassin's Creed* franchise, *Assassin's Creed* (Ubisoft, 2007), massively multiplayer online game *The Secret World* (Funcom, 2012) and the fan film *Predator: Dark Ages* (Bushe, 2015). These new texts are worthy of attention as they demonstrate that the Templar narrative is not solely located in traditional media but has evolved alongside the same culture.

The case studies chosen for this chapter will demonstrate how my concept of the Templar urtext has further expanded through digital participation with the Templar narrative. In further analyzing the warrior monk archetype pillar of the Templar urtext, this chapter can examine how interaction with these different depictions of the Templar expand the Templar narrative in popular culture and further impact the Templar urtext. Due to its thematic malleability, fan participation also enables the Templar narrative to further evolve the previously established Templar aspects of the warrior monk archetype.

The methodology will include similar approaches to Chapter 1, such as the use of textual analysis of the case studies to understand the player and viewer experience. The chapter will also draw on interviews with producers and game reviewers to assess the producer's influences and intentions. However, this chapter will also use web ethnography of YouTube message boards to provide primary evidence to demonstrate how the players' experience has further expanded the Templar urtext.

The chapter draws from fandom studies to approach the transmedia qualities of the Templar urtext, such as the theories of Henry Jenkins's *Convergence Culture* (2006) and Paul Booth's *Game Play* (2015). These studies use the concept of paratextuality to study transmedia texts, which I will also apply to analyze the selected Templar case studies alongside concepts of play and participation. This approach will enable an understanding of how the interaction between the participant and the text influence the perception of the Knights Templar in popular culture and further expand the Templar urtext. After establishing the notions of play and participation, the next section will focus on Templar iconography. The Templar symbol of the red cross on a white background is not just synonymous with the warrior monk archetype but is also a vital visual cue to the Templar urtext. The chapter will address the iconographic connotations of both the bad and good Templar aspect depicted in high-concept Templar hero/villain costumes. This chapter will use academic studies of costume and cosplay to identify how costume influences the depiction of the Templar knight in video games and digital cosplay within MMOG *The Secret World*. This section draws from Paul Booth's case study of the now-defunct Polyvore fashion website in *Playing Fans* (2015) and Barbara Brownie and Danny Graydon's *The Superhero Costume* to determine how Templar iconography further expands the Templar urtext.

The short fan film *Predator: Dark Ages* is the chapter's final case study and provides the means to establish how participation with the Templar narrative expands the Templar urtext by creating new texts. The chapter uses Kurt Lancaster's book *Interacting with Babylon* 5 (2001) to support the case study analysis and determine the significance of performance in expanding the Templar urtext. To further examine the concept the section also draws from Will Brooker's *Using the Force* (2006) and Francesca Coppa's article "Women, *Star Trek*, and the Early Development of Fannish Vidding" (2008) to help bridge the gap between Lancaster's work on performance and support this chapter's attempt to define how fan videos further expand the Templar urtext. Ultimately, this chapter investigates how the Templar narrative moves beyond watching a film to also involve a physical engagement with the Templar mythos. In examining the experience of fans interacting with the Templar narrative of the knight through the acts of play and performance, this chapter ascertains how interaction enables further evolution of the Templar urtext.

Templar Paratexts

The Templars' legacy within popular culture has shifted them from a historical understanding and towards a mythical entity, which places them akin to other medieval mythical characters such as King Arthur and the Knights of the Round Table and Robin Hood. These medieval myths have been transferred across media platforms from literature to film and over to computer games, some acting as standalone games in their own right, such as the game *Robin Hood: Legend of Sherwood* (Spellbound Entertainment, 2002) or *King Arthur: The Role-Playing Wargame* (Neocore Games, 2009), games that incorporate common, popular culture traits associated with those mythical characters. The cover of the computer game *Robin Hood: Legend of Sherwood* provides an example of this, where an Errol Flynn-type character dressed in a green outfit and feathered cap, a trait that was omitted from the later incarnations of *Robin Hood: Prince of Thieves* (Reynolds, 1991) and *Robin Hood* (Scott, 2010). Richard Utz explains that the familiarity of medieval tropes created through new and old media is part of neomedievalism, explaining:

> Neomedieval texts no longer strive for authenticity of original manuscripts, castles, or cathedrals, but create pseudo-medieval worlds that playfully obliterate history and historical accuracy and replace history-based narratives with simulacra of the medieval, employing images that are neither an original nor the copy of an original, but altogether Neo [Utz, 2011, p. v].

Utz's argument is visible in *Robin Hood: Legend of Sherwood's* use of the "pseudo-neomedieval world" depicted in *The Adventures of Robin Hood* (Curtiz, 1938) in its use of the green tights, feathered cap and dexterous swashbuckling performance by Errol Flynn. This Robin Hood imagery is commonly associated with the English legend and is often used to depict the medieval icon in film and animation such as *Robin Hood: Men in Tights* (Brooks, 1993) or the animated movie *Shrek* (Adamson & Jenson, 2001). Kline adds to Utz's notion, writing, "Neomedieval games thus are marked by a double vision, looking toward medieval originals but through intermediate sources like Dungeons & Dragons, with little regard for medieval realities" (2014, p. 4). The notion of attempting to create a medieval reality through intermediate sources is seen through how the thematic Templar narrative of the knight has been included and expanded by film and literature. Films such as *Kingdom of Heaven* have drawn inspiration for their Templar figures from Sir Walter Scott's characters in *Ivanhoe*, instead of attempting to recreate the historical Order of the Knights Templar on screen.

Of course, not all of the neomedieval world computer games are standalone titles; often these film adaptations of medievalist creations release a computer game text of their own. For example, the films *Robin Hood: Prince of Thieves* and *King Arthur* (Fuqua, 2004) have both released computer games based on the film's medieval reality, which enables fans to enjoy this neomedieval world across a convergence of different texts and platforms. Jenkins defines this idea of convergence, writing, "By convergence, I mean the flow of content across multiple media platforms, the cooperation between multiple media industries and the migratory behaviour of media audiences who will go almost anywhere in search of the kinds of entertainment experiences they want" (2006, p. 2). Currently, out of the film texts analyzed in the previous chapter, it is only *Kingdom of Heaven* that ever planned to release a computer game adaptation. According to an article on Gamespot.com, a mobile phone game adaptation of the film was in development where players can take on the role of Orlando Bloom's character, Balian. In 2005, Avery Score posted a review of the early alpha build, stating, "In each of Kingdom of Heaven's 10 levels, you'll find huddled groups of Jerusalem's refugees. Your job is to escort them to safety. Unfortunately, the Saracens keep doing inconsiderate things, like launching volleys of fireballs and arrows at you." Although the review of the game did not offer a detailed insight into the game, it did suggest that the game was never officially released. At the end of the article, Score wrote, "It's often a challenge to deliver involving movie-licensed mobile games, and we're interested to see if the final version of KOH passes the test. Check back in early April for our full review" (2005). As there is no full review for the completed game on Gamespot.com, which along with the lack of other reviews for this game, it suggests that the *Kingdom of Heaven* mobile game was never released. This game, had it been released, would have provided great insight into how the Templar narrative of the knight would have been utilized in this mobile game adaptation. However, the review implies that it is the Saracens that are the enemy in this game, and it makes no mention of the Templars, who are the unquestionable villains of the film version. The game's premise suggests that it approached the Crusades' narrative from a different perspective than that of the film, having Saladin's forces as the villains instead of the Templars. The unreleased *Kingdom of Heaven* mobile game would have stood as a paratext of Scott's original film text, which Booth defines by citing Gerard Genette, stating, "the paratext exists at the 'threshold' of literature, between the 'inside and the outside of the book'" (2015, p. 5). Genette proposes that in regards to literature a paratext:

> comprises what one could call various thresholds: authorial and editorial (i.e., titles, insertions, dedications, epigraphs, prefaces and notes); media related (i.e., interviews with the author, official summaries) and private (i.e., correspondence, calculated or non-calculated disclosures), as well as those related to the

material means of production and reception, such as groupings, segments, etc. [1988, p. 63].

Booth summarizes the concept of the paratext with an example that a book cover "is both part of the book product, and yet substantially different from the content of the book" (2015, p. 5). Although referring to audio commentary and title sequences, Richard Burt states that paratextual elements are "a critical blind spot in medieval film studies" (2007, p. 220). Burt argues that paratextual analysis offers insights "into the way analogies drawn within medieval films between old and new media—book and film, for example— blur" (2007, p. 220). It is this notion of blurring between old and new media this chapter will be addressing through the concept of paratexts to the Templar narrative.

Like the characters of Robin Hood and King Arthur, the Templar phenomenon extends beyond film and literature. Therefore, an analysis of the Templars across different media formats is needed to examine the evolution of the Templar narrative, which is why this section of the chapter needs to address the notion of video games as paratext first. Booth cites Gray to establish the role of paratext within computer games; he writes, "Gray describes licensed video games—promotional games based on films or television series—as allowing players to enter cult worlds and 'explore them in ways that a film or television show often precludes, and/or that amplify the show's meanings and style'" (2015, p. 5). The process of producing content across multimedia formats is what Jenkins explores through the notion of convergence culture. Jenkins explains, "Convergence represents a cultural shift as consumers are encouraged to seek out new information and make connections among dispersed media content" (2006, p. 3). Fans can watch the films, read the books, play the games and are able to create their own texts through fan-generated content.

In studying transmedia convergence culture, Jenkins uses the *Matrix* franchise as a key text of study, an example that offers a framework for understanding the relationship within the Templar phenomenon across different formats of popular culture. Jenkins draws attention to the franchise's multimedia forms of consumption, noting that fans can visit the world by watching the films, playing the computer game and watching the animated short films. He argues:

Each franchise entry needs to be self-contained so you don't need to have seen the film to enjoy the game, and vice versa. Any given product is a point of entry into the franchise as a whole. Reading across the media sustains a depth of experience that motivates more consumption [2006, p. 96].

When examining paratexts, one must acknowledge how far this intellectual concept can go as paratexts ultimately produce paratexts of themselves, and video games certainly create their own paratexts; Booth addresses this concept of video game paratext within paratext. He cites Mia Consalvo, writing, "The paratexts she describes, including video games walk-through guides, cheats, and strategy books, have become essential elements themselves, and a diverse array of paratextual content" (2015, p. 5).

In citing Ian Peters, Booth determines, "paratexts can become as important as—or even more important than—the original text, especially given the commercial value of ancillary products surrounding media texts, such as video games" (2015, p. 6). Booth explains that video game paratexts further expand the source text, and using the video game paratexts of *The Hunger Games* as an example, Booth states, "These video games function as paratexts to further develop the world of Panem (name of the world in *The Hunger Games franchise*)" (2015, p. 135). This notion that the paratext of the video game further develops *The Hunger Games* franchise coincides with the Templar narrative's reoccurring and evolutionary qualities.

Computer games provide the ideal platform to examine the Templar narrative as video games offer consumers a different experience to cinema and literature, as computer games enable a digital engagement with the world of the Templar narrative. Klug and Schell highlight the possibility of engagement with the world of the text, explaining, "Virtual gaming worlds allow participants to experience a universe they may have only imagined" (2006, p. 94). Video games offer a different narrative than that of a film or book; the experience Klug and Schell describe involves participating with the text. Gray explains that there are different types of story narrative and cites Linda Hutcheon to explain:

> The process of adaption frequently moves a story across different modes, opening up new possibilities for both the storyteller(s) and the audiences. In particular she notes three modes of narratives: *telling*, as in novels, which immerse us "though imagination in a fictional world"; *showing*, as in plays and film, which immerse us "through the perception of the aural and the visual"; and participatory, as in video games, which immerse us "physically and kinesthetically" [2010, p. 192].

The participatory mode found in the Templar computer game texts explored in this chapter allows players to take on the roles of both aspects of the knight narrative—the good and the bad knight and explore the games' world of the medieval. When discussing video game adaptation, Gray explains, "it moves the story, its world, and its audience to a different narrative mode, wherein the audience can step into (parts of) the story world" (2010, p. 192). The first case study of the Templar narrative of the knight in a computer game is the worldwide success, *Assassin's Creed,* a game that features an open-world format where the player can visit the Holy Land and explore cities depicted in the Templar film texts. This type of open-world computer game enables players to explore the digital world at their discretion. This computer game open-world format is not unique to the *Assassin's Creed* game, as it features in the popular Simpson's game *Hit and Run*, which Gray uses as an example for how a video game paratext offers greater accessibility. He explains:

> The television show has created many locations, but has rarely shown how they connect. Playing the game, by contrast, allows one to walk, run, or drive between locations, thereby seeing, for instance, how to get from the Simpsons house to Cletus's farm, or what separates The Android's Dungeon and Krusty Studios [2010, p. 193].

This example provided by Gray demonstrates the experience players can have from exploring and interacting with the medieval open-world style of *Assassin's Creed*, enabling players to discover the geography of the journey from Acre to Jerusalem and obtain a deeper relationship with the story world of the fictionalized Crusades setting. Gray describes this style of gameplay as "'sandbox' style … through completing missions advances one through the game to new areas, one has the freedom—with scripted limits, of course—simply to wander the streets and talk to random characters" (2010, Gray). This "sandbox" style is a feature in *Assassin's Creed*, but it only presents the player with the appearance of an ability to freely roam the digital Holy Land as accessibility to areas of the city are barred from the player as more of the cities will be accessible to the player once they have completed the predetermined missions.

The game format of the second Templar case study, *The First Templar*, is in contrast to the style of *Assassin's Creed* in that the format is a more controlled, level-based system where the player must guide their Templar hero through each designated level, with most of the levels taking place in the medieval Holy Land. However, with both examples of Knights Templar-themed computer games, the story and visuals include a heavy emphasis on the player taking on the active role of the Templar knight or interacting with the Templar NPCs in the game. This kinetic interaction with the text's story sets these case studies apart from the passive visual interaction the audience has with the Templar films explored in Chapter 1.

Unlike *The Hunger Games* video games or the canceled *Kingdom of Heaven* mobile game, *Assassin's Creed* and *The First Templar* are original titles and not adaptations from film texts, which make their inclusion as paratexts problematic. To establish whether these games can exist as paratexts in their own right and be considered part of a broader Templar phenomenon, this chapter draws from Gray's argument to define the substance of a paratext. Gray does this by approaching Gerard Genette's theory that a paratext can exist without a text, he cites Genette, writing, "The paratext is only an assistant, only an accessory of the text. And if the text without its paratext is sometimes like an elephant without a mahout, a power disabled, the paratext is without its text is a mahout without an elephant, a silly show" (2015, p. 231). Gray disagrees with Genette's argument, first by criticizing his example as "offensive," and argues, "In positioning the text and paratext as existing in two distinct bodies, Genette precludes the possibility of the paratext being part of the text, much less therefore of it creating the text or even being part of the text" (2015, p. 231).

In a post on the website *Media Commons*, Gray uses the example of a trailer for the low-budget film *C Me Dance* (Robbins, 2009), a film he states he "will never see" (2015), to argue against Genette's ideas. Gray asserts, "as important as I think it is to study paratexts when what Barthes would call their accompanying 'work' is absent, I offer this as an example of how paratextuality is inseparable from the text. If the paratext means something—*anything*—it is part of the text" (2014). Gray claims, "a paratext is not simply the side of a text. Rather, paratexts do the work of texts and are functional parts of them…. Sometimes they do everything the rest of the text does; sometimes they are entrusted to conduct very particular tasks and to play very particular roles in the construction of the text" (2015, p. 232). It is with this approach that the Templar video games explored in this chapter are quantified as paratexts of the thematic Templar narrative within popular culture, as they are part of the evolving Templar phenomenon. There have been no other transmedia Templar studies, which is why analyzing the Templar computer games as paratexts provides an ideal approach for this original transmedia study of the Templar narrative.

This Templar narrative has been reoccurring for centuries and spread across different media formats from literature to film and now to computer games, which adapts and further cements the Templar archetypal roles within the aspects of the bad Templar and the good Templar. The games *Assassin's Creed and The First Templar* cannot exist outside the Templar phenomenon because they include the traits and iconography of the established Templar mythos. This concept coincides with Gray's argument, "we can't truly appreciate that meaning, nor paratexts' role in the construction of meaning in general if we see the paratext as removed from the text" (2014). The Templar video game takes the Templar narrative of the knight to the digital media environment; therefore, the next section explores how the thematic Templar narrative is equipped to create a participatory experience for players and how these computer game texts further add to and evolve the Templar phenomenon within popular culture.

Digital Participation

The *Assassin's Creed* game series as of 2014, according to IGN UK, "exceeded sales of 73 million" (Seibert, 2014) and included nine major games across multiple platforms. The majority of these games allow the player to take on the role of Desmond Miles in the modern world and his Assassin ancestors in the past. This chapter focuses on the original *Assassin's Creed* game due to its setting in the Third Crusade (1189–1192). It is relatively close to the settings of *Kingdom of Heaven* and *Arn: The Knight Templar*, which depict Saladin's conquest of Jerusalem in 1187. This game, however, is the most successful Templar-themed computer game and is the first mainstream game to take the archetypal Templar knight to this new media format. The player takes on the role of the Assassin, Altaïr Ibn-La'Ahad, whose goal is to stop the Knights Templar from finding a powerful ancient artifact. Although set in the Holy Land in the year 1191, the game takes place from within the mind of a present-day man, Desmond. The player experiences the memories of Desmond's ancestor and plays as Altaïr Ibn-La'Ahad, a member of the Assassins. From within the mind of Desmond, the player battles the Templars for possession of the mystical Apple of Eden. The game depicts the Knights Templar as the outright villains; in fact, the game encourages players to kill all the Templars by having unlockable achievement points for killing them all. According to the website Xboxachievements.com, "Throughout the game there are 60 Templars and the majority of them lay within the kingdom. All you need to do is kill every single one of them." Even though this game text is the start of what will be its own franchise, it is adhering to the bad Templar aspect established in literature, and *Assassin's Creed* further demonstrates the malleability of the Templar narrative in that it is capable of migrating across various media formats.

Although the game is set during the Third Crusade, the player does not directly participate in the conflict as Altaïr does not work for either of the two armies. The significance of not being part of these factions is addressed with *Assassin's Creed* Creative Director Patrice Desilets and Producer Jade Raymond for *The Guardian* in 2007. When interviewer Stuart asked the creative director, "How do you present all this in the game without taking sides?" Desilets replied, "Well you start by choosing a third party—this is what the assassins are, they're the third faction in that war" (Stuart, 2007). This interview demonstrates that the game designers for *Assassin's Creed* went one step further than having a third-party villain like *Kingdom of Heaven* but had two other factions to act as hero and villain, the Assassins and the Templars. To ascertain the creative reasoning behind the game's focus on two new rival factions, we can turn to Elizabeth Buzay and

Emmanuel Buzay's critique of neomedievalism in *Assassin's Creed*, who cite from Raymond's interview, stating:

> Knowing that our subject is controversial by nature we have dealt with religion as a purely historical background element.... We have ... worked with cultural experts throughout production to make sure that we treat sensitive topics with respect.... In *Assassin's Creed*, Crusaders (and the Saracens) are not the Assassins' true enemy. War is—as are those who exploit it [2015, p. 123].

The people that exploit war in the game are the Order of the Knights Templar, whose grand master, Robert de Sablé, is referred to by Altaïr as "their greatest enemy" (Ubisoft, 2007). In the game, the Templars are the antagonists to the Assassins, who are spreading their influence throughout the Holy Land through corruption and violence to the detriment of both Christians and Muslims. It is only the Assassins that can halt the Templars' ultimate plan to gain dominance using the mind control power of an ancient artifact. In the same way as *Kingdom of Heaven*, the Templars are used as the enemy of both the Christians and the Muslims, further demonstrating how the Templar narrative of the knight has further evolved to be part of a major computer game.

Like with Scott's usage of the bad Templar, *Assassin's Creed* uses the Templar narrative as a means to maintain a stance of political neutrality. In an interview for xboxgazette.com; Jade Raymond demonstrates this desire for neutrality, stating, "we obviously did not make this game with a political agenda. First and foremost, our goal is to provide a new type of entertainment experience based on crowd gameplay and new levels of interaction with a living game environment" (Max73, 2006). In creating these two factions, the game designers were able to remain neutral by not depicting the Crusaders or Saracens as heroes or villains and therefore not alienate a potentially larger market audience. Buzay and Buzay observe, "One of the striking features at the beginning of *Assassin's Creed* is that the game opens with the statement: 'The game was developed by a multicultural team of various faiths and beliefs'" (2015, p. 123). The game's producers' desire to remain impartial is clear, but what is significant is the Templars' usefulness to provide authors and producers with an ample method to maintain an appearance of neutrality. As the historical Order of the Templars was eradicated in the 14th century and without an overarching authority, the Templars provide an ideal body for appointing unpleasant and evil deeds—a method used by Sir Walter Scott and Ridley Scott.

Unlike previous Templar villain incarnations in fiction, the Templars in *Assassin's Creed* have members of the organization who are Crusaders and Saracens, which break away from the conventional bad colonialist trope depicted in *Kingdom of Heaven*. The diversity of Templar membership is revealed in a conversation between Altaïr and another assassin, Malik Al-Sayf. Malik exclaims, "Crusaders and Saracens working together?" Altaïr replies, "They are none of these things, but something else; Templars" (Ubisoft, 2007). Confused, Malik states, "The Templars are a part of the Crusader Army." So Altaïr confirms, "Or so they would like King Richard to believe." So not only does *Assassin's Creed* use separate factions for the game designers to maintain a claim of neutrality, but it also breaks away from the pre-established racial prejudice trope featured in the bad Templar aspect. Instead, *Assassin's Creed* depicts the Templars as a multiracial organization who all work together to achieve the Templars' ultimate goal of world domination. This depiction is a clear contrast to the villainous Templar Guy de Lusignan from *Kingdom of Heaven*, who openly flaunts his hatred of the Saracens, or *Ivanhoe's* de Bois-Guilbert's discrimination against the Jewish characters.

The main objective for *Assassin's Creed's* protagonist Altaïr is assassinating nine men, which the game is structured around. These nine targets are later revealed to be all Templars, some of whom are based on real historical figures. The secret Crusader Templars that the player must kill include Garnier de Nablus, grand master of the Knights Hospitaller; Sibrand, a German Crusader, founder of the Teutonic Order; William V, Marquess of Montferrat, Regent of Acre. The secret Saracen Templars were Ibn Jubayr, a traveler and poet, who in the game was Damascus's chief scholar; Rashid ad-Din Sinan, who is the leader of the Assassins. Using characters based on real people as the secret Templars gives the game a sense of reality in an otherwise science fantasy realm and cements the game in the historical time frame. This intention is alluded to by Buzay and Buzay, who cite the artistic director, Raphaël Lacoste, stating, "To best portray the Third Crusade, the developers were inspired by both films and history books in an attempt to 'remain as close as possible to the historical reality'" (2015, p. 118). This statement from Lacoste showcases the developer's notion that using real people as antagonists creates a sense of reality and historical authenticity for the gaming experience but while also maintaining the developers' desired appearance of neutrality. Recreating historical figures in Templar garb was a precedent set by *Kingdom of Heaven*. The film depicted the King of Jerusalem, Guy de Lusignan, and the former Prince of Antioch, Raynald de Châtillon, as Knights Templar, which they were not (see Chapter 1 for details).

Apart from the many sequels that followed the success of the original *Assassin's Creed* game, the next standalone, action-adventure, Templar-themed computer game was *The First Templar* (2011), published by Kalypso Media. *The First Templar* offers players the chance to take on the role of Templar knight Celian on his quest to find the Holy Grail. Given that the game's medieval setting is mostly in the Holy Land, the game's previews drew comparisons to *Assassin's Creed*. The comment section of a game trailer uploaded to YouTube by Zeitgeist Game Review in August 2010 demonstrates these comparisons in the vocal and often negative comparisons drawn between *The First Templar* and *Assassin's Creed* franchise. Many of the posts highlight the viewers' disapproval of a game appearing to copy *Assassin's Creed*; for example, Misa Pheonix (2011) posts, "wannabe assasins [*sic*] creed lol" and Jay Defon (2011) "to me this looks like a crappy assissins [*sic*] creed copy." It is plausible that a comparison to the hugely popular *Assassin's Creed* was intentional by the game's publishers, as one of the early shots in the trailer is of the docks in Acre, which look similar to the same location depicted in *Assassin's Creed*. One poster commented on the location similarity, writing, "OK so…. It's my opinion only but that city from 1:06–1:14 looks completely like Damascus from Assassin's Creed?" (Makiturha, 2012). Although the commenter did not see the similarity between both games' Acre, Damascus is still one of the major cities in the original *Assassin's Creed* game and a visually similar setting to Acre. These similarities of pre-established tropes create a sense of familiarity that markets the Templar-themed game as a new text, which is part of the continual evolution of the Templar narrative.

One of the main causes for complaint from *Assassin's Creed* fans in the trailer is a shot from a cut scene of a Templar knight diving off a tall building in the same fashion as Altaïr's leap of faith, which is a common feature in *Assassin's Creed*. Mahmoud Zain (2013) posted, "copying assassins creed in the jump !!"; while LordArcherdon (2011) posted, "It looks like an Assassin's creed reverse-parody sort of thing, right down to the leaop [*sic*] of faith at the end," which implies how iconic to *Assassin's Creed* players that leap actually is. A more levelheaded post from reggiardito (2011) states, "Man, it has nothing to do with AC, but yet still i can't see the title withouth [*sic*] remembering it," this post suggests that in regards to gaming the Knights Templar have become synonymous with *Assassin's Creed*. The apparent similarity identified within *The First Templar* trailer indicated that the more recent game had incorporated immediately recognizable tropes and iconography from the Ubisoft franchise. The trailer demonstrates that the game publishers want to profit from a sense of familiarity with gamers.

Game designer Nikola Ikonomov, though, makes no direct mention of *Assassin's Creed* as an influence in an interview on GamingNexus.com. In the 2010 interview with Charles Husemann, Ikonomov explains, "Because I'm a movie freak, I'll tell you some of the flicks that inspired our team. First on the list is, not surprisingly, Indiana Jones because it defines adventure like no other" (Husemann, May 2010). The next influence he explains is "Ridley Scott, a visual genius, gave us ideas for the representation of the times of the Crusades with his Kingdom of Heaven and the more recent Robin Hood" (Husemann, May 2010). It is implausible to entertain the idea that a game developer would be unaware of a game franchise as popular as *Assassin's Creed*, and it is likely that he simply does not want to claim direct influence from the game. Ikonomov does state, though, "Talking about inspiration, we considered everything that is cool in pop culture. We drew ideas from widely different sources and mediums to create something unique: comic books, art, historical fiction novels, and cult movies" (Husemann, May 2010). So without mentioning inspiration from other games, it is highly likely that *Assassin's Creed* came under the inspiration from "popular culture" (Husemann, May 2010).

Besides the setting and leap of faith, more traits from *Assassin's Creed* appear in the trailer, such as stealth kills and the main protagonist's imagery, depicted as a white, hooded warrior. HoneyReno (2012) highlights this in their post, writing, "Is it just me or does it look like the Templar is doing some instant kill moves from Assassins' Creed." However, the bad Templar aspect of the Templar narrative of the knight's inclusion in *Assassin's Creed* is also hotly debated in the comments section of the trailer uploaded by Zeitgeist Games. LordArcherdon (2011) posts, "PERHAPS IT'S EVIL TEMPLAR PROPAGANDA?" while TubeSakis (2011) jokingly posts, "hey arent Templars the bad guys..? oops thats from another game ^^". The trailer also uploaded to YouTube by Gamerspawn demonstrated similar notions around the depiction of Templar villainy. JewishGun (2012) posted, "I loved Assassin's creed because in that game you kill the Bad guys. in [*sic*] 'The First Templar' you are the bad guy." While Sandro Del Rosario (2012) demonstrates an affinity to Ubisoft's villainous Templar identity, posting, "This game is actually made by templars who want to portray themselves as good because of assassins creed. They trying to hide the truth from us by creating this 'templars are good' propaganda campaign. Its [*sic*] not working. The assassins are winning." The misunderstanding of the Templars as an intellectual property shown in the comments of the trailer for *The First Templar* is important because it demonstrates the malleability of the Templar narrative. Due to *Assassin's Creed's* popularity, the Templar phenomenon has been introduced to gamers under the ownership of Ubisoft. This association demonstrates that reoccurrence and evolution of the narrative are, in part, due to the lack of authority around the Templars' legacy and the prevalence of myths and false depictions in popular culture. The Templar narrative of the knight can be used as a recognizable trope to give an immediate understanding of the text's setting (i.e., the Crusades). However, it also offers flexibility to the text's producers who can include and alter the established aspects of the good and bad Templar knight that best meet their creation's thematic desires.

The familiarity of the Templar narrative in popular culture enables the Templar phenomenon to transcend media formats. The Templar-themed literature, film and computer games are linked together by the inclusion of pre-established Templar iconography and archetypal tropes that act as the green tights motif does for Robin Hood. The Templar texts throw back to one another, adding and changing to the reoccurring Templar narrative. This sense of familiarity within the pre-established aspects, alongside the creation of new Templar traits, further evolves the Templar narrative into a new marketable product that still adheres to the popular understanding of what the Knights Templar stood for. Based on the inclusion of visual tropes from *Assassin's Creed* and the shared notion among the YouTube trailer commenters, *The First Templar* promotes itself by drawing upon the iconography and Templar aesthetics featured within the popular *Assassin's Creed*, a franchise that draws from the villainous Templar aspect of the knight narrative featured in 19th-century *Ivanhoe* and the 21st-century *Kingdom of Heaven*.

Play

Templar enthusiasts can never truly experience the medieval world without traveling back in time, but through playing video games, fans can interact with a digital version of how that world might have been. Playing these medievalist reproduction video games allows players to physically interact with an environment that before could only be read about or viewed on-screen. However, as Klug and Schell explain, the purpose of playing games is "rather than escape, as they do when they read a novel or when they watch a movie, games allow players to become actively involved in the world they escape into" (2006, p. 92). In his study of board game culture, Booth argues that the paratextual game enables players to "push against the boundaries of the original text" (2015, p. 48) instead of watching the original text and being "part of a bounded franchise" (2015, p. 48). Booth cites Silverstone, writing, "play enables the exploration of that tissue boundary between fantasy and reality, between the real and imagined" (2015, p. 48). This act of play with the environment of the game enables fans and players to participate directly with the original text, and "gaming worlds allow participants to experience a universe they may have only imagined" (Klug & Schell, 2006, p. 94).

This section examines the concept of play and how play enables interaction with the thematic Templar narrative. It also explores how the inclusion of the Templar narrative of the knight influences the participatory play of both the avatar that the player controls, as well as the non-playable characters created by the game's producer. The preconceptions of the Order of the Knights Templar, established by the perception of the Templar phenomenon in popular culture, coincides with how the player relates to the game's digital environment. In *Assassin's Creed,* the antagonists are members of the Templar Order, and then the act of playing advances the awareness of the villainous aspect of the Templar narrative. This villainous association was demonstrated in the confusion of playing a Templar shown in examples of the previous section. This notion of how digital gaming stimulates the players' perception of the historical Templar Order is supported by Crawford and Rutter's argument, "new media technologies, such as the Internet and digital gaming, contribute to contemporary mediascapes, providing resources individuals draw on in their everyday lives" (2007, p. 276). This argument suggests that it is how the player associates with the digital avatar that manifests in how the player interacts with the digital reality of the game. This notion of the player identifying and affecting interaction with the game is explained by Nicolle Lamerichs, who states, "a player establishes his or her own identity while interacting with a game and its avatar. This interaction also shapes our interpretation of the fictional material" (2011, p. 11). It is players identifying with the protagonist avatar and interacting with the digital environment of the game, which for *Assassin's Creed* further embeds the villainous Templar aspect.

As explained earlier in the chapter, physically participating within the digital Templar environment allows a deeper engagement with the fictional Templar world. However, for the game to offer this interactive Templar experience, it must not deviate too far from the conceptional Templar tropes established in popular culture or risk losing the game's sense of authenticity. In his study of franchise board game tie-ins, Booth addresses that although play allows the stretching of the boundaries, the game also needs to adhere to the original. He explains, "there must be a certain level of adherence to an original text and at the same time a divergence from that original text in order to create a unique gaming experience"(2015, p. 53). For a franchise game to offer a unique experience the player must be able to push beyond the confines of the consumable text's narrative yet remain true to the essence of the established franchise world, meaning that the popular Templar text must be perceived as authentic.

These tie-in games, according to Booth, need to find "a 'happy medium' … between the authorial intent of the original text and the originality of the players" (2015, p. 53). The Templar video game allows the player to explore the neomedieval world, which should remain truthful to crucial expectations of the Templar narrative such as iconography, setting and story role to maintain its appearance of authenticity. Maintaining a sense of Templar authenticity is less problematic for producers as the Templar narrative offers several interchangeable thematic aspects (see Chapter 3 for the quest of the knight and the quest to follow in the Templars' footsteps). This contrast is due to the malleability of the Templar legacy caused by a lack of authorship, which is why a game where the Templars are heroes can be perceived as a copy of a game where the Templars are the game's outright villains.

The participatory act of play allows players to interact with a Templar environment that they have previously only been able to view passively; this interaction with a digital world coincides with Huizinga's concept of a "magic circle," a concept that Jones links to play by explaining, "play sets its own boundaries and rules inside what he famously calls a 'magic circle,' drawn around themselves by exclusive social groups, those in the game" (2008, p. 14). For computer games, the magic circle would be the parameters of the digital game itself, but for play in general Jones defines it as a "socially collaborative, cultural construct that affects and is affected by material reality" (2008, p. 15). Jones explains the intrinsic connection between the designed space and the act of play in that the space facilitates the act. Jones explains:

> the delineated space of any game is necessarily a social convention. That makes it very much part of the real world. Players come together and agree to stay inside of the circle, as it were, in so far as they remain players, abiding by the rules and working toward the objectives of the game [2008, p. 15].

The concept of play outlined by Booth and Jones is comparable to the creation of the digital play space, but for the digital game, the rules of the game are more restrictive as these limits cannot be broken if players want to play the computer game. Rules and limitations are vital for all games to dictate player interaction. McAllister explains, "The decisions made concerning the limitations of interactivity directly impinge upon a game's 'appeal' and 'gameness' and carry signs of how game developers have conceived of their audience" (2004, p. 36). Combining the approach to determine the concept of play within physical games and digital games runs parallel to the role rules have in maintaining the act of play within the designated space. Juul explains that the common attribute of all games (both physical and digital) is "upholding of the rules, the determination of what moves and actions are permissible and what they will lead to" (2011, p. 48). Jesper Juul argues, "Upholding the rules is an actuality provided by human beings," which does not limit the concept to one medium but encompasses board games, card games, video games and sports. And it is this similarity of convention that enables the "adaption of board games to computers ... possible due to the fact that computers are capable of performing the operations defined in the rules of the games" (Juul, 2011, p. 48). Of course, the interaction levels of a video game such as *Assassin's Creed* are significantly more immersive than a board game, but it is the correspondence of designated play space and abidance of rules that makes the previously mentioned notions of physical gameplay and computer gameplay applicable. This immersive experience enabled the player to participate with the Templar narrative and to expand perception of the Templar phenomenon through digitally interacting with the historical period of the Crusades.

The importance of a designated space in play is addressed by Booth's research into paratextual board games, where he explains, "Paratextual board games like LOTR and The Complete Trilogy reflect this two-fold structure: there is the space of the game itself (the board, the table, the pieces) and space of the cult narrative world, the place of middle earth" (2015, p. 48). Booth adds, "to play Lord of the Rings is to push against those boundaries" (2015, p. 48). For the Templar video games, there is the space of the computer game as well as the connotations associated with the Order of the Knights Templar within the Templar urtext. The digital boundaries of the game are the game's limits (i.e., where the player can physically venture as well as the challenges set for the player). The second barrier type is the cultural barriers of the established Templar phenomenon, which further embed the established Templar narratives or facilitates the evolution of the perceptions of the historic order within popular culture.

The adherence to rules is paramount to continue the participation, as to remain playing players must abide by the rules of the game, and it is through the structure of the designated play space that play is possible. For digital games such as *Assassin's Creed*, these rules are enforced for the player by the game's design as straying from them is either impossible or stops the play. In his examination of franchise tie-in board games, Booth notes the importance of adhering to the rules of the text's original narrative and the game rules within these tie-in board games, noting:

> for paratextual board games, the rules of the game are developed in conjunction with another set of rules: the rules surrounding the cult world upon which the game is based. Every fictional cult world has its own rules that determine such factors as the inhabitants, character relationships, fictional cultures, natural laws and history of the world [2015, p. 22].

For Templar-themed computer games, the rules of the game are those that are designed by the game's producers. They act as both limiters and enablers as they create the text that players can interact with but also set the boundaries for the edge of the designated playing space. The other rules, what Booth would define as "the fictional cult world" (2015, p. 22) in the case of the Templar computer games is the thematic Templar narrative, which has its own set of rules by way of keeping with the archetypal Templar that has been established in popular culture texts dating back as early as the 19th century. For board games though, Booth states, "rules control both the way games are played, and the way cult texts are perceived, so too do rules underline the way that media technologies are used and understood" (2015, p. 23). The video game can, to an extent, control how the player plays the game in both the limits of the digital world (i.e., where the player can go) and by forcing players to adhere to protagonist characteristics.

Although the computer game *Assassin's Creed* features the Templars as the villainous antagonists of the game, it does not include the bad Templar aspect convention of adhering to a racist ideology. The bad Templar's adherence to a racist ideology was depicted in *Kingdom of Heaven* and *Ivanhoe*. It is not featured within the *Assassin's Creed* Templar villain archetype as the game's version of the Templar consists of both Saracen and Crusader members. However, the game does feature the other key traits of the bad Templar aspect, including unjustified violence and disdain of religion. Chapter 1 established how violence is used in the medieval genre as a way of designating the heroic knight from the villainous knight. However, the computer game *Assassin's Creed* depicts its hero as an assassin, a character who leaves a trail of bodies behind him while seeking his goal, but the playable protagonist is still portrayed as a heroic character, as befits the hero's justifiable use of violence.

The Assassin's goodness is established early in the game by explaining to the player in a cut scene that the Assassins must follow a creed, which is a philosophy for order members' code of conduct. The creed itself is three tenets: "Stay your blade from the flesh of the innocent; hide in plain sight; never compromise the brotherhood" (Ubisoft, 2007). It is the first tenet that demonstrates the brotherhoods' morality; the other two do not indicate moral values as they are more ambiguous parts of their ideology. Abiding by the first tenet is forced upon the player because if the player accidentally or deliberately kills a civilian, then his health bar is reduced, and eventually he will be "Desynchronised" and the "memory" will start over as if the character was killed. The game also justifies the killing of the city guard, as they abuse their position and assault the civilians, who need Altaïr to save them from the corrupt guards. To explain the role of violence in depicting heroic knights, Elliott states, "the raw aggression which may well have brought knighthood into existence had to be pared down for the big screen, by the use of vengeance themes to justify them, and by increasing the delay between action and retaliation" (2011, p. 81). Elliott's notion applies to Altaïr's use of violence against the villainous guards, justifying his actions as killing them is an act of vengeance for the citizens, not senseless murder, which is associated with the computer game's villainous Templar characters.

The game further underlines Altaïr's goodness in attributing his Templar enemies with the traits of needless violence, murder and cruelty, traits featured within the bad Templar aspect of the knight narrative. This method of showcasing Altaïr's morality is by the terrible conduct of the first of Templar targets: Tamir, a black-market trader who brutally stabs a merchant to death because he asks for more time to fill an order of weapons. A similar depiction of terrible actions is carried out by secret Templar, Garnier de Nablus, the grand master of the Knights Hospitaller (which was its own international religious order of knights) who carries out cruel experiments on unwilling patients in the Acre hospital. Before the player can assassinate Garnier de Nablus, the player must watch as a prisoner/patient who tried to escape is brought before the grand master and has his legs broken by Hospitaller guards on Garnier de Nablus's orders. Seeing how Garnier treats his "patients" justifies the player's assassination mission as this cruel man needed stopping, and the following violence carried out by the player is a justified necessity.

Unsurprisingly, *Assassin's Creed* carries forward traits of the bad Templar in the Film *Kingdom of Heaven* when the game's producer openly declared the influence of Ridley Scott's film on the *Assassin's Creed* game. Buzay and Buzay cite game producer Jade Raymond, writing that the developers focused on the "epic feeling" of popular movies like *Braveheart* or *Kingdom of Heaven*, saying that this is what "we are trying to achieve in Assassin's Creed" (2015, p. 117). "Epic feeling" is a very loose term which could be attached to a wide range of specifics, such as scale or notions of heroism, including concepts such as good versus evil. Buzay and Buzay believe that Raymond is discussing the game's narrative, writing, "If Assassin's Creed is viewed as a transhistorical epic narrative set in a particular time period, then players can relate this type of narrative to the those of the Middle Ages" (2015, p. 117). The narrative of *Assassin's Creed*, *Kingdom of Heaven* and the popular film *Braveheart* adhere to that story convention of good versus evil and notions of justified violence to distance the actions of the hero from the actions of the villain. The violent evil knight is a common trope within medieval fiction and coincides with Raymond's comment of the game taking influence from *Kingdom of Heaven*. Of course, this does not necessarily mean that this trope was purposely attached to the Templars as part of the Order's established trait of the bad Templar's prone to violence but simply because it is a proven, successful convention of medieval storytelling.

One major feature of the bad Templar aspect of the knight narrative that *Assassin's Creed* shares with *Kingdom of Heaven* is the Templars' apparent contempt for religion. The previous chapter explored how the Templars' Christian faith was depicted within *Kingdom of Heaven* and established that Ridley Scott's Templars openly mocked their own supposed religion. Sibrand, one of Altaïr's targets, demonstrates this open mockery of the Christian faith when this secret Templar and founder of the Teutonic Knights attacks a Christian priest in front of a large crowd, whom he accuses of being an Assassin. However, the real Assassin, Altaïr, is standing in the crowd watching the paranoid Templar accuse a conceivably innocent man. Sibrand openly mocks the priest, declaring, "If you truly are a man of God then surely the creator will provide for you. Let him stay my hand" (Ubisoft, 2007). He then kills the helpless man with his sword. This scene serves two functions: the first being to justify Altaïr's assassination of the man by demonstrating Sibrand's violent exploitation of the helpless but also to portray to the player that the Templars are not Christians.

Sibrand's and the Templar's atheism is further established when Altaïr asks him what awaits him in the afterlife; he replies, "Nothing, nothing waits and that is what I fear." Altaïr asks, "You don't believe?" and Sibrand replies, "How could I given what I know, what I've seen. Our treasure was the proof" (Ubisoft, 2007). Whereas *Kingdom of Heaven* depicts the Templars' open disdain for Christianity, *Assassin's Creed* removes religion altogether by having the Templars as both Crusaders and Saracens who are all atheists. Buzay and Buzay's notion that the "neutrality which Ubisoft's developers vaunt" is further demonstrated by removing the villainous Templar from Christianity and making both Saracen and Crusaders part of the Order of the Knights Templar.

In both Templar games, *Assassin's Creed* and *The First Templar,* there is a familiarity with the established Templar archetypes. These also add elements of control to the player's performance, such as the killing of evil Templars in *Assassin's Creed* or protecting the innocent in *The First Templar.* This reoccurrence of established Templar traits further embeds the Templar narrative within popular culture, despite how removed the fictional Templar is from reality. This idea of creating associations through reoccurrence is explained by Lancaster, who cites Umberto Eco, writing, "The recycling of archetypes ends up creating an 'intense emotion accompanied by the vague feeling of déjà vu that everybody yearns to see again'" (2001, p. 45). This sense of emotion and déjà vu can be seen depicted in the posts on the trailer for *The First Templar*; for example, a posted comment on the trailer uploaded by Zeitgeist Game reads, "templars rule assasins [*sic*] will die GOD WILLS IT!!!" (antec12gtx260, 2011). This post highlights the déjà vu and emotion in the poster's acknowledgment of the deep hatred of the Templars and Assassins from *Assassin's Creed*, which also includes the battle cry of Templars from the film *Kingdom of Heaven.* The comment showcases how the Templar phenomenon has evolved and expanded through three separate texts to create a perception of the Templars which shows little trace of the historical order of knights. The inclusion of separate Templar texts, such as aligning the heroic Templar with the battle cry of Ridley Scott's villainous Templar, further underlines the malleability of the reoccurring Templar narrative.

Despite expressing a similarity in marketing, *The First Templar* game incorporates different traits of the Templar narrative of the knight to that of *Assassin's Creed*. *The First Templar* embraces the good Templar aspect of the Templar narrative, incorporating the themes of chivalry and justified violence explored in Chapter 1. For this level-based game, combat in the game is centered on self-defense and protection of the innocent, while *Assassin's Creed* depicts its Templars oppressing the general populace with cruel acts of violence. These games' use of violence, justified or not, instructs the player in how to control the game's protagonist, being forced to fight off attackers as in *The First Templar* or justifying the killing of evil Templars. The game imposes a playing style upon the players which keeps the desired narrative of the game intact. Therefore, this limiting of player action enables the game to adhere to the overarching themes, which for the Templar-themed games would be adhering to perceptions in popular culture of the Templar phenomenon. Limiting the players' actions to control the narrative is not only key to digital games, but Booth also explains, regarding board games, "by giving players fewer choices, the game locks a particular reading of the narrative into place, closing off players interpretation" (2015, p. 141). By limiting the player actions, the Templar-themed computer games lock the role of the Templar into the archetypal character aspects explored in Chapter 1, the good Templar and bad Templar. *Assassin's Creed* and *The First Templar's* adherence to the thematic Templar narrative of the knight controls how the player plays the game and participates in the digital neomedieval world; essentially the good Templar fights the villains, and the villainous Templar must be fought.

The depiction of the Templars' relationship with religion offers an insight into how the game's designer controls the player's actions. The villainous Templars in *Assassin's Creed* are portrayed as an atheist organization who openly mock the Christian faith, while *The First Templar* incorporates the Templars' monasticism into the mechanics of the game through the playable character's act of prayer. In *The First Templar*, the Templar hero character can heal himself (restore the player's health bar) by using the prayer ability, which takes the form of Templar playable character Celian, kneeling to pray by resting his head upon his sword hilt, which symbolizes a cross. This act of prayer is reminiscent of the stance Arn took when he prayed after battle in the film, *Arn: The Knight Templar*. With the game incorporating a similar motif of prayer in battle, the game is able to invoke the trait of piety associated with the archetype of the chivalrous knight in contrast to the atheist Templar featured in *Assassin's Creed*. *The First Templar's* inclusion of associate traits of the Templar's monastic identity through the game's character healing ability demonstrates the limitations of the game as it fixes a narrative in place. In this case, it would be the limits of the game, forcing the player to become a pious Templar knight, which further embeds the good Templar aspect of narrative into popular culture. These limits support Eco's previously mentioned notion that the reoccurrence of traits creates stronger connotative associations.

Although, through the act of play, players can interact with the thematic Templar narrative of the knight, players are still limited in their experience through the designated play space assigned to the game. This space is not limited to the digital environment created but also the sets of rules that the act of play must adhere to. The rules include both the rules of the game and the conventions of the reoccurring Templar narrative of the knight. In both games, the hero Templar and villainous Templar adhere to the pre-established conventions associated with the Templar narrative by controlling how the player interacts with the digital recreation of the medievalist Templar world. This control is seen in how the Templar hero's healing ability through prayer invokes the widely marketed concept of the Templar hero praying after a battle, which was an image prominent in the films *Arn: The Knight Templar* and *Ironclad*. The use of violence is again noted for its inclusion to justify the protagonist's killing of the villainous Templar, who commit vindictive murders, forcing the player to combat them. The Templar computer games allow players to interact and participate with a world they have only connected with visually. However, this level of interaction is limited, and the player's participation with or in the Templar role is restricted by adhering to the rules of play. Participating with the game further embeds the Templar narrative within popular culture by enabling the player to experience pre-established Templar conventions through a digital medium.

Templar Costume and Digital Cosplay

The Templars' iconic imagery is synonymous with medieval warfare; the iconography of a man in medieval armor with the red cross upon his white mantle is a frequent reference for the Crusades. This ubiquitous imagery identifies the Templar across all media formats, including the film and computer games' texts explored in this project thus far. However, the imagery connotes both heroic and villainous depending on which knight narrative aspect the text is adhering to. This section argues that Templar iconography and the Templar knight are one and the same and share the same malleable component. Therefore, analyzing the imagery of the Templar in their knightly costume is instrumental in defining how the Templar narrative transcends across media formats as it is the connotations of that iconography when associated with either aspect of the Templar knight narrative.

Brownie and Graydon address the importance of costume from the perspective of semiotics in their study of superhero costumes, stating, "For Superman, the costume acts as a record of his alien origin by marking him as other" (2015, pp. 17–18). Of course, the Templars are not superheroes, but what makes the comparison apt is that both Superman and the Templars are marked as other by their iconic costume. The marking of the Templars as others enables the audience to separate the Order from the generic medieval knight; this singles out the protagonist or groups the villainous knights for the audiences, highlighting them with the ubiquitous uniform. Concerning depictions of Superman, Brownie and Graydon stated that marking Superman as other is substantial to signifying his alien identity, but it is "expressed centrally by insignia that Superman wears on his chest" (2015, p. 18). The connotations of Superman's Kryptonian symbol provide an applicable analogy for addressing the relevance of analyzing the iconic Templar insignia of a red cross placed upon a white background, as both are instantly recognizable and have established undertones.

From a historical perspective, the "red cross was a symbol of martyrdom, added to the mantles of the Knights Templar in 1147" (Ralls, 2007, p. 151), while the Templars white surcoat and mantle carried connotations of purity and righteousness. The Templars' use of white to suggest purity runs parallel to observations around the cultural meaning of bright superhero costumes, as Myerly proposes:

> that brightly colored uniform has connotations of trustworthiness in part because it makes the wearer accountable for his or her actions. A brightly colored costume is so noticeable that its wearer would be unable to commit criminal or dishonest acts without being identified by witnesses [Brownie & Graydon, 2015, p. 20].

This notion of bright colors connoting trustworthiness would coincide with the association of the historical Templars' use of white for purity and righteousness and with the good Templar featured in *Arn: The Knight Templar* and *Ironclad*. However, these notions of trustworthiness and integrity are not compatible with the depiction of the bad Templar aspect featured in *Kingdom of Heaven* and *Ivanhoe*, where the Templar iconography connotes rather more sinister themes of oppression, extremism and racism. The contradictory polar associations with Templar imagery further demonstrate how vast the multifaceted Templar narrative has become in popular culture.

The contrasting association of extremism apparent with the Order of the Knights Templar iconography draws further comparison with Brownie and Graydon's study, which addressed the similarities of the depictions of Superman with the depiction of the Ku Klux Klan in Thomas Dixon, Jr.'s *The Clansman: A Historical Romance of the Ku Klux Klan* (1905). Brownie and Graydon cite Chris Gavaler, who explains, "the 'generic formula' of the superhero—'the vigilante hero who assumes a costume and alias'—is borrowed from the behaviour of clansman Ben Cameron" (2015, p. 22). The bad Templar also draws comparisons with the Ku Klux Klan in D.W. Griffith's *Birth of a Nation* (1915) adapted from Dixon Jr.'s novel, which depicts the Ku Klux Klan as knights on horseback who strike a particular similarity to the Knights Templar. The film's poster depicts a Ku Klux Klan member astride his horse dressed in a surcoat of a white cross upon a red background; this is a reverse on the Knights Templars' red cross upon a white background but resonates with the bad Templar's traits of oppression, extremism and racism. When analyzing Superman's negative connotations, Gavaler argues that Superman "closely resembles Grand Dragon, with his consistent and identifiable alter-ego, than previous pulp heroes ... commonly cited as Siegel and Shuster's main influences ... tended to be masters of 'multiple disguises with no single, representative costumed persona'" (Brownie & Graydon, 2015, p. 22). The Knights Templar may not serve as alter ego in the same way as for Superman, but what is apparent is the connotations and thematic links that the Templar costume evokes, which range from chivalrous hero to oppressive extremist.

The five Templar texts that have been analyzed earlier in this chapter and the previous chapter have discussed the two aspects of the Templar narrative of the knight, proposing that the character's actions set them apart. However, when analyzing the Templar imagery, there are three key differences and similarities in comparing the appearance of the Templar costume with the two narrative aspects. The first of these is the softening of Templar iconography in the Templars' costume of the good Templar aspect; most notable is the hollowing of the Templar cross worn upon the chest of Arn in *Arn: The Knight Templar*. Instead of the defined solid red cross that is associated with the order, the cross depicted upon Arn's chest is created through a red outline that leaves a hollow center that is filled with the white color of the Templars' tabard. The good Templar, Celian, in the game *The First Templar*, has his Templar image softened by the use of a black-and-white quartered tabard that is further moderated by inversion of the cross points like the Maltese cross, which is associated with the Knights

Hospitaller and St John's Ambulance, which evokes connotations of charity and healing.

The second is the use of the Latin cross in films *Kingdom of Heaven* and *Ironclad*; although these films feature different types of Templar, one depicts the good Templar and the other the bad Templar. What is significant about the Latin cross is that in both films the Templars represent nationalism; *Ironclad* depicts this positively and draws upon connotations of St George with its Templar hero on the defensive. In comparison, *Kingdom of Heaven* intertwines this nationalism with racism and oppression of the Muslim people. The villainous Templars of the *Assassin's Creed* game are not depicted with the Latin cross, but these Templars are a diverse, multicultural organization and are not associated with the conventional prejudiced Templar archetype. The Knights Templar in *Assassin's Creed* are depicted in the traditional white tabard and with a solid red cross in the style of the Greek cross, which notably has equal length arms.

The third vital iconographic trait is the use of the helmet to distinguish between the good and bad Templar as evidenced in the villainous Templar's portrayal in *Assassin's Creed*, where the Templars hide their identity beneath their great helms, making them indistinguishable from each other. *The First Templar* subverts this for the depiction of the Templar in the good Templar aspect, which always has the hero Templar helmetless. This distinction is not only found in the computer games mentioned but is also in the Templar film adaptations mentioned above; the good Templar in *Arn: The Knight Templar* and *Ironclad* feature their good Templar not wearing a helm, which, of course, enables the main protagonist to stand out from the other knights for the audience (much like Laurence Olivier in *Henry V* [Olivier, 1944]). In contrast to that is the depiction of villainous Templars in *Kingdom of Heaven* who all wear helms in combat (except for Guy) when attacking the Muslim merchant, which makes it difficult to single them out as individuals and with the identical uniform masks them as part of a collective.

With the villainous Templars hiding their faces, the audience or player is made aware that there is something sinister about these knights as there are connotations of wrongdoing: "people who wear a mask to protect their identity are usually people who are undertaking villainous or morally questionable acts" (Brownie & Graydon, 2016, pp. 37–38), which is why, according to Brownie and Graydon, Clark Kent's mother "would never include a mask as part of her son's Superman costume…. Martha Kent recognises the associations between moral ambiguity and the mask" (2016, p. 38). This notion of masked identity enabling immoral action is addressed in *Kingdom of Heaven*; when the Templars attack the Muslim merchants, Raynald informs Guy that no one in Jerusalem will know he is there and then mocks, "you are at Nazareth praying" (Scott, 2005). Guy can join in the violent crime with the knowledge that there will be little consequence due to the anonymity offered to him through the uniform of his Templar costume, while the actions of the hero Templars are just and do not need their identities masked. From looking at the differences and connections between the costumes of the good Templar aspect and the bad Templar aspect of the knight narrative, it is apparent that the appearance of the Templar iconography and costume contributes to the multiple conflations of the Templar phenomenon. This repetition of altered Templar symbols further embeds the fictional Templar archetypes with the associated iconography.

The play experience of the games explored offers players minimal opportunity to tailor the look of their character's costume; in the same way, the player is forced to play their character in line with the rules of the game in both digital limits and playing style. However, *The First Templar* offers some element of customization, as the game enables the player to unlock three different costumes for their digital character to don. This customization is limited though, as the costumes are all of a similar style and only differ in color aesthetics, and the player must wear the outfit in its entirety. There is no ability to customize a unique collaboration of items such as armor, trousers or weapons to create a personalized Templar avatar. *The First Templar* provides the player with a heroic Templar character whose costume matches that role; even with the limited customization, Brownie and Graydon propose that costumes carry a set of rules for behavior, explaining, "Any costume, as it is associated with a particular role, is accompanied by a set of unwritten rules dictating how the wearer must act" (2016, p. 34). Citing Miller, they further explain that all clothes affect identity; they state, "Dress is part of the expectations for behaviour that define a person's role within the social structure" (2016, p. 34). In limiting the player's customization of the character costume, the producers further tailor the play experience by compelling the player to conform to the rules of the digital world but also how to play with the Templar character. Not only does the producer incorporate the good Templar aspect of the thematic Templar narrative, which limits the game's playing style, but also does not offer the player a real customization of costume. The change of outfit only provides different versions of the brightly colored, good Templar imagery, an image that the player must conform with to play the game. The player must adopt the identity and play style of the good Templar aspect of the Templar narrative of the knight.

Although the opportunity for customization is limited in *The First Templar*, the PC game *The Secret World* provides a flexible mode for customization of character costume. Unlike the previous computer games discussed, *The Secret World* is a massively multiplayer online game that incorporates the Templars as a joinable faction for the players to select. *The Secret World* is themed around conspiracy theories, both historical and modern, where players enter the secret world within ours to fight against supernatural forces for the fate of the Earth. In an interview for gamingillustrated.com senior producer Ragnar Tornquist explains that for the game they aimed:

> to make a world that feels exactly like our world, but with a dark twist to it. It's important for us that players are drawn into the reality of our setting, in order to believe in the story and the characters, and to make the more fantastical and horrific elements more solid and believable [Gibson, 2012].

The Secret World did not share the same success as *Assassin's Creed* upon release as the only sales of the game were disappointing: "The game sold only 200,000 copies since its June 29th launch, despite more than half a million players having signed up for the beta" (North, August 2012). The article for destructiod.com also states that because of the poor performance "the company will be cutting costs and staff. Games industry says that they saw a loss of $49 million, compared to $3 million the previous year." The game found greater success later that year by ditching the monthly subscription fee and making the game a one-off purchase. In an article posted on pcgamer.com on January 12, 2013, it explained that since the change of approach, "Funcom noted The Secret World's activity levels rose 400 per cent as a result of the model change" (Petitte, 2013).

In *The Secret World,* players of the game can fully customize their digital avatar, including the physical appearance as well as clothes and physical abilities. Players can unlock various items of clothing throughout the game, and, if they are part of the Templar faction, players can dress their avatars in clothes that resemble Templar imagery without dressing themselves as a knight; thus the game's character customization is a form of digital cosplay. Daisuke Okabe states, "Cosplay is an abbreviated term for costume play. The term originally referred to period dramas and historical plays…. The term has gained currency in Japan since the 1970s to describe the practise of dressing up as characters from anime, manga, and games" (2012, p. 225). However, when examining the concept of cosplay, Booth provides a more current definition of the activity, explaining, "Cosplay, as a fan practice that plays with fashion and media representation, emphasizes the fan's body as a site of transformative power" (2015, pp. 151–152). The customization of the game's avatar enables players to extenuate aspects of their digital character, instead of conventional cosplay when fans physically create and wear costumes; the cosplay aspect of this game is the transformation of the costume of the player's digital avatar. This idea of digital cosplay provides players with the same transformative possibility which, Booth explains, "parodies this transformative potential of the body by erasing the fan identity from the fashion. Rather than 'inhabit' the fashion, as cosplayers might, these participants in the digital environment hail the aesthetic itself as emblematic of media play" (2015, p. 152). Booth's notion that digital cosplay parodies the transformation is apparent in the Templar-style costume that players can construct in the game, creating a personal self-identifying digital avatar that the player can participate with while also benefiting from limited restrictions to the play.

To put into context the concept of digital cosplay, Booth uses as a case study the outfits designed digitally by users on the now-defunct website Polyvore. The website was a fashion database that allowed users to create their looks from the database and showcase where they could be ordered. An example Booth analyzes is the image of the digital cosplay uploaded by gapech97 that uses the fashion database to recreate outfits inspired by the film *The Breakfast Club* (Hughes, 1985). Booth explains, "different outfits for each of the film's main characters emphasize the way gapeach97 imagines the character, but little is revealed of the person or of the underlying film" (2015, p. 152). All we can ascertain from the image is what clothes the user identifies with that film as he later identifies: "For digital cosplayers, the practices engendered by the website may have less to do with the media text than with the fashion collected from around the web" (2005, p. 152). The uploaders level of interest in *The Breakfast Club* text may not be evident in Booth's example, but an outfit uploaded to Polyvore by catherinefox9 for a *The Secret World* Templar outfit alongside an image of a female Templar character demonstrates not only an interest in the fashion but also in the game text itself. The uploader also states:

> My new obsession is The Secret World, the only MMO that I've enjoyed for more than a day. The Templar are my faction, and this outfit is inspired by them. The Templar are a unique blend of class and badassery [*sic*], and I tried to embody that here with touches of gold with black and buckles [catherinefox9, 2015].

The user states that they are a fan of the game and have used the website to create a reflection of the game's character. Booth defines this as "textual nostalgia—without the identifying text, it would be hard to identify this outfit as representative" (2015, p. 155). A similar relationship occurs with the customization of character clothes in *The Secret Templar* as players cannot dress up as medieval Knights Templar but as modern-day equivalents, and while the costume is inspired by the Knights Templar, they would be hard to identify as such without the knowledge of the character being in that faction.

The Secret World allows the players to unlock specific outfits if they collect a specific number of abilities. These collections of abilities are called "decks," and once completed the player unlocks a costume that encompasses those specific abilities. This concept of deckbuilding and related costume customization is similar to Jen Gunnels's notion of cosplay identity cited by Duffett: "aspects of the character are specifically tied to donning the costume. He may not believe that he carries specific aspects of character identity over into everyday life, yet they are available when in costume" (2013, p. 189). The digital cosplay of *The Secret World* ties specific abilities to the character's costume, which then enables players to participate with the game and experience what would be impossible outside the digital world. The deckbuilding in *The Secret World* offers players the chance to tailor their character to specific abilities, but they are also limited in their style of play due to each deck requiring specific weapon choices. For example, if a player chooses to build a paladin deck for their Templar character, then they must be proficient in swords and pistols as the paladin abilities can only be used by these choices of weapons. It is in this way that the game's rules control how the players play the game. Although there is the appearance of customization of character, if the player wishes to unlock a specific character type and represent them through costume, then they must conform to the established character requirements.

The digital cosplay of *The Secret World* includes aspects as outlined in Booth's study of Polyvore, which he defines as being "less fannish and more fashion because it attempts to counter the pathologization of Polyvore's polysemy" (2015, p. 152) but also influences how the player's costume influences how they play the game. This notion is comparable to Lamerichs's thought that in cosplay "the values or features of a character are projected onto the player by the spectators and him or herself" (Brownie & Graydon, 2016, p. 110). Not only must the player's digital avatar conform to a particular playstyle, but when interacting with other players, that deck type will be expected to perform a specific task role in the gaming group. For example, a player using the paladin deck would be a "damage dealer," and a player using the Crusader deck would have the role of "debuffing."

Digital cosplay in *The Secret World* can affect the play experience for the player through the use of costume to define which deck they are using, which ties the notion of performance into participating with the game, an aspect that Booth observes within digital cosplay. Booth states, "The body is less crucial in digital cosplay, and the performativity that digital cosplay enables becomes less an aspect of the fan and more an aspect of the clothes. As a form of media play, then, digital cosplay hinges on both the novel potential of cosplay and the nostalgic element of pastiche" (2015, p. 164). Booth's notion concerning the Polyvore website users' capacity to transform consumable products to create new interpretations of character costume is not only apparent in the way catherinefox9 creates a wardrobe for her *The Secret World* character on Polyvore but the way players are able to purchase clothes in-game to dress their identity and not represent the traditional Templar costume. In resemblance to Booth's example for the creation of Loki, the player can create "a novel version of the character that simultaneously emulates … color, style, and personality" (2015, p. 155) but of a modern-day fantastical Templar dress that combines the familiar traits of the cross and colors white and red with current fashion to create a parody of the Templar iconography synonymous with the Templar narrative of the knight.

Cosplay is about the physical transformation of the fan's identity and incorporates fan performance to embody the character of play. Booth states that there is a "muted sense of performance" within digital cosplay but notes that it "represents the power of the fan to create meaning out of the human experience of online shopping" (2015, p. 163). However, despite the customization within *The Secret World,* the player's ability to play is limited by the game's association of costume and roles similar to the use of the traditional Templar dress associated with the good and bad Templar within the film and game texts explored. The digital performance is limited as players must abide by the rules of the game and can only access specific costumes through an associated playing style. In using digital cosplay, players can mirror the performance transformation of physical cosplay through the appearance of their video game avatar. In doing so, they would further embed the Templar narrative in popular culture via personalizing the Templar iconography in their individual Templar character.

Although digital cosplay enables players to tailor their character to adhere to their perception of the Templar phenomenon, they are still bound by the limits of the game. As in *The Secret World* players must adhere to the traditional playing style associated with their created costume that limits the player's control when participating with the Templar narrative in a digital environment. The limitations of costume customization are factored within the digital limits of the game in the same way as the rules of the computer game influence the player's interaction with the digital world. Although performance cosplay within the digital space allows the player to self-identify with the digital avatar, the player cannot truly kinetically participate with the fantastical Templar world as their level of interaction is encompassed by the limits of the game's fixed narrative and the pre-established conventions of the Templar narrative. However, the personalization of Templar iconography enables a greater sense of immersion for the player and also enables the Templar narrative to be further evolved by the player's creation of a new Templar character by using archetypal Templar imagery.

Performance Through Fan Film

Through the medium of computer games, players can be a Templar in a digital world; however, that experience is hindered as the game compels the player to adhere to the limits and boundaries of the game. Even games with the sandbox-style gameplay, such as *Assassin's Creed*, control and influence how the player plays and interacts with the digital avatar. Although players can experience the thematic Templar narrative of the knight in a medieval setting, it is controlled by the limits of the digital creation and the direction of the game's narrative. The relationship between customer and producer can be understood from a hierarchal perspective, which Abercrombie and Longhurst argue, "present a 'continuum' of audience experiences and identities, ranging from the 'consumer' at one end, to the 'petty producer' at the other end of the scale" (Hills, 2002, p. 29). It is the customer end of the hierarchal scale that this section will address, examining how fan-generated content can further evolve and extend the Templar phenomenon in popular culture, incorporating the existing Templar archetypes of the narrative.

When examining the relationship of fans with products, it is imperative to acknowledge the perception of this hierarchal chain as representative of subject authority, as it can propose a diminishing of the validity of fans' expertise. Hills is critical of the hierarchal perception of fandom, writing, "This view of the consumer is an essentially negative one: consumers lack the developed forms of expertise and knowledge that fans, enthusiast and cultists all possess in ever-increasing and ever-more-specialised forms" (2002, p. 29). Despite the implications of fans lacking the authenticity of the text producers within the concept of fandom, Hills highlights the active and less passive perspective that Jenkins sees of the relationship between fans and texts. Hills cites Jenkins, writing that he has addressed television fan culture "through what he concedes is a 'counter-intuitive' lens, beginning from the position that '[m]edia fans are consumers who also produce, readers who also write, spectators who also participate" (2002, p. 30). This approach to perceiving fan activity moves away from the idea of the passive consumer and fans actively engaging and producing their own content. This act of fan activity can also demonstrate a place within a hierarchal relationship with the new text conveying a sense of authenticity to the original due to the inclusion of basic tropes and themes known, due to their fan knowledge. The fan texts, perceived as authentic, will further evolve the Templar narrative in popular culture as they will be included as pre-established tropes but a unique take on the Templar fiction.

The active relationship fans have with the object of their fandom involves fans creating their own texts from fan fiction, art and fan film that can be a new take on the text or a homage to the original. To define this creative interaction, Booth highlights Fiske's concept of a "Producerly" text; "with producerly texts, viewers can 'construct narratives,' produce their own meanings and find their own values, but can still appreciate the construction of the text, the artificially created narrative" (2010, p. 36). It is this idea of participation with the Templar narrative that this chapter proposes will further cement and evolve the Templar phenomenon within popular culture. The chapter has explored the transmedia properties of the Templar narrative within the participatory engagement of consumable computer games, proposing how the act of play further embeds the connotative Templar within popular culture, despite the limitations of the game mechanics. This section examines the other end of Abercrombie and Longhurst's scale to look at how the Templar narrative of the knight is embedded further and evolved through the fan's creation of new Templar texts.

Fan fiction allows fans to actively participate within the world of their fandom, which Lancaster suggests is the closest fans can get to entering the reality of the fictional space. Lancaster explains, "If fans can't live in the imaginary fantasy, they can at least participate in the culture of creation. By writing fan fiction and publishing web pages, fans immerse themselves in the *Babylon 5* universe" (2001, p. 132). This level of participation, suggested by Lancaster, is higher than that of the participation fans can have with role-playing games and computer games since these readily available consumables all come with rules and restrictions. Fans who perform in role-playing games are restricted by adherence to established rules, which Lancaster explains, writing, "players buy a rulebook, which describes how participants play the game. Without the rules there can be no performance" (2001, p. 38). Computer games also restrict limitation regarding the player's adherence to a preexisting digital landscape, be it sandbox-style or level-based. To define fan participation through creation, Lancaster cites Jenkins, writing, fandom "becomes a participatory culture which transforms the experience of media consumption into the production of new texts, indeed of a new culture and a new community" (2001, p. 132). Although the production of fan texts enables less restriction on participation, Lancaster argues that there are still restrictions imposed upon fan texts. He argues, "performances occurring within fandom … rely on the circulation of the performance's originating production. Only by relying on the representation of the original … can fans 'play' with it: reperform it and make it into a new kind of performance" (2001, p. 133). Lancaster's notion of restriction in fan texts implies that Templar fan fiction should conform to the pre-established conventions of the Templar phenomenon in popular culture because without these archetypes the new text would lack the authenticity of the phenomenon that the fan text is attempting to adapt. Although the fan text need adhere to the ubiquitous archetype and iconography, that does not mean the fan text need copy the original and that this fan creation can further evolve the Templar narrative by such divergence. The divergence by fan fiction is a factor addressed by Coppa, who suggests that fan fiction is not restrained by a necessity to represent the original. Coppa states:

> The existence of fan fiction postulates that characters are able to "walk" not only from one artwork into another, but from one genre into another; fan fiction articulates that characters are neither constructed or owned, but have, to use Schechner's phrase, a life of their own not dependent on any original "truth" or "source" [2006, p. 230].

Coppa here suggests that fan fiction is about breaking away from the conventions of the original and exploring different themes with the new text. She states, "decontextualizing of behaviour echoes the appropriation and use of existing characters in most fan fiction; in fact, one could define fan fiction as a textual attempt to make certain characters 'perform' according to different behaviour strips" (2006, p. 230). The notion of reshaping behavior is shared by Lancaster, who cites from Schechner, "Restored behaviour is living behaviour treated as a film director treats a strip of film. These strips of behaviour can be rearranged or reconstructed; they are independent of the casual systems that brought them into existence" (2001, p. 146). The notion of established behaviors being rearranged indicates how fan fiction further embeds the ubiquitous Templar in popular culture by reaffirming the Templar narrative. It assists in the Templar phenomenon's continual evolvement due to a new direction or focus that these texts have with the Templar narrative. The consumable texts inspire the fan producers who, Lancaster explains, "become high-tech nomads, poaching images and texts as a means to perform in their favourite fantasy universe. The spectator becomes the performer" (2001, p. 151). It is from the perspective of what the fan producers poach and reimagine within their new Templar film texts that this section explores, expressly, how the reoccurring Templar narrative of the knight is incorporated into fan film and how the pre-established conventions of the Templar narrative influence the new fan-produced Templar text.

Will Brooker describes fan films as "simply a branch of fan fiction and has a very similar relationship to the primary texts: a creative departure that stays within a recognisable framework, an experiment that sticks to acceptable rules, a filling in of gaps within the official narrative" (2002, p. 173). Brooker explains that there are different types of fan film, giving the example that (The Force.net) "The TFN theater site organises its offerings to some extent distinguishing 'Animation' from 'short film,' 'music video,' 'coming soon'—which indicates a trailer, rather than the full movie and FX project" (2002, p. 178). These types of fan productions are towards the professional end of Abercrombie and Longhurst's scale of fandom in that fan film requires technical ability and often the support of a production team. This type of high-tech fan fiction is analyzed to understand how the conventions of the Templar narrative transfer to a fan production, where the consumer can produce their own inclusion to the Templar phenomenon in popular culture.

Fan films came about in a form that Coppa describes as a "vid or a songvid" (2008, p. 1). She explains, "Vidding is a form of grassroots filmmaking in which clips from television shows and movies are set to music" (2008, p. 1). Jenkins states these types of fan film "are edited together from found footage drawn from film or television shows and set to pop music" (2006, p. 155). Coppa links the origin of "vidding" to how "Second-wave feminism had popularized ideas of female independence and sexual subjectivity, priming woman to take control of the camera" (2008, p. 3) and argues, "Vidders locate the origin of this distinctive female filmmaking practice within *Star Trek* fandom" (2008, p. 3). Coppa notes, "To be a vidder is to work to reunite the disembodied voice and the desiring body, and to embark on this project is to be part of a distinctive and important tradition of female art" (2008, p. 20). Jenkins informs, "Though the gender lines are starting to blur in recent years, the overwhelming majority of fan parody is produced by men, while 'fan fiction' is almost entirely produced by women. In the female fan community, fans have long produced 'song videos'" (2006, p. 155). There are many examples of vidding using clips from Templar film texts on YouTube; for example, *Arn: The Knight Templar—Only One* was uploaded by MrsPygmyPuff20 and focused on the tragedy of Arn and Cecilia's separation by war. It also ends on a happy note as Arn isn't mortally wounded during the film's climactic battle. The songvid gives Cecilia equal screen time to Arn, an approach not shared by the feature film, which emphasizes more on the good Templar aspect of the Templar narrative, focusing on Arn's struggles in the Holy Land. A songvid uploaded by teresatesssa called *Eva Green—Sibylla—Blue eyes* uses clips from *Kingdom of Heaven* to tell the story from Sibylla (played by Eva Green), the Queen of Jerusalem's perspective, often depicting her from a position of strength, looking down at Balian and Guy from horseback or the battlements. This songvid breaks away from the film's theme of the good knight versus the bad knight, with Sibylla merely a political pawn, and instead depicts her as a queen who is caught up in a love triangle between two knights. Coppa states, "a high percentage of vids are still engaged in fleshing out marginalized female perspectives" (2008, p. 20). This notion is mirrored in the *Kingdom of Heaven* songvid but also can be seen in the *Arn: The Knight Templar* song, where Cecilia's character is given equal exploration to Arn.

Fan film can produce a more ambitious product but will require significant resources. Brooker cites from an email from *Star Wars* fan Nathen Butler; explaining the difficulties of fan production, he says, "unless you have a lot of backing and a great crew, your scope is limited by what you can or cannot do on film and post production" (2002, p. 174). The authenticity of the product, especially one set in an iconic medieval period, will require a certain amount of plausibility in the costume and set design, which will require a significant budget to create a new Templar narrative text. The short film *Predator: Dark Ages* (2015), written and directed by James Bushe, is almost half an hour long and pitches the good Knights Templar in a battle against the alien hunter from the *Predator* franchise. The film aimed for high production value and was subsidized using crowdfunding website Kickstarter, which was set up by Simon Rowling in June 2014. The ambitious producers were hoping to raise between £10,000 and £20,000 but added, "£5000 is our back-up, to make an epic extended trailer or micro short film!" (Rowling, 2014). The project was able to raise £5,525 from Kickstarter, and according to an interview Bushe gave to avpgalaxy. net on June 2015, "originally if we got 5K (our minimum we were going to shoot a high concept trailer)" (Hicks), but the project ended up being a short 25-minute film. Bushe explained that the short film was only possible, as after "the campaign finished, one of our backers, Tim Clayton, asked us what we needed to at least shoot a version of the short. We told him and he offered to come on board as Exec producer and basically gave us another 7–8K to film it" (Hicks, 2015).

The Kickstarter page describes the film as a "Predator fan film set in the Dark Ages" (Rowling, 2014), which is contradictory as the short film focuses heavily on the Knights Templar and includes established tropes from the Templar warrior monk archetype. Further contrast to Rowling's statement on the Kickstarter page is a short synopsis, stating, "Templar Knights are put to the ultimate challenge, to hunt The Predator. Testing not only their skills as fighters but also their faith" (www.kickstarter.com), although the title states a prominence for the role of the Predator, the synopsis focuses more on the Templars, referencing their dual identity of warrior monks. The Kickstarter page organizes its pledge amounts into an ascending numerical value from £5 up to £1,000 but also names them with stereotypical medievalist titles such as "Page Boy," "Archer" and "Knight's Templar." These different pledge levels all reward the backer with different rewards and privileges; these range from "A special Thank You [*sic*] shout out on Twitter and Facebook!" to "An Executive producer Credit. Plus all downloads and an invite to production meetings." For the latter privilege, you would need to pledge £1,000, which one backer did; £500 is needed to achieve the pledge level "Knight's Templar" and be gifted "A Templar

Knight's helmet, signed (if preferred) by cast and crew" (Rowling, 2014). It is unclear what the Templar Knight's helmet offered looks like as there is no photo included, but it is likely to be a great helm, which is the type of helmet worn by the Templar knight protagonist in the film. This reward, as well as the emphasis of popular medievalist traits to secure funding and alongside its Templar-heavy synopsis, demonstrates that this film is also aimed at Knights Templar fans. These Templar traits suggest that the film is not only a *Predator* fan film as page creator Rowling suggests. If the funding requested was aimed solely at *Predator* fans, then surely the themes around pledge levels would have recognized this with *Predator*-type titles instead of a clear focus on Templar-associated conventions. This crowdfunded film is a new Templar text that further evolves the Templar narrative by repurposing Templar archetypes for a science fiction horror setting.

Bushe stated that he "never had any plans originally to make a Predator fan film. I have been a huge Predator fan since I first saw it when I was 10" (Hicks, 2015). Bushe had ambitions of making a *Predator* major motion picture, stating, "I already had this medieval Predator idea in the back of my head, waiting to take to Hollywood" (Hicks 2015), but he decided to move forward with his vision when he "realised this probably wouldn't happen and I discovered Phillip Lane and his Predator costume I decided maybe a fan made trailer of my film idea would at least get it out there" (Hicks, 2015). In an interview for cultfilmreviews.co.uk in November 2015, Bushe explained, "I also have a big love of medieval/period films like Braveheart and Kingdom of Heaven etc" (CD). Bushe's influence from *Kingdom of Heaven* can be seen from the original plans for the film, as Bushe had initially planned to set the film in Jerusalem. Bushe stated that the initial idea of Jerusalem "was the perfect setting we really wanted, for the Crusades War and of course the extreme heat. But with our small budget it just wasn't possible" (Hicks, 2015). Instead of setting this Templar project in the Holy Land as recent Templar game texts have, the film is set in the English countryside, which is not due to the creative team not knowing the conventional setting for a medieval Knights Templar story but a reflection of the challenges fan filmmakers face when creating their new text.

Filmmakers often use ambitious fan films as a way of demonstrating their skill, according to Brooker, who states, "Amateur filmmakers increasingly see their projects as calling cards and potential springboards to careers in the movie industry" (2002, p. 175); a well-executed film like *Predator: Dark Ages* would act well as a showcase for the filmmaker's skills. According to its YouTube page, the short film has over 1,000,000 views and was the winner of "best fan film" at the Tri-Cities International Film Festival. Bushe demonstrates his vision for the progression of the project when he states, "A lot of people have said they would love to see a different era of history, which would make for a great miniseries or something. But time and funding is the main problem we would face. Unless Fox got involved of course" (Hicks, 2015). Like Brooker's notion, Bushe's aspirations move beyond creating a fan film but of a collaboration with mainstream media and projection above the idea of a petty producer of fandom texts. Bushe's professional credits are noted when introduced in the interview, with Hicks introducing him, stating, "James is a multi-award winning filmmaker, having written, produced and directed a number of short films that have featured in various film festivals…. He is also one of the founders of Fascination Pictures" (2015). The Fascination Pictures website showcases several short films that they have produced, which include a trailer for a planned film called *Vatican Knights*. In a trailer uploaded to YouTube in 2008 to the Fascination Pictures account called Vatican Knights (VK) trailer, the synopsis states the film is "about a group of elite soldiers that have to battle a horde of the undead." The trailer informs that James Bushe directs the film, and despite being set in modern times incorporates a similar theme to Bushe's *Predator: Dark Ages* in that the focus is on a group of knights battling monsters.

IMDb states that VK was a 15-minute short film with an estimated budget of £1,300 but is unclear whether a finished film was released as only the trailer is available online. However, the trailer is an early indication of Bushe's intention of incorporating medieval and horror themes together. Aside from including an elite knightly order with close links to the Vatican, it is unclear what other conventions of the Templar narrative Bushe included in the film. A more detailed analysis of *Predator: Dark Ages* is possible due to the successful fundraising and higher profile for the production. However, Bushe does state his interest in "Medieval/period films like Braveheart and Kingdom of Heaven etc" (CD, 2015); *Predator: Dark Ages* appears to draw inspiration from the Templar film text *Ironclad*, despite Bushe making no mention of the film's influence on his own Templar film.

Bushe's film incorporates the good Templar as its protagonist, but instead of using the good Templar aspect of the Templar narrative as inspiration, it appears that Bushe has lifted the character straight from Jonathan English's *Ironclad*. The apparent similarities start with the hero Templar looking very similar to that of James Purfoy's Thomas Marshall, while Bushe's good Templar is called Marshall Thomas and identically to Purfoy's character he is also referred to as "Marshall" throughout the film. The inclusion of Purfoy's Marshall coincides with Coppa's notion, "fan fiction articulates that characters are neither constructed or owned" (2006, p. 230). Although Bushe does not openly state his influence from English's Templar film, knowing his "love" for *Kingdom of Heaven* and his previous work depicting of a knightly order similar to the Templars suggest at the very least he has an awareness of the *Ironclad* film. The similarity was questioned in a comment on the *Predator: Dark Ages* YouTube page by Anthony Pinon (2016), who wrote, "is this supposed to be Marshall Thomas from Ironclad?"

Further similarities are apparent during an early scene in Bushe's film, in the scene which suggests that Marshall Thomas will leave the Order after this mission, and the Templar priest questions this, saying, "I hear you are to leave the Order after this mission." He responds with "Your grace my men have seen too much too much death; some deserved, some not." The priest then says, "Many return from defending our faith only to find themselves questioning it" (Bushe, 2015). This dialogue scene mirrors that of an early scene between *Ironclad*'s Marshall and a priest, where the priest says, "I know the Templars placed a heavy burden on you, I know you are deeply scarred. The cross on your tunic is a symbol of your faith in God's will, you should be full of the torment it now bears upon you. When you arrive at Canterbury, I am requesting your leave from the Order of the Knights Templar." And when Marshall meets with the Archbishop of Canterbury, the Archbishop addresses this absence, stating, "Some men have returned from defending our faith, only to find themselves questioning it" (English, 2011). Although not directly indicated by the director, the line of the priest in *Predator: Dark Ages* and that part of the story are lifted directly from *Ironclad*. This dialogue, along with the hero's look and name, indicates that not only has the Templar hero aspect been incorporated into the fan production of *Predator: Dark* Ages, but the film suggests an influence of James Purefoy's portrayal of the Templar hero character.

In incorporating what is arguably a copy of the good Templar aspect from *Ironclad* within his fan film, Bushe is staking his claim of ownership of Purfoy's character in his low-budget Templar text. The notion of ownership of popular fictional characters is addressed by Booth, who cites Jenkins when explaining, "once television characters enter into a broader circulation, intrude into our living rooms, pervade the fabric of our society, they belong to their audiences and not simply to the artists who originated them" (2010, p. 36). In taking ownership of another's original content, using *Babylon 5* as an example, Lancaster defines the fan producer as "Performing as textual nomads staking individual authorial claims, fans poach the primary text of *Babylon 5* in order to enter its universe" (2001, p. 134). Lancaster explains that the performance is acted through "poaching images and texts as a means to perform" (2001, p. 151), and it is through the poaching that "the spectator becomes the performer" (2001, p. 151).

Bushe however, does not only take ownership of the conventions of the Templar aspect depicted in *Ironclad*, but he also incorporates elements from the villainous Templar aspect, which coincides with Coppa's notion that fan fiction is to "make certain characters 'perform' according to different behavioural strips" (2006, p. 230). Bushe's Templar hero incorporates the racism and religious prejudices associated with the villainous Templars featured in *Ivanhoe* and *Kingdom of Heaven*. To defeat the predator, Templar Marshall must work with Sied, a Saracen. When introduced to Sied, Marshall is quick to protest his involvement, stating, "What help could a Saracen give me?" He then adds "Brother, he cannot be trusted, he is a savage; they all are" (Bushe, 2015). In the heated confrontation, Marshall is stopped from physically attacking Sied. This attitude of prejudice is depicted in the villainous Templar characters of Guy de Lusignan and de Bois-Guilbert but has not been associated with the hero Templar. For example, when Arn meets Saladin, the two are respectful of each other and do not focus on racial or religious difference. In the closing scene of *Predator: Dark Ages*, Marshall and Sied have a newfound respect for one another by battling the predator. Marshall shows his gratitude by saying, "Thank you for coming back," to which Sied replies, "Where would be my honour if I did not" (Bushe, 2015). Bushe has used the polar opposite Templar traits of the thematic Templar narrative of the knight to create a story arc for his Templar hero, thus further adding to the Templar narrative by merging parts of the two aspects to create his own version of the Templar hero knight. It is through Bushe's act of performance with the Templar texts that Bushe can visit that medieval world and is able to incorporate the good Templar aspect of the narrative text and then further expand the Templar conventions in popular culture through his Templar hero's behavior, which amalgamates different aspects of the Templar narrative.

Bushe's film is a variation from the two aspects of the knight narrative by including aesthetics from the bad Templar aspect. Within his Templar hero, he demonstrates how the perception of the Templars has further evolved in popular culture through the malleability of the contradictory Templar narrative aspects. Bushe's merging of the two aspects of the knight narrative coincides with what Coppa perceives as the attractiveness of creating fan fiction, as it enables making "certain characters 'perform' according to different behaviour strips ... or able to walk out of one story and into another" (2006, p. 230). Fan fiction showcases the fan producers' desire to state their claim of ownership and gain some authority over the myth by diverging from the established associated conventions, a divergence that Bushe takes in his version of the good Templar aspect, which is a Templar protagonist that incorporates characteristics associated with the bad knight Templar aspect. Bushe's take on the Templar hero demonstrates the evolvement of the Templar narrative, which runs parallel to the changes made by Ubisoft to the Templar villain archetype in the *Assassin Creed* franchise, which shows how the Templar narrative further expands the Templar phenomenon within popular culture.

Conclusion

The reoccurring thematic Templar narrative traverses multiple media formats and forms of consumption due to the thematic narrative's malleable quality. The chapter has identified the multitude of Templar texts as paratexts to approach the Templar narrative's transmedia qualities of my Templar urtext concept. Although the texts exist on their own, they collectively incorporate the pre-established aspects of the warrior monk archetype and expand on the perception of the Knights Templar in popular culture. For producers of new Templar texts, the Templar narrative provides identifiable tropes and iconography established within popular culture. However, due to contradictory perceptions, the Templar narrative gives the producers the flexibility to expand the thematic narrative within new media formats. These developments still coincide with the popular perceptions of the Templars and expand the Templar urtext.

The globally successful computer game, *Assassin's Creed,* provides this study with the most significant example of how the Templar narrative of the knight expanded through transmedia forms into a participatory format. The game's producers drew from the Templar narrative of the knight to define the game's villains by using traits of the villainous Templar aspect depicted in *Ivanhoe* and *Kingdom of Heaven.* In this alternative media, the producers evolved essential traits for the digital Templar villain to meet the game's desired perspective of neutrality, meaning the Templar were neither Crusader nor Saracen but a diverse atheist organization. The malleability of the Templar narrative enables the producers to include aspects of the warrior monk archetype that suited their project's requirements but further expanded the perception of the Templar by depicting the Christian warrior monks as diverse atheists. This change to the archetype further embeds the established Templar perceptions in popular culture, and due to the game's popularity, it associates the historical order with a new image of the Templar archetype.

Although *The First Templar is* a far less successful computer game compared to the *Assassin's Creed* juggernaut, the game holds significance as an example of how, as a participatory media format, *Assassin's Creed* further embed their game's perception of the Templar phenomenon in popular culture. From examining the message boards of promotional video trailers for *The First Templar* on YouTube, the accusations of copying from *Assassin's Creed* fans was evident as the incorporation of the Templar narrative has made the game's villainous Templar synonymous with digital gaming. Despite the claims of intentional copying, *The First Templar* focused on the good Templar, choosing to allow the player to control a Templar hero protagonist. Many of *Assassin's Creed* fans disliked this as they perceived the digital Templar as a villain, demonstrating how the Templar narrative has evolved across media formats. Although one game was ultimately far more popular than the other, the thematic Templar narrative is seen in the way in which games that showed apparent similarities provided polar opposite playable characters.

The Templar-themed computer games offer a more immersive experience than literature and film as the gamer can participate with the digital recreation of the Templar historical setting. In participating with the Templar-themed text players were able to interact with the Templar narrative through the act of play although not able to divert from the designed game narrative as the game's rules, such as the digital constraints and the game's adherence to the Templar narrative, prevent such divergence. The game's adherence to the Templar narrative conventions ensures that a degree of passivity is retained albeit with the possibility to experience it at the player's leisure. The producers of *The First Templar* incorporated the religious aspects of the warrior monk archetype by creating "prayer" as the Templar protagonist's healing ability. The limitations of participating with *Assassin's Creed* is shown through the game's use of the villainous Templar's unjustified violence to highlight the virtuousness of the Assassins.

Although the computer games mentioned above enable the exploration of a digital world, it is limited due to the constraints of the game's rules and adherence to the pre-established Templar conventions. The exploration falls short of players identifying with a Templar due to the necessity of playing a predetermined character devised by the game's producer. However, this gap in the experience is bridged in the computer game *The Secret World*, which offers players the ability to practice digital cosplay with the mechanization for a level amount of customization. Digital cosplay enables the player to perform digitally as their avatar. Although this is limited to the game's prerequisite playing style of needing to play to unlock character costume, the costumes once obtained allow the player to recreate the essence of the archetypal Templar costume in a neomedieval stylized sense. The digital cosplay possibilities in *The Secret World* might not allow the player to fully shape the identity of their digital avatar but will allow players to echo the performance quality of cosplay in enabling players to create different and unique depictions of their Templar characters.

While *The Secret World* enables greater participation with the Templar narrative through a digital avatar, the interaction is regulated by the rules of both the digital world and the pre-established conventions of the

Templar urtext. The migration of the Templar phenomenon to computer games has further evolved the Templar narrative through reworkings of the established aspects of the knight narrative. Digital cosplay incorporates elements of performance which enable the player to take on the role of their digital avatar and personally identify with the Templar narrative, although the digital constraints of the game limit the performance within the thematic narrative.

Participation with the Templar narrative demonstrates how the pre-established Templar archetype has been further embedded in popular culture but also further evolved to suit the mechanisms of the digital medium. The symbolic transformative qualities of performance demonstrate how the Templar narrative can be further evolved through altering the iconography in digital cosplay and in a greater sense through the creation of user-generated content. This Templar-themed generated content enables the pre-established traits to be revisited and the narrative altered from the new perspective to the Templar-themed text. The malleability of the Templar narrative is demonstrated by further evolution of the narrative by user-generated content, be it reediting of themes in a Templar film text via songvids or a reworking of Templar narrative aspects in a crowd-funded film. The fan film *Predator: Dark Ages*, was a crossover of the director's genre interests and allowed the fan film producer the freedom to explore different aspects of the Templar character by merging traits of both the good knight and the bad knight. The fan producer utilized established aspects and iconography of the Templar narrative of the knight to situate the film in the Templar urtext but also further expand the perceptions of the Knights Templar in popular culture.

The two aspects of the thematic Templar narrative of the knight originated within literature and then embedded further in popular culture through film, but through participatory mediums such as computer games and user-generated content, these aspects have evolved further still. The case studies examined demonstrate how the malleability of the Templar archetype broadens through performance and play—further expanding my concept of the Templar urtext.

CHAPTER 3

The Mythical Quest

From Fictional Medieval Origins to Conspiracy Narrative

The part of the Templar urtext that this chapter is examining is the grail guardian archetype, which is adapted and reused as part of the reocurring Templar narrative. The chapter aims to identify how the concept of the thematic Templar quest narrative has evolved over the centuries to include two aspects: the quest of the knight and the quest to follow in the Templars' footsteps. Both parts incorporate the structural elements of a quest narrative as established in myth, as well as incorporating supernatural and fantastical elements. The case studies selected are the low-budget cult film *Monty Python and the Holy Grail* (Gilliam & Jones, 1975) and the action-adventure blockbuster *Indiana Jones and the Last Crusade* (Spielberg, 1989), which show the quest of the knight. The 21st-century Hollywood conspiracy films *The Da Vinci Code* (Howard, 2006) and *National Treasure* (Turteltaub, 2004) show the quest to follow in the Templars' footsteps.

These case studies have been selected because they demonstrate my concept of the Templar urtext and also show how the quest narrative has evolved over the centuries. This chapter aims to understand why these films incorporate, adapt, and evolve the grail guardian archetype of the Templar urtext. By examining the grail guardian archetype, this chapter explores how these different texts build on the Templar urtext and expand the popular perceptions of the Templar phenomenon in popular culture. The methodology to approach this will include textual analysis of the case studies but also an analysis of the producer's influences and intentions. The chapter will draw on interviews and production sources to understand creative decisions, complemented with academic sources used to highlight how the Templar narrative has evolved.

The chapter will firstly examine the concept of the quest as a story itself. This study will be done by approaching the structuralist concepts of

Joseph Campbell alongside Norris J. Lacy's work on the MacGuffin. These concepts provide the ideal starting point for analysis as they focus on Arthurian myth and are concepts clearly referenced in the work of George Lucas and Steven Spielberg. After introducing the quest as a story structure, the chapter then examines the quest of the knight. This aspect of the Knights Templar quest narrative is a formulaic tool used by filmmakers to retell the grail narrative and further cement the Templar narrative within popular culture. The chapter examines the Templars' first appearance in popular culture in Wolfram von Eschenbach's 13th-century poem *Parzival* to provide context for the appearance of the quest of the knight. However, to explain this aspect of the quest narrative, this chapter will not be analyzing conventional Arthurian grail myths as case studies but instead using *Monty Python and the Holy Grail* and blockbuster *Indiana Jones and the Last Crusade as* they are synonymous with the Holy Grail. These film texts offer a different depiction than the traditional grail stories. To demonstrate how story producers incorporate aspects of the Templar quest narrative within their variation of the grail story, I will draw upon Donald L. Hoffman's work on *Monty Python* and Rebecca A. Umland and Samuel J. Umland's study of grail adaptations in Hollywood. It should be noted that neither film features the Knights Templar by name, but both films show the influence of the Templar quest narrative on the iconography and themes of the story.

The second half of the chapter will examine the second aspect of the quest narrative, the quest to follow in the Templars' footsteps. This aspect of the grail guardian archetype sees the protagonist revisit the past through researching a Templar conspiracy story. The Templar conspiracy narrative reaffirms faith within Christianity, emphasizing Christ's legitimacy and linking America's divine purpose to its founding. The chapter will introduce Templar conspiracy myths and draw from Timothy Melley's study of conspiracy theory to study the myth in popular culture. The analysis of this aspect of the quest builds upon the typological theories of Aronstein and Torry (2009) to establish how the quest narrative has continued to evolve within popular culture, building upon the established grail story which is part of the Templar urtext guardian archetype. The prevalence of this aspect of the quest narrative is demonstrated through two case studies: *The Da Vinci Code* and *National Treasure*, chosen due to their popularity and focus on conspiracy, myth and history. These case studies highlight how the Templar quest narrative has evolved and has helped to renew popular interest in the Knights Templar in the 21st century.

The Quest

The first type of Templar quest draws upon the supernatural powers of the grail created from the Arthurian legend, while the second aspect uses the Templar myth as the supernatural environment that the protagonist must venture forth into on the quest. The first quest type focuses on the search for the grail, while the second quest is for a symbolic grail in the form of beneficial revelation. The Knights Templar have been associated with the grail quest since its 13th-century version within Wolfram von Eschenbach's *Parzival*. This inclusion by Eschenbach not only located the grail within the real world but also situated the Templars within the supernatural. The Templars' role in the grail quest created the origins for the reoccurring Templar narrative within popular culture, placing them in medieval literature as the guardians of the grail. Of course, not all grail stories included the Templars, but that role is the origin of the Templar quest narrative and the start of the merge between the Templars' historical reality and historical myth.

This chapter proposes that there are two types of Templar quest narrative because this narrative is a major feature in opposing genre narratives, such as medieval historical/Arthurian or mystery adventure/thriller. Although this type of Templar narrative can appear in the different cinematic codes of variations of the genre, it is also the use of time periods that outlines the separate quest types, such as the medieval past and the modern day and the roles of the story's protagonist. Simply put, the first type of quest narrative incorporates the role of the questing knight, seeking the grail or a long journey. The second type of quest narrative, set in modern times, involves the protagonist venturing back into the past by uncovering the Templars' lost secret. The final difference between the two types is the goal of the quest, as, in the quest of the knight, the item sought has no intrinsic value in the same way as the story tool known as a MacGuffin. Lacy defines the concept as "a McGuffin [*sic*] is something—a person, an object, an event—the primary purpose of which is to motivate the characters and therefore the plot, whether or not that 'something' possesses any implicit significance" (2005, p. 54). This type of quest narrative can also function as the emotional motivation for the character, one that drives them forward in their character arc.

For example: in the *Arn* series, the titular character must crusade to the Holy Land to atone for his sins for sex outside of marriage with his lover Cecilia. Arn's mission is to protect Christians and the Christian Kingdom of Jerusalem, a duty which he fails due to the Christian armies' defeat at the Battle of Hattin by Saladin. Arn's failure in his quest has no bearing on the plot; he still returns to his homeland, but he has returned as a battle-hardened warrior able to defeat invading forces. Arn's quest to the Holy Land is in itself irrelevant to the plot; even if history were rewritten and Saladin were defeated, Arn would still return home as the battle-hardened warrior. It is in this way that the quest narrative works as a mechanism for the character's emotional journey. In the case of *Arn: The Knight Templar*, Arn goes from an innocent young man to a veteran knight of the Crusades. This example is in keeping with the concept of the Mac-Guffin as the quest has no actual impact upon the narrative but only serves as a means of facilitating Arn's emotional change. The importance of character change while obtaining the goal is called by Christopher Vogler "The Road of Heroes." He explains, "Heroes are symbols of the soul in transformation, and of the journey each person takes through life. The stages of that progression, the natural stages of life and growth, make up the Hero's Journey" (2007, p. 37). The quest as a narrative documents the character's growth through the stages of the search for that goal, which provides an ideal backdrop to the quest of the knight, illustrating the hero's journey through the given character arc.

The concept of the quest as a story links to the early storytelling of heroic myth ranging from Perseus in Greek mythology to Beowulf of Scandinavia. These narratives incorporate the quest as a thematic tool that is still one of the major formats of storytelling. The Templar narrative originally appeared in the Arthurian grail myth, which means that the Templar quest narrative is tied to the format of mythic storytelling identified through Joseph Campbell's structuralist theories. Vogler explains that Campbell "found that all storytelling, consciously or not, follows the ancient patterns of myth and that all stories, from the crudest jokes to highest flights of literature, can be understood in terms of the Hero's Journey" (2007, p. 4). Part of Campbell's theory is that the hero leaves the ordinary world and ventures into the fantastical, a story tool that is apparent in both types of Templar quest narrative. For the quest of the knight, it is more literal; the questing knight leaves his homeland and journeys to a dangerous foreign land, exemplified in *Monty Python and the Holy Grail*. In this adaptation, Arthur and his knights battle the deadly Rabbit of Caerbannog, a deadly rabbit that demonstrates the fantastical of the supernatural world the hero must venture within.

The journey into the supernatural world is part of the mythic story format, and as the Templar quest narrative derives from the King Arthur grail myths, it is fundamental to the Templar narrative. The second type of quest narrative features this fundamental story step, but the protagonist takes the journey into the fantastical world by traveling into the Templar past. Not literally, but by investigating the Templars' past, the hero must travel from the ordinary world to the Templars' past to achieve the quest.

The Templar myths (the grail, Freemasons) are drawn from the past into the modern world via a conspiracy that hides a revelation, one which the modern-day hero must uncover to rediscover faith in America/Christianity. The mythology of the Templar conspiracy links the medieval mythic past to the modern world, a fantastical world which the hero must delve into to complete the quest.

The Templars and the Holy Grail

The Templars first appeared in popular culture as the guardians of the grail in the Arthurian grail myths and created the foundations for mythic variants of the quest narrative, which were further diluted after the Order's sudden extinction. The mythic stories associated with The Templars form one half of the cornerstone for the Knights Templar's place within popular culture, the other half being the villainous/chivalrous knight explored in the previous chapters. The importance of this aspect to the Templars' infamy is expressed by Haag, who explains, "The Secrecy of the Templars, their hybrid, nature as monks with swords, the exotic worlds they encompassed, their romance and sudden fall, and the mysteries left unanswered by the disappearance of their archives, have enlarged them in popular imagination where they survive and flourish" (2009, p. 282). The sudden fall of the Templars in 1312 left unanswered questions about the Order, and with no Templars left to dispute them, many narratives of conspiracy and myth were able to flourish.

However, before the Templars' infamous fall, the warrior monks were infused into medieval romance literature as guardians of the grail. Haag notes, "The first mention of the Templars in literature came in about 1220 in *Parzival* by the German knight and poet Wolfram von Eschenbach" (2009, p. 253). The Templars' appearance in this Arthurian poem marked the start of the Templar narrative, a story theme that would become an encompassing phenomenon that grew over the centuries, as this chapter will explore. Wolfram's work built on the unfinished work of Chrétien de Troyes, who was "a poet from northern France who wrote Perceval, or Le Conte du Graal, under the orders of Count Philip of Flanders" (Müller, 2002, p. 177). The significance of the difference in Wolfram's version, Müller explains, is "Wolfram almost tripled the length of Chrétien's romance (from about 9,200 to 25,000 lines), completed the story in detail, added the early history of Perceval's father, and even gave a preview of the following generation of characters" (2002, p. 177). The differences to both grail stories, Umland and Umland explain, are that in Wolfram's *Parzival* "the knights who do guard it [the grail] are referred to as Templars, and Wolfram expands upon the history of the grail family naming the current King Anfortas" (1996, p. 13). Haag suspects that Wolfram drew direct influence for his grail Templars from Wolfram's visits to the Holy Land; he writes, "Eschenbach had visited Outremer in about 1200 and he set sections of his poem in the East" (2009, pp. 253–254). Haag notes that his "Templars are pure warriors, defenders of the sacred territories which contain the Grail, just as the real Templars defended the Holy Land" (2009, p. 254). It is this inclusion of detail around Percival's father and introducing the next generation of characters that the Knights Templar appear within the grail romances, which create a Templar narrative where the lines of myth and reality of the Templars start to blur.

It is worth noting that Wolfram's *Parzival* "is neither a paraphrase nor translation" and "changes so many large and small details that his *Parzival* becomes an independent work" (Müller, 2002, p. 177). Müller highlights the difference of each version's description of the grail, writing, "Even his description and interpretation of the Grail are original: his Grail is a mysterious, powerful stone with divine origins, whereas Chrétien represents it as a Golden Vessel" (2002, p. 177). Haag states, "there was nothing explicitly religious about Chrétien's grail; he did not write about it as the cup or chalice at the last supper" (2009, p. 255). Haag argues that the grail was about the "cultural and spiritual quest ... regardless of its religious overtones, that has belonged to secular writers, never to the Church" (2009, p. 255). It is in this aspect that the Holy Grail and the Knights Templar are similar as they both have Christian implications, but the writers use both for narratives not associated with Christianity. This separation between knight and religion was also established as an aspect of the Templar knight narrative. It highlights how the fictional Templar hero and villain distance themselves from the Christian religion by either rejecting the faith's elite community or openly disrespecting and distorting the Christian faith.

Associations with Jesus Christ and the cup from the Last Supper were not part of the Chrétien grail story; this connection came from a later medieval version by the French poet Robert de Boron who imbued the myth with Christian iconography. He "made the grail cup from which Christ drank at the last supper, a cup that also held Christ's blood collected by Joseph of Arimathea" (Umland & Umland, 1996, p. 13). The inspiration behind the grail may not have been from Christian influence, and Umland and Umland believe that the grail has pagan influences. Umland and Umland argue, "It is possible that Chrétien was influenced by stories of nourishing vessels of Celtic origin (e.g., cornucopias and horns of plenty), but he is the first to connect it to an elaborate ritual (the grail procession) with spiritual overtones" (1996, p. 13). Wolfram redefines the grail, noting, "*Lapsit exillis*, the name given to the grail, is a stone that was once set in Lucifer's crown but which fell with him from heaven, and which serves as an elixir of life" (Haag, 2009, p. 254). Of course, including the Templars into a story will carry Christian connotations, but the inclusion of the cup of Christ in the story shows how quickly the Templar narrative envelops new thematic links. This will further fuel what centuries later will be the fictional Templar phenomenon.

Given the substantial number of grail stories, writers focus on various aspects of the established grail lore, such as Robert de Boron's inclusion of Christ iconography instead of Celtic myth. This is also true of the later film adaptations; for example, *Indiana Jones and the Last Crusade* focuses on the healing power of the grail, which gives the grail knight eternal life. *Excalibur* (Boorman, 1981) draws upon the ideas of the cornucopia, which enables the grail to heal the decimated kingdom of Arthur as well as the king himself. Although Boorman's adaptation focuses on the original concept of the grail as a cornucopia, Boorman's grail still incorporates Christian iconography such as the blood of Christ during Percival's vision. This vision appears to Percival as he is at the threshold of death as a blinding light transports him into the grail castle where he witnesses a magnificent floating chalice that pours a red liquid that resembles blood. Upon witnessing the golden chalice, Percival hears a mysterious voice that asks him, "What is the Secret of the Grail?" (Boorman, 1981). This sequence draws upon the grail's later associations with Christ and also with Wolfman's grail castle, also known as the "Temple," which Guerber describes, writing, "Some idea of its unrivalled loveliness may be faintly gained from the description which tells that 'The temple itself was one hundred fathoms in diameter. Around it were seventy-two chapels of an octagonal shape'" (1922, p. 247). Although, unlike Wolfram's account, Boorman's Excalibur features no Templars or guardian grail knights. Aberth argues that Percival's vision of the grail "is emblematic of the religious emasculation that takes place throughout the movie" (2003, p. 23); however, this version's grail does evoke associations with Christ. Boorman's version links the grail directly to Arthur, as the grail's secret is that Arthur can heal both himself and the land, but does demonstrate the contrasting grail themes as the film also evokes Christian iconography through Percival's vision of the golden chalice connoting the transubstantiation of Catholic Mass.

Eric Rohmer's 1978 adaptation of Chrétien's grail romance, *Perceval le Gallois*, depicts the grail like the original romance, seen as part of a spiritual ritual procession as witnessed by Percival; the film features no Templars as part of the grail ritual as they did not become associated with the grail until Wolfram's later account. Rohmer used an expressionistic style for his grail film by capturing the entire film in a studio with sets constructed to resemble medieval manuscript illustrations and artwork. In an interview with Nadja Tesich-Savage, Rohmer explains that instead of filming on location at historical sites, his vision was to "attempt to create a film according to period's own conceptions of itself" (1978, p. 52). Although Rohmer's vision was to adapt Chrétien's grail romance and emphasize the iconography and cultural visuals of the period, his grail film also contrasts the pagan influence and spiritual properties in Chrétien's grail romance with the Christian themes of the later versions with the inclusion of Percival's vision of Christ's crucifixion. In the interview with Tesich-Savage, Rohmer explained that the film's "end will be very Christian, closing with the Passion played with full force" (1978, p. 56); however, this inclusion was accused of being an "awkwardly tacked-on ending" by critics (Callahan, 1999, p. 50). Callahan argues that the Christian-themed ending is appropriate for the adaption as its inspiration "grows directly out of Chrétien's romance" (1999, p. 50). The line Callahan refers to is translated as "After the service he venerated the cross and weeping for his sins humbly repented" (Satines, 1990, p. 418).

One of the most significant variants to the grail story was the inclusion of Sir Galahad, who would replace Sir Percival as the story's protagonist. Despite replacing Percival in literature, Galahad was not often the main protagonist when the stories were adapted to film. Umland and Umland press that when being depicted in film:

> the quest tend[s] to rely upon these early medieval versions of the quest for the holy grail and bypass the later versions (best known perhaps by Malory's *Queste del sanc Graal*) in which Galahad, a product of the imagination of Cistercian monks, largely usurps Perceval's role as grail knight *par excellence* [1996, p. 14].

Galahad's usurpation demonstrates how the different versions of the grail alternate with the writer's vision, and with Galahad written as the most pure and perfect Christian knight, the grail story is further embedded within Christian themes.

The significance of the inclusion of Galahad with the Templar narrative can be seen in one of the most iconic film grail adaptations: *Monty Python and the Holy Grail*. The film features King Arthur, Percival and multiple knights searching for the grail; the film also features Sir Galahad, an inclusion that is rare among modern retelling. Umland and Umland clarify that Galahad's lack of appearance in modern retelling is due to his "purity and his perfection render him a less sympathetic character than his precursor, Perceval ... when Galahad appears in Hollywood productions, he is most often presented satirically and only in passing" (1996, p. 14). Satirical characters are the only depictions for Monty Python's knights, and this includes Galahad, but what makes this film's inclusion of Galahad significant is Galahad's infusion with the Templar narrative and iconography. The character of Sir Galahad dresses in traditional Knights Templar garb; over his armor he wears a white mantle with a large red cross in the center and even carries a white shield with a red cross emblem upon it.

The similarity of costume between Sir Galahad and the Knights Templar also runs parallel by the vows of chastity taken by the Templars' monkhood and Sir Galahad's piety drawing a direct comparison. As with the rest of the Arthurian concepts, Galahad's great Christian piety is parodied so that instead of something to be admired, as the Cistercian monks would have envisioned, it is something to be mocked. One scene that typifies this inversion for comedic effect is when Sir Galahad is vulnerable and squeamish when accosted by a castle of lustful women, and the comedy is "because the chastity is not based so much on an ascetic ideal as it is on the men's squeamishness; Galahad seems less chaste than frightened" (Hoffman, 2002, p. 142). Despite the ridiculous nature of the film, *Monty Python and the Holy Grail* parodies and subverts the Arthurian conventions. The film is a more valid example of the Templar quest narrative despite not featuring a Templar by name, as the Templar quest narrative incorporates through the amalgamation of Galahad with the warrior monks.

Monty Python and Templar Iconography

Monty Python and the Holy Grail was the second film released by the comedy team, while its first film, *And Now for Something Completely Different* (MacNaughton, 1971), was an anthology of previous sketches; the second film would feature an entirely new format and content. The film was a box office success, grossing $5,028,948 worldwide, far extending the film's modest budget of $400,000 (The Numbers). The film has a cult following and is still shown for audiences at dedicated events decades after its original release. The crux of the comedy is subverting Arthurian and medievalist themes, which gives the material a timeless factor. Founding member of the comedy team John Cleese explained the timelessness of the film in a November 2017 interview for courier-journal.com: "Cleese said that 'Holy Grail' remains a comedy milestone because, foremost, it's funny. Just as important is that its setting in ancient history allows viewers to see it without being distracted by dated references" (Puckett). This grounding of the comedy within the medievalist realm inspired the film to include common medieval associations aside from Arthur, such as the *Black Knight*, grubby peasants, witchcraft and the meddlesome French. The Templars do not appear as grail guardians in the Monty Python version of the grail story, but the influence of the Templar quest narrative is apparent in both the iconography and character in the film's depiction of Sir Galahad. Monty Python's unique version of the grail story includes many established medievalist conventions but uses comedy to subvert the audience expecta-tion and provides a parody of the Arthurian grail story. Therefore, for the parodic context the Templar narrative is combined with the pious Galahad to construct what Umland and Umland summarize as "a fop and dandy" (1996, p. 14).

Monty Python's parody with Arthurian conventions is not only the subversion of pre-established themes but also the subversion of the epic nature of the grail story with an unauthentic, low-budget aesthetic and use of cartoon animation. This parody of conventions is illustrated by the film's version of the grail reveal, which is not taken from early stories but the search for the Holy Grail charged to Arthur by the appearance of a cartoon God in the sky. Hoffman suggests, "The scene is then more a parody of the audience's expectations than it is of the actual scene" (2002, p. 140). Hoff-man's assertion is that Python's version draws from the later versions of the grail's association with Christ and the "assumptions about the quest as a define mission" (Hoffman, 2002, p. 140). The film moves Arthur and his knights away from Camelot, which prevents the grail from appearing to them there. This removes the "Pentecostal imagery of the first appearance of the Grail at Camelot, the prophecies of Siege Perilous" (Hoffman, 2002, p. 140). The removal of the appearance from Camelot focuses the story away from Galahad, who does not take up his usual grail role, but as the grail appears to King Arthur, the quest is then focused upon him.

Guerber explains the significance of Galahad with the grail story in recounting the Arthurian myth. He writes, "one of the empty seats was marked 'Siege Perilous.' Marvelling as to what this could mean, the nobles eagerly questioned Merlin, who told them that that seat was reserved for a knight who should be absolutely pure, so that did any other adven-ture himself upon it he would straightway be swallowed up by the yawn-ing earth" (1922, p. 291). According to the myth, only Sir Galahad could sit upon the Siege Perilous due to his unwavering piety and perfection, but in this version, Galahad is a Templar hybrid, and therefore, his usual lead role is made redundant in favor of inverting the chaste, pious warrior with a frigid knight with a fear of women. The appearance of the grail typifies the uniqueness of this grail story, one that uses its low budget to address the ridiculousness of the narrative further. As Hoffman explains, the deliver-ance of the divine quest "reproduces a certain kind of Moses on Sinai sub-limity, but then undercuts that sublimity completely by reducing God to a cartoon" (2002, p. 140). This undercutting envelops the comedy of authen-ticity of both aesthetics and parody of Arthurian concepts.

Even Arthur's kingly origin is made comedic through parody. Day cites from the film, writing, "Arthur, his eyes turned heavenward, launches into a description of how he received his kingship by the supernatural sanction of 'the lady of the lake, her arm clad in the purest shimmering samite,' ... Arthur is, nonetheless, abruptly cut short by Dennis' derisive squawk, followed by one of the funniest lines in the movie: 'Strange woman lying in ponds distributing swords is no basis for a system of government'" (2002, pp. 129–130). King Arthur's origin and the medieval convention of rule through divine right is made comedic, and "Dennis's dismissal of them seems that much more bizarre and jarring" due to "the presence of anachronism in the juxtaposition" (Day, 2002, p. 130). *Monty Python and the Holy Grail* incorporates the established conventions of the Arthurian myth but repackages them for comedic effect. The peasants' freethinking and rejection of Arthur's right to rule is a subversion of Arthur's pre-established, unchallenged divine authenticity of the grail myth. The amalgamation of the Templar quest narrative with Galahad also demonstrates this comedic subversion. The iconography and ideology of the Templar knight are fused with Sir Galahad, who is not the protagonist but a comedic, frigid, virgin knight; it is the film's playing with pre-established ideas that enables the comedy to remain timeless.

The ending in *Monty Python and the Holy Grail* shows perhaps the subtlest inversion of an Arthurian grail convention, due to the suddenness and unsatisfying conclusion. The film ends with Arthur at the head of an army charging the French fortress that holds the grail, only for Arthur and his knights being arrested by police officers due to the murder of the modern-day historian by the mythical Sir Lancelot. The final shot of the film is a police officer blocking the camera with his hand while King Arthur and his knights are bundled into a police van. The significance of this ending, which leaves the quest incomplete, coincides with Chrétien's original and unfinished grail story. Hoffman argues, "This inconclusive conclusion is, however, a strange replication of the original quest narratives. From Chrétien's uncompleted Perceval on to the extraordinary regenerating series of incomplete conclusions that followed, it is almost a feature of the Quest that it remains unachieved" (2002, pp. 146–147). Monty Python's version of the grail quest reproduces aspects of the myth, but in coherence with the assertions proposed in the previous paragraph, the convention of the futility of the quest is juxtaposed with the historical inaccuracy of failing due to prevention by a 20th-century policeman; thus the quest is unfulfilled.

The concept of the failed quest is one of three quest character arcs that Kennedy proposes; these are not to be confused with the Templar quest narrative as that is a reoccurrence of themes and iconography, while Kennedy's proposal supports types of quests as character arcs. This can be perceived as a more detailed look at the quest as a character arc that Christopher Booker outlines as "a long hazardous journey to reach it becomes the most important thing to him in the world ... the story is shaped by that one overriding imperative; and the story remains unresolved until the objective has been, triumphantly secured" (2011, p. 69). Kennedy proposes, "One type concerns the quest to correct mistakes that we have made in life.... A second type concerns the quest for the ideal; related to that should be consideration of the fine line between idealism and fanaticism.... And a third type ... is a quest for something that turns out to be futile and that can be dismissed as a waste of time and energy" (2009, pp. 10–11). The very self-aware ending of the film coincides with Kennedy's character arc of the notion of the quest as futile. However, the sudden and ridiculous ending does not make the film's earlier scenes dissatisfying. The film from quest set up is structurally a 91-minute series of sketches held together with a loose narrative of a quest for the Holy Grail. This loose, overarching narrative serves well to thematically link the series of jokes together but also firmly sets the film within the first type of Templar quest narrative. Monty Python demonstrates the influence of the Templar quest narrative; despite not featuring the Knights Templar by name. It does, however, feature the Templar iconography of the iconic red cross on white mantle and monastic chastity depicted within the squeamish Sir Galahad. The film's playful inversion of Arthurian conventions as shown in examples given, such as the sudden ending or peasants questioning Arthur's legitimacy, demonstrates that this comedic approach gave the film a timeless appeal. It is this parody of Arthurian conventions that made Galahad an amalgamation with Templar iconography and ideology. This enables this case study to show the influence that warrior monks extinct from the 14th century still have in popular culture through this aspect of the Templar quest narrative.

Indiana Jones and the Last Crusade

The second case study that demonstrates the Templar quest narrative of the knight is the third installment of the Indiana Jones franchise, *Indiana Jones and the Last Crusade*. Despite not being set in the medieval past but the 1930s, this film depicts Indiana Jones and his companions as grail knights and incorporates the Templar quest narrative with Templar iconography in depicting a grail guardian knight. This case study demonstrates how the Templar quest narrative of the knight is featured in popular culture not merely within a medieval setting but an association that is intrinsically linked to grail myth reset in Spielberg's 1930s' adventure.

Indiana Jones and the Last Crusade took $474,171,806 worldwide (Box Office Mojo); the film was not only a financial success but a critical one. Sullivan asserts that although *Raiders of the Lost Ark* (Spielberg, 1981) "has come to occupy the primary place in the public's imagination as the jewel in the series crown" (2015, p. 158), he suggests that *Indiana Jones and the Last Crusade* is the finest film of the franchise. He cites Robinson's review in *The Times of London* that judged Indy III as "Probably the best written and generally most accomplished of the series" (Sullivan, 2015, p. 158). Despite the Holy Grail featuring in the title, the grail quest is sidelined for a more human quest; Sullivan explains, "they use the Grail as a means-to-an-end, one whose attainment stands metaphorically for the film's most important theme, namely the quest of a son for, and reconciliation with, a distant father" (2015, p. 158). Despite the film's central empathic human theme, *Indiana Jones and the Last Crusade*, like the two previous installments, focus around the hunt for a supernatural object. In an interview with *Vanity Fair* in February 2008, executive producer George Lucas explains, "Indiana Jones films are supernatural mystery movies. They're always going after some supernatural object" (Windolf). Essentially, the Indiana franchise focuses its narrative around a quest for the MacGuffin, which coincides with the first type of Templar quest narrative, as the object of the quest is redundant in the wake of the emotional journey of the character.

The prominence of the MacGuffin as the focal point of the *Indiana Jones* franchise is demonstrated by Lucas' difficulty in fashioning one for the fourth installment. In an interview for *Entertainment Weekly* in April 2008, Lucas said, "When we go to [the idea of making a fourth] one, I had already said, 'No. I can't think of another MacGuffin'" (Daly). Lacy argues that in medieval literature, "The Grail unarguably functions as a true McGuffin [*sic*].... But despite its obvious value, I suggest that it is a McGuffin because its effect, if not purpose, is to provoke, stimulate, and sustain action, much of which actually has no connection" (2005, p. 61). The transfer of the grail from a literary MacGuffin to film MacGuffin proposed an early challenge for the production, as Lucas in a *Vanity Fair* interview explains:

> The Holy Grail has mythical connotations, has been ascribed with several powers, but nothing very specific. So we had a time when we were going to do it and we rejected it, and we thought we better add to it some sort of healing property, to give it something to grab onto—which have been alluded to in the history of the Holy Grail [Windolf, Feb, 2008].

The healing process Lucas refers to is that of the wounded Fisher King by Percival or Galahad, depending on which version you read. The powers and appearance of the Holy Grail are adapted to suit the film's story, drawing upon a large amount of folklore similarly to how producers draw upon the reoccurring Templar narrative to suit their desired narrative themes. However, seeking the grail is not the focus of the film's personal story, but as Sullivan explains, "Rather they use the Grail as a means-to-an-end, one whose attainment stands metaphorically for the film's most important theme, namely the quest of a son for, and reconciliation with, a distant father" (2015, p. 158). The quest for the grail in actuality is a search for Indiana's father and the healing powers of the grail seen as symbolic of healing the relationship between Indy and his father. Focusing the third Indiana Jones film around the Holy Grail was never deemed a direct intention by Lucas and Spielberg, as Lucas said in an interview with *Entertainment Weekly*:

> I said, look, let's just try the Holy Grail. Ohhh, it's too cerebral, we'll never make it work.... So we turned it into a tangible magic cup with healing powers, instead of an intellectual thing. It wasn't until the idea of introducing the father came along that we kind of pulled [the third movie] out of the fire. Because it then shifted from being *about* the MacGuffin [Daly, April 2008].

Lucas' crediting of the change of focus from the mythical artifact to the relationship between Indiana Jones and his father is further demonstrated by the success of the film overseas. Sullivan cites from the *New York Times*, writing, "'Sean Connery is a good actor to Americans, but a superstar to the rest of the world...' And that the film did, in fact, earn much more overseas ($297 million) than domestically ($197 million) undoubtedly had at least something to do with Connery's star power among foreign audiences" (2015, p. 168). Spielberg himself was concerned about addressing the quest for the Holy Grail as the grail was firmly cemented in popular culture through Monty Python. In the interview with *Entertainment Weekly*, he stated, "Of course, I was worried that people would hear Holy Grail, and they would immediately think about a white rabbit attacking Monty Python. My first reaction was to say, everybody run away! Run away" (Daly, April 2008). Spielberg's concerns about *Monty Python and the Holy Grail* show how embedded the low-budget comedy became within popular grail associations despite its unconventional take on the myth. This notion of an unconventional grail myth runs parallel in this case study. Spielberg's version offers an alternative take from within the 1930s' adventures of Indiana Jones, but like Monty Python it still incorporates the Templar quest narrative of the knight.

The Indiana Jones films are not set in the medieval period but pre–World War II, which differs from the qualifier of the quest of the knight being set in a medieval/Arthurian world. However, Aronstein would argue that the Indiana Jones films are reimaginings of medieval romances. She outlines, "The tales of Indiana Jones are tales of knighthood, modernizations of medieval chivalric romances" and that in the film, *Indiana Jones and the Last Crusade* "his achievement of the Grail makes him just that—and not just any knight, but the best knight in the world" (1995, p. 3). The association of an Arthurian grail quest with Indy's quest is made apparent within Boam's original screenplay, which has Henry Jones declare to Indy, Sallah and Brody: "We are like the four renowned grail heroes of legend. (glances at Sallah) Bors, the ordinary man. (Looks to Brody) Perceval, the Holy innocent. (Looks at Indy) Galahad, the valorous knight. (then; meaning himself) And Lancelot…. Galahad's father. The Old Crusader. Who was turned away because he wasn't worthy. And perhaps neither am I" (1988, p. 120). This seemingly on-the-nose piece of dialogue supports the intention for Indiana Jones to not merely follow in the footsteps of the knights but that he is himself one. Indy's knightly prowess is further demonstrated in a literal sense by using a flagpole as a lance while riding a motorcycle during a chase scene with Nazi soldiers. Despite the non-medieval setting, *Indiana Jones and the Last Crusade* is still encapsulated within the first type of Templar quest narrative due to the Arthurian reimagining of Indiana as a grail knight. Also, in sync with the quest of the knight, the quest for the grail serves as a plot device for the underlying focus of family reunification. Therefore completing the objective of the grail, as with the previous case study, it has no impact but is the motivator of the story.

The other crucial aspect of determining *Indiana Jones and the Last Crusade* as following the Templar quest narrative of the knight is in its lacking one of the primary signifiers for the quest type following in the Templars' footsteps. This key determining signifier is the notion of American exceptionalism, which the second half of this chapter explores in greater detail. However, with *Indiana Jones and the Last Crusade*, Wasser proposes that the film "has hardly any references to American exceptionalism, which is also in contrast to its contemporary action films" (2010, p. 143). Wasser believes that Spielberg wanted "to put distance between the Indiana Jones character and white male dominance" (2010, p. 142). Friedman addresses the criticism that Spielberg's Indiana Jones series has received by citing McBride, writing:

> McBride severely chastises Spielberg for skilfully manipulating audiences into "identifying with this ruthless figure and finding him heroic," for cynically exploiting him for "purely visceral thrills," for presenting his violence and greed in a "winking tongue-in-cheek style," and for "anesthetizing the audience's moral sense" over a "casually amoral" character who "loots Third World Cultures" [2006, pp. 115–116].

In contrast to the colonial criticism of the franchise and to set the third installment apart from the 1980s' genre conventions, Spielberg "denied himself the opportunity for egregious colonialism of the previous two

Raider movies by safely confining most of the story's action to Europe and the United States. The violence is mostly white on white. Indiana Jones even meets the ultimate Aryan: Adolf Hitler" (Wasser, 2010, p. 142). This notion of Spielberg's desire to move away from American exceptionalism and right-wing ideology suggests why the Templar narrative is apparent within the film, but the film does not mention the Order directly by name due to the Order's association with the extreme ideology that the works of Sir Walter Scott personify.

Despite not mentioning the Templars by name, Haag argues that the third Indiana Jones film is significant in bringing the Knights Templar to the forefront of popular culture. He argues, "with Spielberg's film *Indiana Jones and the Last Crusade* (1989), an order that had officially died out seven hundred years ago suddenly came to feel part of Zeitgeist" (2009, p. 331). Haag further explains his point by listing the increase in Templar novels that followed on after *Indiana Jones and the Last Crusade* and before the international bestseller, *The Da Vinci Code* (Brown, 2003). Haag informs, "In the next decade, Katherine Kurtz, an American novelist, ... launched a series of heroic Templar fantasy novels; British writer Michael Jacks penned various Cadfael-esque murder mysteries starring a Templar called Sir Baldwin; and Swedish author Jan Guillou entered the fray with a trilogy about a Swedish Templar" (2009, p. 331). What Haag does not address though with this notion is why the Templars are never actually mentioned by name in *Indiana Jones and the Last Crusade*; instead Spielberg introduced a Templar-esque copy called The Knights of the Cruciform Sword. This omission of the Templar name is due to the desire for the inclusion of a third rival faction in a later draft of the script called the Brotherhood of the Cruciform Sword.

This rival faction would include characters who were agents of the Sultan of Hatay and include the grail knight guardian whose appearance was a slight change to the iconic red cross on white background. The symbol of The Knights of the Cruciform Sword is a red cross on a white background but with two additional bars; the highest one is curved into a semi-circle to give the impression of the grail. The knight himself wears full armor as expected of the conventional knight, but like the stereotypical Templar knight, the Knight of the Cruciform Sword wears a white tabard over his armor which displays the red cruciform symbol of the knightly order. When highlighting the specifics of Templar fiction texts, Haag explains that the film "has a suggestively Templar theme and features a scene in which the weary Templar like guardian of The Holy Grail looks forward with quiet relief to ending his 800-year watch.... Even though the sets are full of eight-pointed stars and talk of chivalrous knights abounds, the Templars are not mentioned once" (Haag, 2009, p. 341). The inclusion of the quasi

Templar knight shows the role of the Templar quest narrative within the film. Lucas and Spielberg chose to incorporate Wolfram von Eschenbach's Templar grail knight and the iconography of the Templar knight. However, they infused the role of the Templar guardian with other characters in the narrative to create a third rival faction in claiming the grail.

The inclusion of the Brotherhood of the Cruciform Sword came from the uncredited script rewrite by Tom Stoppard. Stoppard made many changes to the original Jeffrey Boam screenplay; one of the significant changes was the role of Kazim and his new role within a new third party, The Brotherhood of the Cruciform Sword. In an online article for *Creative Screenwriting*, Mike Fitzgerald analyzes Stoppard's influence on the script and the importance of the change to Kazim's role. Fitzgerald explains:

> in the earlier draft he works for the Sultan of Hatay, who is also hunting for the grail. When the Sultan allies with the Nazis, Kazim basically becomes a Nazi grunt. The revised version thickens the plot by having Kazim instead serve the Brotherhood of the Cruciform Sword, a group avowed to protect the grail [March, 2016].

This inclusion of a third party seeking the grail not only heightened the conflict with new obstacles for Indiana but changed the connotations of the Templar's role within the film. In the original Boam script the knights are simply referred to as "Grail Knights," and according to the original script uploaded to *Creative Screenwriting*, "he is dressed as what he is: A grail Knight" (Boam, 1988, p. 217); the only detail of the knight's image given is "the chalice symbol on the [*sic*] his breastplate" (Boam, 1988, p. 217). The description of the knight offers little insight into the inspiration behind the grail knight; however, a conversation between Indy, Brody, and Elsa offers hints of the knights' origins and Templar influence. Brody explains that the knights "were the ones said to have actually found the grail seven hundred years ago," which Elsa follows by commenting, "That's right. They formed the order of the Grail" (Boam, 1988, p. 40). These lines of exposition demonstrate the Templars' early influence on the generic grail knight. Although the Templar Order was functioning 700 hundred years ago, it was founded 100 years earlier. However, one of the Templar myths within popular culture is that the Templars found the grail and like Boam's grail order, created an order to protect it.

The inclusion of a Templar-esque order of knights is in no way a coincidence, and it must be stated that Lucas and Spielberg were aware of the Templars' appearance within the grail quest. Gordon claims that Lucas "researched grail lore" (2008, p. 138), and this knowledge of the Templars' role within the lore is displayed during an interview with Spielberg and Lucas. During a discussion on the mythology of the Indiana Jones

MacGuffin and the Holy Grail, Lucas stated: "We may have exaggerated some of its powers, but basically there are people who believe there is a Holy Grail, brought back by the Knights Templar" (Daly, April 2008). The crusading connotations of the Knights Templar are also infused with Spielberg's grail knight; Indiana himself refers to one of the knights as a "knight of the first crusade" (Spielberg, 1989). This coincided with Lucas's opinion that the Templars brought the grail into Europe from the Holy Land, and it indicates that Lucas and Spielberg wanted for their adaptation on the grail myth to include the Templars' role of grail guardians and the iconography associated with the order.

The incorporation of the Templar-like grail knight owes much to the Wolfram grail stories and runs parallel with the story's thematic focus on family but also to Chrétien de Troyes's grail story that Wolfram's work builds upon. Sullivan notes that by using the grail as the MacGuffin, the film can be more faithful to the mythical literature. He states, "In associating the Grail with the reunification of father and son, the filmmakers stumble upon a connection between the Grail and family that is at the very heart of many medieval Grail romances" (2015, p. 169). Sullivan highlights the similarity between *Indiana Jones and the Last Crusade* and Chrétien de Troyes's *Percival*, noting the narrative of *Percival* being the "hero who seeks the Grail is both the maternal nephew of the old Fisher King as well as related to many of figures most instrumental to directing him to the Grail" (2015, p. 169). The conclusion of Indiana Jones' quest mirrors this as the father figure is healed through the success of the grail quest. For *Indiana Jones and the Last Crusade,* the healing is both physical and spiritual, due to healing the relationship between a father and son as well as a mortal gunshot wound to Henry Jones. The thematic healing of the father and son, as well as the literal healing of the father figure, further demonstrates the validity of including this case study within the parameters of the quest of the knight narrative.

However apparent the influence of these early grail texts may be on *Indiana Jones and the Last Crusade*, Sullivan asserts, "there is no indication that Chrétien or Wolfram or any other author of a medieval Grail romance directly influenced the filmmakers in the formulation of their own Grail. Instead the decision to make the Grail a source of eternal life seems to have been a rather spur-of-the-moment one that Lucas proposed to make the Grail more appealing" (2015, p. 159). In terms of the quest as a character arc, Kennedy suggests that *Indiana Jones and the Last Crusade* can be defined as "The Quest for the ideal" with the theme of "the fine line between idealism and fanaticism" (2009, p. 10). This is reflected in the inclusion of the Nazis as the opposition grail seekers who want the grail to dominate civilization, while Indiana only wants the grail to save his father's life. The theme of Nazi occultism is not unique to this film and was a significant theme in the franchise's first installment: *Indiana Jones and the Raiders of the Lost Ark,* but for this installment Kennedy suggests, "The film's plot may have been influenced by a book written by Otto Rahm, one of Hitler's SS officers. *Rahn's Kreuzzug gegem den Gral (The Crusade for the Grail),* written in 1933," which Kennedy claims was "influenced by Wolfram's *Parzival*" (2009, p. 20). The notion of the film's influence by Nazi occultism is shared by Umland and Umland, although they claim the influence is from a different source. Umland and Umland suggest that *Indiana Jones and the Last Crusade* draws its influence from Trevor Ravenscroft's *The Spear of Destiny* (1973); the book "examines the occult beliefs in the spear as used by artists from Wolfram to Wagner and by the Nazis as well" (1996, p. 15). The theme of Nazi occultists is a significant theme within Indiana Jones, Umland and Umland cite from Pollock's biography of George Lucas stating that influence for the film is "Trevor Ravenscroft's *Spear of Destiny,* which allegedly documents the Nazi interest in religious relics with putative occult powers" (1996, p. 169). Although Kennedy and Umland and Umland cite different influences on *Indiana Jones and the Last Crusade,* what they both acknowledge is the inspiration of the Nazi fascination with the occult.

The suggestion of inspiration by Nazi occult texts offers an insight into why Lucas and Spielberg included the Templar quest narrative and Templar iconography in Boam's original script before being repackaged in the later draft. The switch from naming the grail knight as a Templar takes away the right-wing and racist connotations of the Templar narrative (as explored in Chapter 1) and allows the Knight of the Cruciform Sword to represent goodness and stand as the polar opposite to the Nazi grail seekers. This follows Sullivan's argument that the Nazis are used in Spielberg's film to create a polar opposite to the good of the grail. He argues, "the filmmakers chose not to explore the complexity of the actual historical Nazi evil with their own, cartoonish film-Nazis but rather to let them stand-in for a general, a vague badness in contrast with the inherent goodness of the Grail" (2015, p. 163). This notion of the grail representing goodness offers insight into why the Templars' quest narrative was included but did not recognize them by name, as the Templars are also associated with the same aspects of villainy as the film's Nazi archetype. It is not only the right-wing connotations that the Templar narrative shares with the film's villains but also associations with the occult, as that was one of the unproven charges levied against the Order which led to their downfall.

The occult became associated with the warrior monks when the Templar leaders were arrested in 1307 and charged with heresy. Haag explains that the accusation was that when "being inducted into the order, initiates were required to deny Christ, spit on the cross and place obscene kisses about the body of the receptor" (2009, p. 218). These accusations would be abhorrent to a medieval order of the church, but the association with the occult and witchcraft came from worshiping "a strange idol which looked like a human head with a long beard called Baphomet" (Haag, 2009, p. 218). Newman clarifies, "most Templars, even the ones who had been tortured, claimed to have no idea what the inquisitors were talking about. However, the ones who did tell of an idol described it differently" (2007, p. 338). It is worth noting, "it is generally agreed that 'Baphomet' is a corruption of the name 'Mohammed,' and linguistically; that is probable" (Newman, 2007, p. 338). The implausibility of the accusations against the Templars is strengthened by Haag's fact: "Heresy was the one possible charge that the king could successfully level against the Templars, and so heresy it had to be" (2009, p. 219). The Templars were vulnerable only to accusations of heresy due "to a loophole in the law going back to the time of the Cathars" (Haag, 2009, p. 219). These unfounded accusations of heresy provided a cornerstone in the emerging reoccurring Templar quest narrative, which was not disproven until the discovery of the Chinon Parchment in the Vatican archives in 2001. Haag informs that it "reveals that the Pope found no heresy among the Templars and granted absolution to its leaders" (2009, p. 232). However, the Templars' relationship with the occult has been embedded within the Templar mythos and explored in literature centuries after their trial and abolishment.

The Templars' occultist link resurfaced in the 1531 German book *De Occulta Philosophia* by Heinrich Agrippa. Haag argues that due to their mention in this book "the Templars were raised from the depths of half-forgotten failures and became the focus of the darkest disturbing forces in the European mind" (2009, p. 257), an association which has inspired numerous works throughout the 20th century and into the 21st century. The occultist Templar is the major theme of the 1972 Spanish film *Tomb of the Blind Dead/La Noche del Terror Ciego* by Amando de Ossorio, which features blood-drinking, undead Templars, who don their armor and steads to terrorize and murder a group of teenagers. As fantastical as the plot sounds, the "film was successful enough for de Ossorio to make three more: *Return of the Evil Dead (1973), The Ghost Galleon (1974), Night of the Seagulls (1975)*" (Haag, 2009, p. 341). This trope of the undead Knights Templar recently reappeared in the 2017 film *The Mummy* (Kurtzman), which featured the undead Templars as minions of the antagonist. These supernatural Templar monsters show how the Templar villain aspect of the narrative has been sensationalized into a movie monster and also demonstrates how Templar iconography and a reoccurring Templar narrative are interchangeable. The Templars' association with the occult is an inspiration behind the monstrous undead Templar of the *Tomb of the Blind*

Dead films but also infiltrates into the quest narrative with the juxtaposition of the Templars alongside the Nazi villains. The association of the occult with the Order of the Knights Templar remains despite the accusations remaining unproven. This adds weight to the assertion that the Templar narrative has been able to continue expanding due to the Order's extinction in 1312, leaving no officials to dispute such associations to the occult.

Indiana Jones and the Last Crusade falls into the category of the quest of the knight narrative despite not being set in a medieval/Arthurian world. Due to the film's depiction of Indiana and his companions as grail knights, the inclusion of grail themes, such as the healing of the father and son's relationship and the physical healing of the father figure, Spielberg's adaptation is encompassed within the parameters of the Templar quest narrative. In a similar fashion to the Monty Python case study earlier in the chapter, where Templar iconography and associated traits were parodied without the Order's mention, *Indiana Jones and the Last Crusade* incorporates the Templar quest narrative and iconography but also without the name. The fictional Knight of the Cruciform Sword replaces the Templar name, which was created in a later script draft to serve a dramatic function. This knight plays the role of the Templar grail guardian, which first appeared in the 13th-century poem *Parzival*, with a slight variation on the iconic Templar regalia. This sleight of hand with the name enables the film producers to use the Templar quest narrative of the knight without other aspects of the Templar narrative encroaching and causing the film's themes to clash. The traits of the bad Templar aspect of the narrative draw connotative comparisons with the film's Nazi villains, who are intended to represent oppositional evil to the goodness of the grail and the knight guarding it. It is in this way that Spielberg and Lucas were able to use the Templar quest narrative without thematically undesired connotations bleeding into the Templar quest narrative, which depicts the Templar knight as the guardian of the grail.

The Templar Conspiracy Theme

The first half of this chapter focuses on the Templar quest aspect of the knight, which originated back in the 13th century as part of Arthurian poetry, then used case studies from the 20th century to demonstrate how this concept is apparent within popular culture. The Templar narrative has become a malleable concept over its reoccurrence that has enabled the narrative to incorporate several aspects of the Templar phenomenon within the key narrative aspects. The case study, *Indiana Jones and the Last*

Crusade, demonstrated the malleability of the Templar narrative through the inclusion of the Templars' mythical association with the occult into the grail narrative. The Templar phenomenon became malleable due to the extinction of the original and purest form of the Knights Templar back in the early 14th century. This meant that without the original denotive Templar, the conative Templar myths have been unhampered and grown into a reoccurring malleable narrative. It is this significance which enables the Templar narrative to be reoccurring and thus creates a second aspect to the pre-established 13th-century Templar quest narrative.

The reason for analyzing the quest narrative with two aspects in mind is due to the moving of the story's setting away from the past and into the modern world. The protagonists are not themselves knights like the first aspect but seek the Templar knights and research the forgotten history of the Templars. These key variations within Templar narratives mean that the Templar quest narrative should be analyzed from the perspective of two aspects, although not a completely different type of Templar narrative, as the second aspect incorporates joint signifying traits of a shared quest narrative. The quest of the knight depicts the knight's quest into the world of the supernatural to find a treasured item, which is akin to the traditional mythic tale. However, the quest to follow in the footsteps of the Templar follows the protagonist's quest into the past world of the Templar to rediscover a lost truth of value to society. It is the rudimentary similarities of these two aspects that encompass them within the Templar narrative of the quest, which demonstrates the significance of the malleability to the reoccurrence of the Templar narrative.

The case studies chosen to establish the second quest narrative are the 2004 film *National Treasure*, directed by Jon Turteltaub and starring Nicolas Cage, and the 2006 film *The Da Vinci Code,* directed by Ron Howard and starring Tom Hanks, as well as the previous novel by Dan Brown. These case studies were chosen due to their popularity and financial success as both films were worldwide successes at the box office, with *National Treasure* taking $347,512,318 (Box Office Mojo) and *The Da Vinci Code* doubling that, taking $758,239,851 worldwide (Box Office Mojo). *The Da Vinci Code* novel was no less popular as "By the time the film version was released in May 2006, the book had still not left the New York Times bestseller list since its release" (in 2004) (Johnsrud, 2014, p. 103). Johnsrud cites from Dan Brown's official website to highlight, "as of 2009, the novel had sold more than 80 million copies worldwide" (2014, p. 103).

Similar to the first aspect's use of the grail theme as the focus for the quest, the second aspect uses the conspiracy as an impetus for the quest. *National Treasure* focuses on the conspiracy that the Templars took a secret treasure to North America to wait for the creation of the United States of

America; this conspiracy is the crux that sends the protagonist, Ben Gates (Nicolas Cage), on his quest. *The Da Vinci Code* uses the conspiracy theory surrounding the Templars' sudden disappearance due to their secret knowledge, which Robert Langdon (Tom Hanks) quests to discover. These narratives are both set in the modern day and depict the protagonist on a quest into the past to rediscover a forgotten truth, which is why this aspect is not a quest of the knight but the quest to follow in the Templars' footsteps. The forgotten truth discovered in *National Treasure* is the desire for the American Founding Fathers to redistribute the world's wealth, and in *The Da Vinci Code* it is the renewed faith in Christ due to his human lineage on earth. The conspiracy, like the grail in the first aspect, acts as the motivation to set out on the quest, and by venturing into the Templar past, the protagonist will solve the conspiracy, and instead of a healing grail, the protagonist will find a forgotten truth that will benefit Western society.

Despite *National Treasure* and *The Da Vinci Code's* worldwide popularity, both films were very successful in the United States, with *National Treasure* making almost half of its revenue, taking $173,008,894 domestically (Box Office Mojo). *The Da Vinci Code* took $217,536,138 domestically; although dwarfed by the $540,703,713 (Box Office Mojo) it took from the foreign market, the domestic takings were still more than double any other country's box office. The popularity of *The Da Vinci Code* and *National Treasure* in the United States is arguably influenced by the American production (*National Treasure* is a Disney picture) and Hollywood stars Hanks and Cage as well as the latter's setting around American landmarks and historical events. However, the films also benefit from including the prominent theme of the conspiracy theory, which was ever-present in wider society post 9/11. Oliver and Wood examined the conspiracy culture within American society and analyzed data collected from "four nationally representative surveys" that "were fielded in 2006, 2010, and 2011 as modules in the Cooperative Congressional Election Studies" (2014, p. 955). Oliver and Wood concluded that they:

> do see that both the willingness to agree with conspiracy theories or see them as valid explanations for political phenomena are quite commonplace in the American public. Not only does half of the American population agree with at least one conspiracy from a shortlist of conspiracy theories offered, but also large portions of the population exhibit a strong dispositional inclination toward believing that unseen, intentional forces exist and that history is driven by a Manichean struggle between good and evil [2014, pp. 963–964].

These findings offer insight into the interest and popularity of the Templar conspiracy theme and propose that the conspiracy theory narrative, in general, is part of the American political climate and American popular culture. It is this Western interest in the theme of conspiracy that has enabled the Templar quest narrative to branch into a second aspect because the quest for truth-seeking in a post 9/11 West coincides with the mystery surrounding the demise of the Templars hundreds of years ago to form a new type of Templar quest narrative. The mystery around the Templars' demise is fueled with ongoing uncertainty since the Order's 14th-century extinction. The post 9/11 climate concept of venturing into the dangerous unknown is not about traveling to a foreign land but peeking behind the curtain of your own country. This notion of hidden within plain sight conspiracy coincides with the change of the quest narratives focus of grail seeking in a supernatural world to revisiting Western history to discover a revelation.

Conspiracy theory narratives are generally themed around concepts of an unnoticed elitist suppression of powerless citizens. To define the perception of conspiracy theory in American society, Oliver and Wood would cite Davis (1971), defining, "Americans periodically have organized themselves around narratives about hidden, malevolent groups secretly perpetuating political plots and social calamities to further their own nefarious goals, what we would define as 'conspiracy theory'" (2014, p. 952). These oppressive fantasies described above differ to the revelations discovered within the Templar conspiracy theme, which once revealed would vindicate Western culture does not reveal it as oppressive. These positive revelations demonstrate the divergence of the Templar quest to follow in the Templars' footsteps from the conventional American conspiracy narrative. The Templar conspiracy revelation acts like the grail, which like the wondrous item, would benefit mankind. It is this positive outcome that links the two aspects of the quest narrative together.

The positive Templar revelation is the outcome of this aspect's case studies, *National Treasure* and *The Da Vinci Code*, which both reveal in their story's conclusion the vindication of Western culture by reestablishing America as the shining light of democracy and belief in the historical existence of Jesus Christ. The concept of the positive Templar revelation is emphasized by Aronstein and Torry, who argue, "both the Da Vinci Code and National Treasure employ Templar legend to revive optimism, rediscover 'original truth,' and restore faith—whether in a miraculous divine (*The Da Vinci Code*) or America's privileged destiny (*National Treasure*)" (2009, p. 226). The Templar quest narrative of following in the Templars' footsteps introduces a revelation that justifies and is a revival of the audience's traditional belief in religion and American patriotism through the protagonist's journey into the historical world of sensational Templar myth.

America's Templar Link to the Past

Following in the Templars' footsteps incorporates myths from the already rich tapestry of Templar fantasies to merge with the growing post 9/11 interest in a conspiracy theory to forge a Templar revelation that offers a link to a medieval past. The Templar conspiracy theme became "identified with American history, this legend of the Templars' hidden truth merged with the myth of America's privileged destiny" (Aronstein & Torry, 2009, p. 226). This merging of mythic histories to create the conspiracy stands apart from the conventional paranoid conspiracy theory, dated back to post–World War II America. To introduce the concept of conspiracy theory in America, Timothy Melley cites Richard Hofstadter, writing, "this way of thinking insists that important events are controlled by 'a vast and sinister conspiracy, a gigantic and yet subtle machinery of influence set in motion to undermine and destroy a way of life'" (2000, p. 1). Hofstadter's account of conspiracies paints a disastrous, doomed way of life which contrasts with the optimistic link to a medieval past and vindication for Western values that the Templar revelation provides at the quest's end.

The interest and popularity in such negative conspiracies, such as the surrendering of belief to an all-powerful shadowy organization, according to Melley, is in part due to conspiracy bringing people a sense of ease. Melley explains, "the idea of conspiracy offers an odd sort of comfort in an uncertain age: it makes sense of the inexplicable, accounting for complex events in a clear, if frightening, way" (2000, p. 8). These frightening conspiracies are commonly used to explain the political climate and tragedy around instances such as JFK's assassination and the events of 9/11 and the post–9/11 invasion of Iraq. Ray Pratt notes, "Before Osama Bin Laden and the Al-Qaeda network there were irrational, 'paranoid' fears of men-in-black with license to kill, black helicopters under UN control taking over America, and fears of 'mad cow' disease" (2003, p. 255). These fears listed, point to the level of distrust towards the American government, which focused on the threat of the conspiracy within.

In the wake of the 9/11 attacks, there has been an "upsurge in trust in government since then, fears directed at government men-in-black are now projected onto networks of Islamic radicals who may, in fact, be hiding within the borders of the United States" (Pratt, 2003, p. 256). This notion of the outside threat hiding among us is still prevalent today, with the fear of ISIS terrorists infiltrating into Europe as refugees. The conspiracy theory has been and remains a significant theme of film and TV texts since the Second World War. Melley highlights, "Numerous post-war narratives concern characters who are nervous about the way large, and often vague, organizations might be controlling their lives, influencing their actions, or even constructing their desires" (2000, pp. 7–8). Television conspiracy thriller shows such as *24* (Cochran & Surnow, 2001–2010), *Prison Break* (Scheuring, 2005–2017) or the more recent *Designated Survivor* (Guggenhiem, 2016–2019) draw upon the themes of shadowy political groups influencing the unaware public. Conspiracy science fiction/fantasy shows such as *The X-Files* (Charter, 1993–2018), *The 4400* (Echevarria & Peters, 2004–2007) and *Supernatural* (Kripke, 2005–2020), draw upon those same themes but with fantastical villains, such as aliens, a terrorist organization from the future and a race of shape-shifting monsters called Leviathans who have infiltrated the positions of the most powerful in America.

What connects both the entertainment texts and current popular conspiracies is the feeling of powerlessness. Pratt cites Fenster to explain this reoccurrence of notions of feeling powerless: "just because in some specific cases 'overarching conspiracy theories are wrong does not mean they aren't onto something'" (2003, p. 258). The same could be said of the fantastical villains of the science fiction texts; they are, of course, dark fantasy, but the popularity of such shows indicates the anxiety around shadowy threats to the American nation. Pratt summarizes Fenster's theory, explaining, "if people feel powerless it is, because to ever greater degrees, they are powerless. Actual power proceeds from agencies and entities ever more removed from popular control or effective monitoring by elected officials" (2003, p. 259). These notions of powerlessness within the conspiracy theme reveal the Western culture to be corrupt and oppressive, while the Templar revelation vindicates the West of such negative perceptions. The Templar conspiracy theme does not focus on the infiltration of oppressive shadowy groups as in conventional post 9/11 conspiracy fiction but the rediscovery of the Templar shadow of history, a discovery that is liberating by offering renewed faith in Western history and reaffirming of Western culture.

The Templars' association with America is due to the marketing of 18th-century Freemasons and the myth of the hidden Templar treasure in the United States. Despite the historical inaccuracy of these links, the Templar appropriation has created what Aronstein and Torry would describe as a typological link, which makes the Templars part of America's link to the Holy Land. Aronstein and Torry explain that Templar and American myth merge through what they explain as the Puritans' belief in "Typology." They explain:

> Typology as hermeneutical strategy began with the desire to discern a prophetic unity between the old and New Testaments. Thus Old Testament events and figures were to be understood proleptically as forecasting their more perfect embodiment in a divinely ordered historical sequence governed by the movement from the initial instance, the *type*, to the fulfilment, the *antitype* [2009, pp. 228–229].

This process of interpreting religious occurrences alongside historical events created the beliefs of America's divine destiny. Aronstein and Torry clarify this notion, stating, this "understanding saw in the New World the site of antitype of the Exodus crossing of the Red Sea, the puritans the antitype of the nation of Israel fleeing the European 'Egypt/Babylon' for a new Israel in America" (2009, p. 229). By employing this method of addressing history, the Puritans would deem the Knights Templar the Type and would name the American Freemasons the Antitype, which would mean that the Freemason founding fathers were predestined to create the new Israel and demonstrate America's divine right and concept of exceptionalism. Aronstein and Torry identify the extent of this version of America as in "the New World God's plan is both made manifest and fulfilled; similarly, the versions of Templar romance that relocate both Templars and treasure to the New World identify America as the end of history, the repository of truth and revelation" (2009, p. 229). This concept of the Templars as America's typological link to the past demonstrates how the Templar quest narrative of following in the Templars' footsteps provides a positive revelation by claiming America's historical legitimacy.

The concept of America's typological ideology is further established through the prominence of "the Jeremiad" in the Puritans' later generations. According to the concept of typology, the Puritans saw themselves as the new Israelites, but the later generations were faltering in their interest of the utopian mission and became the typological manifestation of the decline of the Judean people as described in the Old Testament text, the Book of Jeremiad. Madsen interprets Clergyman John Cotton's 1641 sermon to explain how the narrative for God's chosen people had changed to focus on the negative; she writes:

> Cotton argues that fellowship with Christ in suffering is an assurance of ultimate deliverance from application. God punished His chosen people because they are so special to Him and because they have been entrusted with a unique spiritual destiny. Affliction can then be seen as a sign of God's ultimate favour but also of His immediate wrath; suffering is a sign that changes must be made to renew personal and collective faith in the terms of the covenant [1998, p. 25].

The American Jeremiad reminded the later Puritan generations of their mission and their divine destiny but also of the perils of failing to build the protestant utopia. Geraghty proposes that the "American Jeremiad was optimistic and promised success to those chosen to build a new Zion; most importantly it showed non-puritans the infallibility of the puritan cause and affirmed exultation" (2007, pp. 72–73). The American Jeremiad shows a desire to remind future generations of the original mission and America's biblical legitimacy as the new Israelites, sentiments that echo through the empowering Templar revelation. The second aspect of the Templar quest narrative shows a secular retelling of the essence of the American Jeremiad due to the Templars' typological links to America and the benefits that the West would gain if these forgotten values are rediscovered. The Templar conspiracy is a vital theme used in the Templar quest narrative as this link adds significance to the Templar revelation due to the perception of Templar history being part of fundamental American history and religious truth.

Holy Blood *and* The Da Vinci Code

The Da Vinci Code draws from the Templar conspiracy theme to underpin the scope and magnitude of the conspiracy, using the perception of the Templars as guardians of the Holy Grail, infused with the Order as victims of the Catholic Church in their downfall. The combination of two features of the Templar phenomenon demonstrates the malleability of the Templar narrative with this forging of a Templar revelation. Although Brown's novel incorporates the concept of the grail, it is still part of the second aspect of the quest narrative due to its modern-day setting. Also, due to the idea that the grail is not a physical item but a mechanism to represent the lineage from Jesus's marriage to Mary Magdalene (i.e., the bloodline of Jesus Christ). In the book this invention is argued academically, with its crucial argument being use of language. This key aspect Lacy explains as "according to the novel rests on a linguistic 'error' involving 'San Greal,' which, we are informed, should actually be 'Sang Real'" (2004, p. 87), which translates to royal blood. It is essential to establish first that Brown's narrative was not unique but a concept published widely in *The Holy Blood and the Holy Grail* by Baigent, Leigh and Lincoln in 1982 but repackaged in popular fiction in 2004 through *The Da Vinci Code*. Partridge asserts that there is "evidence to suggest that the plot of The Da Vinci Code is lifted almost wholesale" (2008, p. 121) from Baigent, Leigh and Lincoln's work. Partridge summarizes the connections in that Brown's novel "draws explicitly on popular conspiracies about western Christianity and, as Baigent, Leigh & Lincoln had done, includes within its theories about the Priory of Sion and the Knights Templar, which have been popular with occulture since the 1960s" (2008, p. 121). Despite Brown's inspiration, this notion that Holy Grail was a misprint for Royal Blood underpins the entire conspiracy. Newman debunks this, stating, "there are a number of problems with the theory, the most important being that this only works in modern Spanish," also noting, "in no other language of the Middle Ages can 'Holy Grail' be twisted to mean 'Holy Blood'" (2007, p. 365). This clever use of wordplay that underpins the theory fails to replicate into any language that of the Middle Ages and debunks the theory that the medieval scholars made a typo. The concept of the Holy Grail as the blood of Christ is no more real than Excalibur, the Percival myths or the magic healing properties of Indiana Jones' grail.

Although as Aronstein highlights, the nonfiction book *Holy Blood, Holy Grail*'s "exposure of the massive cover-up of an explosive truth, of a suppressed history, is nothing new; in fact, many of its methods and some of its conclusions closely mirror those early occultist texts, most notably occultist A.E. Waithe's *Hidden Church of the Holy Grail*" published in 1909 (2015, p. 115). Despite not pioneering these fantastical theories, Baigent and Leigh attempted to sue *The Da Vinci Code*'s publishers for plagiarism. They were unsuccessful with this due to the difference in genres of the books. Brown's book was a work of fiction using the themes of the historical narrative, while Baigent, Leigh and Lincoln's work was 'history.' Aronstein cites from *Baigent and Leigh v. Random House* to explain that the court argued, "there is no copyrights on ideas expressed in a work which claims to be a book of history" (2015, p. 112). They concluded: "the Claimants had no exclusive property rights as they could not 'monopolize historical research or knowledge'" (2015, p. 112). That is not to say that Brown did market his book as pure fiction; he presented the fantastical theories as historical fact.

While the clever wordplay with Sang Greal underpinned the theory's claim of plausibility, the other pillar of this Templar revelation is Brown's assertion that the fraudulent organization, The Priory of Sion has legitimate ancestry to Crusader Franks. Brown introduces this organization just before the preface of *The Da Vinci Code,* stating, "Fact: The Priory of Sion—a European secret society founded in 1099—is a real organization. In 1975 Paris's Bibliothéque Nationale discovered Documents known as Les Dossiers Secrets, identifying numerous members of the Priory of Sion, including Sir Isaac Newton, Botticelli, Victor Hugo and Leonardo Da Vinci" (2003, p. 11). These facts, Brown asserts, are the creation of French fraudster Pierre Plantard in the 1950s. Master of the Temple Church London, Robin Griffith-Jones explains that Brown's statement of fact is entirely false. Griffith-Jones explains Plantard's creation stating, "After the war he was imprisoned for fraud and embezzlement. On his release he renewed the promotion of his social and political agenda, and founded the Priory of Sion.... Plantard named the Priory after the hill 'Mont Sion' close to Annemasse," which was a French town (2006, pp. 15–16). Griffith-Jones explains that the organization links itself to the Crusades; Mount Sion in Israel was an afterthought and "saw the advantage in claiming connection" (2006, p. 16), creating a dynastic link between himself and the throne of France. Brown mentions the discovery of "Les Dossiers Secrets," but

Griffith-Jones asserts, "To press his claims, he and his associates deposited in the Bibliothéque Nationale a cache of *printed* documents to which they themselves gave the title *Les Dossiers Secrets*" (2006, p. 16). Griffith-Jones draws his readers' attention to the fact that these documents were not written on parchment as you would expect from a long-lost document but typed on paper (2006, p. 16). This discredited organization, the Priory of Sion, has nothing historically to do with the Order of the Knights Templar, but the Order was repackaged in the book *Holy Blood, Holy Grail* to make the Knights Templar the military arm of the Priory of Sion. The significance of this is that this merger between the organizations further extends the malleable Templar conspiracy theme, which has grown to encompass the fraudulent Priory of Sion within the rich tapestry of fantastical Templar myth.

For the Templar revelation to justify Western values, the conspiracy underpinned by clever language play needed the appearance of the legitimacy provided by an assertion that a 20th-century organization had actual links to the Crusader kingdoms and the Knights Templar. To add greater emphasis to the importance of creating a credible perception of the Templar conspiracy, Brown uses his fictional characters to add authority to the Templar myth narrative that the protagonist and reader must delve into on the quest. Aronstein highlights:

> Brown goes out of his way to establish Langdon and Teabing's academic credentials; in the words of Langdon's publisher as he responds to the Harvard symbologist's book on the Sacred Feminine, "You are a Harvard historian for God's sake, not a pop schlockmeister." Langdon calms him down by presenting a bibliography of books written by established academics—his network—including Sir Leigh Teabing, a "royal historian" [2015, p. 120].

In Brown giving these characters authority over the reader and history, Brown is underpinning the importance of ensuring the conspiracy is credible, which will strengthen the message of the Templar revelation.

Aronstein suggests that Brown's fictional narrative further strengthens the theories of Baigent, Leigh and Lincoln and elevates the Templar revelation to a positive message of the legitimacy of Western Christendom. Aronstein proposes, "it is precisely this fictional status that allows Brown to elevate Holy Blood, Holy Grail's theories to 'fact.' If the fiction lies within the pages of his novel, the facts must lie outside those pages" (2015, p. 119); this enables Brown to quickly re-establish historical events using his character's authority, which is essential to elevate the Templar revelation's positive message. For Brown, the Templar conspiracy theme needs to be perceived as credible; otherwise, the revelation at the end of the quest narrative does not have the required payoff in that, if there is no perception of a metaphorical grail of wondrous forgotten truth, then it will not provide the desired positive gravitas.

In Brown's novel, the protagonist and reader are drawn into the supernatural world via venturing to the forgotten Templar past when Langdon explains to Sophie Neveu his view on the legendary Templar history and its origins within the fictional Priory of Sion. Langdon recounts that the Priory of Sion was created in 1099 by Crusader Godefroy de Bouillon (although Brown mischaracterizes Bouillon as a French king) after his army conquered Jerusalem. Langdon explains, "the Priory learned of a stash of hidden documents buried beneath the ruins of Herod's temple, which had been built on top of the earlier ruins of Solomon's temple." According to Langdon, to recover those documents "the Priory created a military arm—a group of nine knights ... commonly known as the Knights Templar" (Brown, 2016, p. 213). Unconvinced by Langdon's fantastic story, Sophie asserts, "I thought the Templars were created to protect the Holy Land." Langdon debunks this notion with the argument that the historical reality is "a common misconception. The idea of protection of pilgrims was the guise under which the Templars ran their mission. Their true goal in the Holy Land was to retrieve the documents from beneath the ruins" (Brown, 2016, p. 214). Langdon dismisses the historical reality of the origin of the Knights Templar in 1119, 20 years after the conquest of Jerusalem by the first Crusaders, with the argument that it is a common misconception. This conversation is adapted into a short scene in the film version where Langdon simplifies the account of the alternative history. He responds to Sophie's assertions, stating in a sinister tone that the Templars' origin "was a cover to hide their true goal, according to this myth. Supposedly the invasion was to find an artefact, lost since the time of Christ. An artefact it is said the Church would kill to possess" (Howard, 2006). This section of the book and film scene demonstrates how the second aspect of the quest narrative requires the protagonist (and audience/reader) to venture into another world, not a physical new environment such as the first aspect of the quest narrative but a metaphorical New World. This New World of forgotten Templar history enables the protagonist to find the metaphorical grail of the Templar revelation. This goal is formed by creating a plausible grail through language, promoting a fraudulent 20th-century organization and giving characters the academic credentials and authority that the Templar conspiracy is lacking.

In *The Da Vinci Code*, the Templar revelation of Jesus Christ's earthly lineage attempts to renew the lost faith of the audience, which is experienced by protagonist Robert Langdon and his quest companion Sophie Neveu (played by Audrey Tautou in Howard's film adaptation). Langdon is more the skeptic in the film than the novel as Aronstein and Torry note that when the "true" history of the Templars and the Priory of Sion is debated in the novel, it "unfolds as a tag-team effort as Teabing and Langdon expand upon and support each other's assertions. While Teabing is the acknowledged expert, Langdon, through his own research into the imagery of the sacred feminine, has also clearly drunk the Kool-Aid" (2009, pp. 233–234). However, in Howard's film adaptation, Langdon takes nothing at face value and calls Sir Leigh Teabing's claim that Mary Magdalene was the wife of Jesus Christ "an old wives' tale. There's virtually no imperial proof" and notes that there are "only theories" (Howard, 2006). The film depicts Ian McKellen's Teabing as an eccentric and not the royal scholar of Brown's novel, but it is he who leads the protagonist and audience into the fantastical world of the Templar mythical past where the Templar revelation asserts a vindication for traditional Christian values, further extended through the protagonists rediscovering their lost faith.

Despite uncovering the Templar revelation that leads Langdon and Sophie to Rosslyn Chapel in Scotland, Mary Magdalene's tomb has been moved, which leads Sophie to conclude that without the sarcophagus, "there's no way to prove that I am related to her." Langdon responds with, "Ok maybe there is no proof and maybe the grail is lost forever, but Sophie, the only thing that matters is what you believe" (Howard, 2006). Langdon no longer needs proof that the Templar conspiracy is real and places his emphasis on the importance of faith, which appears to undercut the novel's focus on establishing historical evidence. However, Langdon's conclusion further strengthens the attempt of legitimizing the Templar conspiracy due to the premise that damning evidence which discredits the holy blood theory is irrelevant in contrast to the importance of faith in the myths and fantasy narrative presented by Brown.

The film's final revelation of Sophie's heritage as that of Jesus Christ and Mary Magdalene validates the use of the Templar conspiracy to link the modern to the distant past, as the woman who does not believe in God becomes a physical manifestation of the divine. Aronstein and Torry explain, "Sophie represents the continuity of history, an unfolding of divine lineage from Christ to the present. A woman with healing hands, heir to the sang real, she reanimates the divine in a world that has lost touch with religious truth" (2009, pp. 237–238). Sophie is depicted as the antitype of Christ, demonstrating the typological aspect to the Templar revelation. This acts as a metaphorical grail in the following in the Templars' footsteps narrative, which shows a thematic difference to the quest aspect of the knight but still enables this modern grail narrative to fall into the overarching Templar quest narrative. The Templar conspiracy theme is a crucial part of this second aspect as it provides a mechanism for the protagonists to venture into the fantastical world of the past to reaffirm the legitimacy of those Christian values using the Templar revelation as a means. The aspect of following in the Templars' footsteps is a metaphorical concept; however, in the final scene, it is physically carried out by Robert Langdon. At the close of *The Da Vinci Code*, Langdon traces the location of Mary Magdalene's tomb, located under the Louvre in Paris, and kneels outside the Louvre to pay his respects to the Holy Grail as he believes the Knights Templar would have. This conclusion provides a physical and symbolic action of following in the Templars' footsteps through Langdon's act of respect to where he believes the tomb is located.

Aronstein and Torry state that *The Da Vinci Code* revelation within the Templar conspiracy "restores faith ... in a miraculous divine" (2009, p. 226) through the Catholic Church's cover-up of the humanization of Jesus Christ. The novel and film attempt to provide a sense of plausibility in parts of the Templar myth with the use of the Sang Greal, linking the Order to a modern-day organization and presenting the holy blood theory as possible historical fact. This creates a Templar revelation that proposes the existence of Jesus Christ on Earth through his bloodline, the Sang Greal. *The Da Vinci Code's* narrative contrasts to the theme of powerlessness within the conventional post–9/11 conspiracy narrative, and through the narrative's reworking of parts of the Templar phenomenon, the story's conclusion provides a case for its vindication of Western values. This would coincide with Aronstein and Torry's perception of the Templar conspiracy narrative as casting "therapeutic narratives aimed at healing an American public mired in a post–9/11 paranoia" (2009, p. 226). The Templar conspiracy theme within the quest narrative shows similarity to the secular retelling of the essence of the American Jeremiad in that it reaffirms America's faith in Jesus Christ and that the religion's dominance with the foundation of the United States project is not fallible faith. In similar fashion to the words on the dollar bill, "in God we trust," the Templar conspiracy reaffirms that the truth is what you believe.

The Templars, the Freemasons and the United States

National Treasure draws upon three aspects of the Templar myth to create the film's Templar revelation: these are the secret Templar treasure, the Templars starting the Freemasons, and the Templars escaping to the New World. The film's use of three Templar myths for the narrative's Templar revelation further unpins the malleability of the Templar phenomenon. The most concise way to explain how these three Templar myths interlock together is to explain how the Templars became associated with the Freemasons, a group that started as a stonemasons' guild. The simple answer is because the Freemasons pretended to be descended from the Templars so that they could market themselves to the upper classes. According to Frank Sanello, the Templars were not even the Freemasons' original claim of descendance; he wrote:

> The Templars were still the *betes noires* of French history in the minds of roy-alists and defenders of Phillip the fair like Ramsey, so in his speech to prospec-tive members, the chevalier claimed the Knights Hospitallers were the Masons' historical antecedents. The only problem with Ramsey's creative mythmak-ing was that the source of his myth, the Hospitallers, were very much alive and operational in their genuine reincarnation as the Knights of Malta [2005, pp. 221–222].

According to Sanello, Freemason Andrew Michael Ramsay was a cheva-lier and "of humble origins but had powerful patrons." So, it was his wish to "continue the mythologizing of the Mason's roots. He placed them higher up the social ladder than mere stonemasons and connected them to the monastic warriors of the Crusading era. Ramsey believed a more exalted pedigree would appeal to French aristocrats" (2005, p. 221). Unable to claim descendance from the Hospitallers, the Freemasons changed their claim to be descended from the Knights Templar and "since they had been exter-minated, The Templars were in no position to deny they were the original Masons" (Sanello, 2005, p. 222). The disappearance of the Templars in the early 14th century left a vacuum in historical memory, one that the Free-masons were able to exploit to further their agenda; the silence of these long-gone warrior monks enabled the Order to be misappropriated and the Templar narrative to re-emerge and develop origins for new narrative aspects.

    This new form of masonry became very fashionable; Sanello explains, "The Templar form of Freemasonry proved wildly popular, transcending borders and Oceans…. The Templar version of Freemasonry competed with the earlier British Version and the first Templar lodge was founded in England in 1778" (2005, p. 227). Newman claims that the link between the Templars and Freemasons can be traced back to "1750, when Baron Karl von Hund invented the 'Templar Strict Observance.'" In order to legitimize his creation, he claimed that it was "the successor to the Knights Templar" (2007, p. 403). Haag, however, supports Sanello's account by recounting Ramsay's claim that the Freemasons descended from Crusader knights in "his Oration to Saint John's Lodge in Paris, variously dated 27 December 1736 or 21 March 1737" (2009, p. 262). Newman concludes her section on the connection between the Freemasons and the Templars by stating, "no reputable historian of the freemasons believes that the group was founded by the Templars" (2007, p. 404). Similarly to the wishful claims of the existence of the grail as Christ's bloodline, the Freemasons' claim of Templar ancestry has no substance when the claims are examined beyond the surface.

The Templar treasure is linked to the Freemasons through the claims of George Frederick Johnson, a Frenchman who pretended to be Scottish. Haag explains what he calls "Johnson's concoction of history," writing:

> On the night of his execution, James of Molay was said to have ordered a group of Templars who were somehow still at large to enter into the crypt of the Paris Temple and make off with the treasure, which consisted of the seven-branched candelabra stolen from the Temple by the Roman Emperor Titus, the crown of the Kingdom of Jerusalem and a shroud [2009, p. 264].

Haag casts clear doubt on this theory through its implausibility; Newman states, "One of the most popular theories is that they went to America, sometimes via Scotland, sometimes Portugal. And they took their treasure with them" (2007, p. 361). The myth is not only that the Templars escaped to America with their vast fortune intact, but as she explains, the "Templar treasure was then buried under New York City and the Templars battened down to wait for the founding of the United States so that their beliefs could live again" (2007, p. 363). This fantastical myth is the crux of the conspiracy that drives the protagonist on his quest in *National Treasure*, which brings together the Templar and American history through the Masonic myth that the Freemasons orchestrated the American Revolution. The reality differs drastically from the myth; Haag explains, "the role of the Freemasons has been exaggerated. A few Freemasons may have participated in the Boston Tea Party" and "Of the Committee of Five who drew up the Declaration of Independence, only one, Benjamin Franklin, was a Freemason" (2009, p. 273). This myth of the Freemasons' influence draws directly to them the conspiracies of the Templars' survival and thus links the Templars to American history.

National Treasure

The influence of America's divine mission and the Puritans' dream is still rooted in the American identity, and this concept of creating a Puritan utopia can be found within the powerful institutions of American society. The sentiments of the American Jeremiad and the divine mission can be attributed to presidential speeches, such as George W. Bush's 2004 inaugural speech, where he said:

> America is a nation with a mission, and that mission comes from our most basic beliefs. We have no desire to dominate, no ambitions of empire. Our aim is a

democratic peace, a peace founded upon the dignity and rights of every man and woman. America acts in this cause with friends and allies at our side, yet we understand our special calling: This great republic will lead the cause of freedom [*The Washington Post*, Jan. 20, 2004].

The notions expressed by President Bush echo that of the Puritans' mission to create heaven on earth and even suggests connotative, typological links to the Israelites regarding his words, "our special calling." The sentiments of divine favor and the unfinished American mission link with the imagery on the dollar bill, which demonstrates that the Puritan beliefs are still at the core of America's political culture. These Puritan ideals are encapsulated by the imagery on the one-dollar bill, the unfinished pyramid and the eye of providence also known as the all-seeing eye, which connotates God watching over America as it carries out its still incomplete mission. The note also bears the words "in God we trust," as well as the Latin "Annuit Coeptis" that translates to "He Favours our Undertaking," which highlights the influence of the Puritans' belief in being God's chosen.

The dollar bill is used as an early symbol within the film *National Treasure* to visually show legitimacy to the link that connects the United States of America to the medieval Order of the Knights Templar. In the opening scene of *National Treasure* where a young Ben Gates is shown a dollar bill by his grandfather, who claims, "The Freemasons amongst our founding fathers left us clues." He then points to the reverse of the bill explaining, "the unfinished pyramid, the all-seeing eye, symbols of the Knights Templar" (Turteltaub, 2004). While it is true that the Freemasons use the iconography of the all-seeing eye, it should not be confused as a Masonic symbol upon the dollar bill as it has been used as a Christian symbol long before the Mason's adopted it. This misconception has fueled the theory that the Freemasons founded the United States.

This scene evokes the Masonic myth of their influence within the founding fathers but also the typological link between the Templars and Masons, the Type and Antitype, which is parallel to the Puritan's belief that they were the new Israelites. These associations of the Templars with America's divine mission are part of the Templar conspiracy theme, which, like with *The Da Vinci Code*, is used as a mechanism for enabling the protagonist to venture into the supernatural world of the quest. Upon completion they will be rewarded with a metaphorical grail symbolized with the Templar revelation. In this aspect of the quest narrative, the Templars are not seeking or guarding the grail but are a shadowy memory of forgotten values and once rediscovered will vindicate America's faith in Christ and their Western patriotism.

The Templar conspiracy theme of the quest narrative echoes the sentiments of the American Jeremiad in that as the Jeremiad was used to steer

Puritans back towards the divine mission, the Templar revelation reintroduces Americans to the ideals and Puritan values of America as the blueprint to creating a utopia. Aronstein and Torry conclude their clarification of typology by highlighting the uniqueness of the Templar conspiracy in that "traditional conspiracy narratives feed paranoia by showing that apparently random events are part of a planned and malevolent deception … in which the hero's knowledge is suppressed" (2009, p. 230). However, the "Templar conspiracy tales lead us back to a truth that will set us free" (2009, p. 230). Both *The Da Vinci Code* and *National Treasure* draw upon these notions of positive outcomes created through the use of the following in the Templars' footsteps quest narrative. It proposes a legitimacy to America's place in the world instead of the feeling of suppression and hopelessness associated with conventional conspiracy narratives.

The prominence of typology within the Templar conspiracy theme is further reflected through the opening and closing of the film *National Treasure*. The opening scene of the film shows a young Ben Gates "initiated by his grandfather as 'knight' pledged to the values and purposes of the Templar/Masonic lineage whose narrative the grandfather has related" (Aronstein & Torry, 2009, p. 238). This would make Ben Gates the "Antitype" to America's Founding Fathers and demonstrates the magnitude of importance in his quest. After Ben's grandfather explains the legend of the treasure, the young Ben asks his grandfather if they are knights, which causes him to smile, and he asks the boy if he wants to be, and Ben nods enthusiastically. Ben's grandfather asks him to kneel, places a blanket around him like a robe and dramatically states "Benjamin Franklin Gates, you take upon yourself the duty of the Templars and the Freemasons and the family Gates; do you so swear?" to which Ben replies, "I so swear" (Turteltaub, 2004). The film then cuts to adult Ben now played by Nicholas Cage on the verge of solving the first clue. Ben Gates is now the *antitype* of the Templar and Masonic orders, having been sworn into this new order of questing knights by his grandfather, and is teamed up with fellow treasure hunter Ian Howe, played by Sean Bean, who soon establishes himself as the film's antagonist.

What is significant about Howe's role is that he is the opposite to Gates; he is a wealthy criminal who has financed the expedition to the Arctic but tries to kill Gates when he refuses to follow the second clue and steal the *Declaration of Independence*. Gates and Howe draw upon the themes of the good Templar and bad Templar featured in the Templar knight narrative (see Chapter 1), as both are seeking the treasure and following in the footsteps of questing knights. Hannum draws attention to Gates' justification for the theft of the *Declaration of Independence* (which contains the next clue to the treasure), noting that Gates references the principles

America was founded upon. Hannum states, "Ben draws from the text of the Declaration of Independence to offer a classic transcendent rights argument" (2012, p. 154). Hannum references from Ben Gates, citing the declaration, "when a long train of abuses and usurpations, pursuing invariably the same Object evinces a design to reduce them under absolute Despotism, it is their right, it is their duty, to throw off such Government, and to provide new Guards for the future security" (2012, p. 154).

To protect the declaration from falling into the hands of the villainous Howe, Gates calls upon the logic of America's Founding Fathers to justify his actions, noting that it is the duty of Americans to action against threats to the United States. Hannum notes Gates' second justification for the crime, quoting Gates' toast "to high treason. That's what these men were committing when they signed the Declaration. Had they lost the war, they would've been hanged.... So, here's to the men who did what was considered wrong in order to do what they knew was right" (2012, p. 154). Here Gates further justifies his actions to the audience by comparing himself to the American revolutionaries, noting that their treason alongside his (i.e., stealing the declaration) is with honest intentions, similar to the good Templar's use of violence to defend the weak and punish the wicked, further demonstrating the flexibility of the reoccurring Templar narrative.

Howe's methods are unjustifiable uses of violence and theft for his own personal financial gain, while for Gates finding the treasure is not about seeking riches but clearing his family name and sharing the treasure with the world. Gates asks that the government "Give it to the people. Divide it amongst the Smithsonian, the Louvre, the Cairo museum. There's thousands of years of world history down there. And it belongs to the world, and everybody in it" (Turteltaub, 2004). Gates also asks that the Gates family get the credit for finding it. Howe, as the villainous questing knight, seeks the treasure for personal power and uses violence in his attempts and is thus condemned to incarceration by the FBI at the film's close. Gates, however, demonstrates his chivalric intentions of the betterment of the world and to restore honor to his family name. These are the motivations of the good Templar, and therefore, his actions are justified by his exoneration by the American government for his nonviolent but criminal methods.

While the Templar revelation's vindication of America's privileged destiny is uncovered by venturing to the forgotten historical link to the Templars, Aronstein and Torry propose that the film is not merely referencing a generic sense of pro–American sentiment but draws links to actual moments in recent history. This is done by addressing two critical moments in history; the first commentary is suggested at the opening of the film. At the opening of the film, after Ben Gates' grandfather explains the secret history of their family and the Templar treasure, Ben Gates' father, Patrick, interrupts the tale and pours scorn on the idea, stating, "You know what that dollar represents? The entire Gates family fortune; six generations of fools chasing after fool's gold." Aronstein and Torry note that it is the date of the opening scene in 1974 that is important, explaining that that was the year of "Richard Nixon's resignation in disgrace of the Presidency following the Watergate revelations, the year between the American withdrawal from Vietnam and the 1975 fall of the South Vietnamese government" (2009, p. 239). This setting for the opening has connotations of the political climate of the 70s and also the identity crisis of American citizens. Aronstein and Torry assert that this is further addressed by the negativity of Patrick Gates. They note, "Patrick's cynicism reflects the cynicism of a generation that has lost its faith in America's millennial potential, in its 'national treasure'" (2009, p. 239). This represents the perception of the waning belief of the American people with the Puritan utopian mission, and like the Jeremiad, the Templar revelation will reaffirm the audience with those traditional American values.

The conclusion of the film shows Ben Gates rejecting the 10 percent finder's fee of a treasure worth $50,000,000,000, which symbolizes the possibility for the redemption of America, a country exonerated from the accusations of corruption from their recent interventions in the Middle East and a glimpse of what the Puritans envisioned. Aronstein and Torry draw on this conclusion to argue that the film "offers its viewers a narrative therapeutically aligned with the eventual justification for invasion and occupation offered by the Bush administration following the failure to locate weapons of mass destruction in Iraq" (2009, p. 243). They propose that the specific act of Ben Gates donating the treasure to museums around the world "suggest[s], at the simplest level, an America devoted not to material appropriation, but rather to global distribution, to the spreading of wealth through global corporate expansion" (2009, p. 243). Further interpretations and comparisons between real-life events at the time of production and the film are made by Eric Lott, who suggests that Turteltaub depicts 9/11 in the mise-en-scène of the secret cavern underneath the Trinity Church in Manhattan. Obviously, there is the coincidence of the location, but Lott proposes that the collapse of the rickety wooden structures they descend and "one of Ian's men falls through a landing to his death—and the whole episode has the air of a displaced representation of the Twin Towers trembling and then crashing to the ground" (2008, p. 113). This scene may be Lott's interpretation, but it further demonstrates how the current political climate overshadows this film's narrative, thus underlining the Templar revelation's need for vindication in America's mission. However, Lott notes that the secret treasure is hidden underneath Manhattan, drawing parallels to the view, "the US as a storehouse of expropriated global wealth" which is "hidden under Wall Street rather than distributed to its citizens" (2008, p. 114). This notion would tie into Aronstein and Torry's theory that Gates' request to redistribute the wealth to the world demonstrates a desire for the world and Americans to rediscover their faith in the United States as a democratic global power and not the exploitative imperialist invader perceived in the political climate.

The film's conclusion provides the case for exoneration of America's modern-world criticisms, offering a glimpse at how America could be instead of the reality. The Templar conspiracy theme is a vital part of the second quest narrative as it provides the story with a new destination for the protagonist to venture to, as this travel to a new land is truly the essence of the quest narrative. The conspiracy theme is the driving force behind the quest because it is what leads the protagonist to the Templar revelation, which will reframe the perception of the ideals that America was supposedly founded upon. The Templar conspiracy theme uses the myth of the Templars' link to the Freemasons and the Founding Fathers to set up the importance of the Templar revelation. Similarly, with *The Da Vinci Code*, it proposes that the historical link to the Templars is vital to heighten the vindication of American Western values. The quest narrative of following in the Templars' footsteps uses the established Templar myth to create a fantastical world that the protagonist enters to rediscover a symbolic grail in the form of a revelation that reaffirms the values that the United States was founded upon, a revelation that does not lead to a discovery of powerless oppression but a reaffirmation of the historical signification of America's destiny through its typological links to Israel within the Templar myth. What makes the Templar myth so compatible with those ideals of a Puritan utopia is that the connotative Templar myth supersedes the Templars in a denotative sense due to their extinction in the 14th century. The Freemason's link to the Templars and therefore to America's Founding Fathers is further embedded into popular culture through the reoccurring Templar narrative due to centuries of plausible deniability caused by the silence of Templar historical authority.

Conclusion

This chapter examined the grail guardian archetype from the Templar urtext, tracing the evolution of the quest narrative from the quest of knight aspect's origin in the 13th century up to the quest to follow in the Templars' footsteps in the 21st century. The chapter began by examining the first aspect of the Templar quest narrative, which is the quest of the knight, which was analyzed alongside unconventional but hugely successful and iconic grail films *Monty Python and the Holy Grail* and *Indiana Jones and the Last Crusade*. The benefit of using those case studies instead of conventional Arthurian literature is that neither case study directly mentioned the Knights Templar. However, both studies demonstrate the influence of the Templar quest narrative through the use of iconography and associated Templar character archetypes. These unconventional grail stories demonstrated the fluidity of the Templar narrative through its relevance within a satirical series of sketches and a 1930s' adventure movie.

The case study of *Monty Python and the Holy Grail* incorporated the visual aesthetics associated with the Templar knight through the character of Sir Galahad, who wears the iconic white surcoat with a red cross. The incorporation of the Templar quest narrative also attributes Sir Galahad with stereotypical Templar traits, making him chaste and pious. The comedy of the film often stretches from the parody of Arthurian conventions, and Sir Galahad's fear of women provides a parody of the Templars' notoriety as chaste monks. *Monty Python and the Holy Grail* does not follow the usual conventions of the grail quest, preferring to deliberately diverge from audience expectation and therefore does not feature the Templars by name. The film's comedic theme of satirically inverting Arthurian conventions demonstrates the influence of the Templars in popular culture through the incorporation of Templar iconography and the parody of the Templars' monkish piety within the reimagining of Sir Galahad.

Indiana Jones and the Last Crusade moved the grail away from the medieval/Arthurian world and into the 1930s for Spielberg's version of the grail story. Despite not being set in a medieval time frame, this film is incorporated within the first aspect of the quest narrative due to the depiction of Indiana Jones and compatriots as knights of the Round Table and grail literature's themes of healing both physically, as seen with Henry Sr.'s wound, and symbolically with Indiana's reunion with his father. Indiana Jones provided a clear example of the influence of the Templar quest narrative similar to Monty Python as even though the Knights Templar are not mentioned, the contribution of the quest narrative is illustrated through the film's use of Templar iconography and their role as grail guardians. This reimagination of the Templar grail knight was the creation of scriptwriter, Tom Stoppard, who rebranded the grail guardian as The Knights of the Cruciform Sword. These knights hold small differentiation with the Knights Templar due to a similarity of roles with Eschenbach's 14th-century Templar guardian and a slight change to the red cross on their white surcoat to further emphasize the grail.

Lucas demonstrated his knowledge of the Templars' role as grail guardians in a 2008 interview, a role that was altered for the film to create another party to oppose Indiana Jones' grail search and to accommodate the film's thematic grail depiction as the ultimate good. This desire to depict the grail as the ultimate good is underlined in the contrast of incorporating the Nazis as the ultimate evil. A rebrand is essential as having the Templars depicted in a positive way would be problematic due to their pre-established perception as the villainous knight in Sir Walter Scott's *Ivanhoe*. The Nazis in Indiana Jones are motivated by an interest in the occult, an association that is shared by the conative Templar myth, and therefore such a villainous perception would undermine their depiction as a human manifestation of the grail's goodness. *Indiana Jones and the Last Crusade* highlights the inspiration the reoccurring Templar narrative has within storytelling, an inspiration that has further embedded the Templar narrative within popular culture. The reoccurrence of the Templar phenomenon is due to the malleability of the narrative as shown with the variations taken by Lucas and Spielberg on the Templar identity, where they were able to make the Templar quest narrative work within the desired themes of their film.

The second half of this chapter examined the other aspect to the Templar quest narrative, following in the Templars' footsteps. The second aspect is set in the modern day, a setting that visually distances itself due to the medieval/Arthurian setting of the first aspect of the quest narrative. Despite distinguishing settings, the other key variation is the change of the protagonist's role, from questing as knights in the first aspect to following in the Templars' footsteps and venturing into the mythical Templar past. Both aspects follow a quest story structure of venturing into unknown territory. The first aspect follows a literal journey to a dangerous land, while in the second aspect the supernatural world is the forgotten mythical Templar past. Most importantly, though, is that both aspects feature the quest for the grail, often a literal grail for the first aspect, but the second aspect is the quest to find a metaphorical grail. This metaphoric grail is in the guise of a Templar revelation; this revelation is the renewed faith of Western culture, ultimately vindicating the original mission for the creation of the United States and the legitimacy of the Christian faith in Jesus Christ. The revelation is the discovery found at the quest's end, and inspired by the Templar conspiracy is a malleable theme that can draw inspiration from a plentiful abundance of Templar myths and misrepresentations that have been formulated in popular culture for centuries.

The reoccurring Templar narrative of the quest shows how the Templar phenomenon has evolved since it was first planted within popular culture as part of Wolfram von Eschenbach's *Parzival*. The Templars' cultural origin as grail guardians is shown in the first aspect of the quest narrative, which draws upon their links to the Holy Grail and Arthurian literature as knight protectors. The second aspect of this narrative demonstrates the narrative's malleability and builds upon the myth established in the first aspect of the quest, that of the knight, and brings it into the modern day. In this setting, the protagonists must venture back into the Templar mythic world to find a symbolic grail in the form of a Templar revelation. Templar mythic history provides a link to the past, where venturing will provide vindication for Western culture. Both quest narrative aspects share fundamental parallels; they include a search for a valuable article, and both rely on the connotative Templar associations for inspiration as a story formula. The Templar quest narrative shows how the narrative has evolved over the centuries and remains a reoccurring phenomenon within popular culture. The Order's extinction in the 14th century has left room for interpretation and allowed for an open text that the Templar quest narrative has extended by creating new stories; this enabled the once pious warrior monks to be represented by ideas and themes that were established long after their disappearance.

CHAPTER 4

The Quest for Truth

Play, Performance and Participation Within the Tourist Site

Chapter 3 defined the two aspects of the Templar narrative of the quest in popular culture using case studies from popular films. This chapter will continue the analysis of the grail guardian archetype by examining how this part of the Templar urtext has expanded and evolved through physical immersion in places linked to the Templar narrative. The Templar quest narrative focuses on the journey into the fantastical medievalist world to obtain an item of terrific value. Following this, in the same way as Chapter 2 examines the Templar knight narrative's place in popular culture through fan participation, the quest narrative also needs to be analyzed in terms of fan participation through tourism and visiting related sites. Fan tourism is the ideal fan practice to examine as the fan can participate in the fictional world of the text by traveling to the real site featured in the text and emulate the truth searching of the text's protagonist. The chapter's case studies will be *The Da Vinci Code* and *National Treasure* fan tourist experiences at the Rosslyn Chapel in Scotland and Independence landmarks of Philadelphia in the United States of America. The film *National Treasure* includes the Independence landmarks in Philadelphia as locations for the protagonist to retrace the Templar past, with sites such as Independence Hall hiding a secret clue to the Templar treasure. *The Da Vinci Code*, novel and film set their climax in Rosslyn Chapel as the burial place of Mary Magdalene (the Holy Grail), a site that is already associated with mystery and the Templar myth.

The case studies chosen for this chapter will demonstrate how my concept of the Templar urtext has further expanded through physical participation with the Templar narrative via fan tourism. In analyzing the grail guardian archetype of the Templar urtext, this chapter will examine how participation with the quest narrative further expands and evolves the Templar narrative in popular culture and further impacts the Templar urtext.

Fan tourism enables the Templar enthusiast to recreate the thematic journey of the protagonist and venture on their own quest to obtain new knowledge of a text and a closeness to the story world via a physical experience. As I outlined in the introduction, I traveled to several fan tourist locations, immersed myself in the site and collected data on the tourist experience. The methodology to approach this will include methods of primary evidence-gathering used in fan tourism studies such as taking notes on site and using photographs to document the fan experience. To further document the tourist experience, I took photos of the film's filming locations to compare the location to its on-screen appearance and interacted with site officials such as park rangers and tour guides. This chapter on Templar fan tourism also uses autoethnographic methods by drawing upon tourist reviews, social media posts and photos to underpin how participation strengthens the Templar myth through the thematic narrative of the quest.

To examine how fans have forged a deeper understanding of the Templars through the thematic structures of the quest narrative the chapter uses academic studies to analyze the fan tourist experience. The chapter draws from Lincoln Geraghty's work on fan geographies in *The Smallville Chronicles: Critical Essays on the Television Series* (2011), which incorporates Foucault's concept of heterotopia to understand the relationship between real sites and their fictional counterparts. Geraghty's chapter provides a useful method to analyze the conflicting mythical and historic realities within my case studies. To help frame primary data taken from the immersive fan experiences I visited, the chapter draws from Will Brooker's chapter in the edited book *The Blade Runner Experience: The Legacy of a Science Fiction Classic* (2005) and Matt Hills's book *Fan Cultures* (2002). These sources feature studies of fan tourist sites that provide a useful framework for this chapter. Immersion enables fans to build their own vestiges of the Templars, which demonstrates how the Templar narrative has been emended and evolved within popular culture. The final section of the chapter explores how the acts of play and performance further enhance the fan tourist experience. For this section, the chapter draws from Lancaster's book *Interacting with Babylon* 5 (2001), also using Stijn Reijnder's article, "On the trail of 007: media pilgrimages into the world of James Bond" (2010) to ascertain how the more immersive qualities of play and performance impact the evolution of the Templar urtext.

The concept of participation with text narrative was explored in Chapter 2, and the importance of analyzing the quest narrative from this perspective is evident through Gray's dialogues on fans interacting with a text narrative in three ways: telling, showing and participation (2010, p. 192). This chapter analyzes how fans can participate with the Templar texts by visiting the space or location of their fandoms. This visit is done symbolically as these sites are signs for the historical past and also literally as the fan travels to a historic geographic site. The real-world sites associated with the Templars are historical sites and provide a crossover experience for fan tourists with heritage tourism. These spaces provide tourists with physicality to the Templar myth, where the heritage sites stand as a shared space, where the historical and mythological coexist. Templar fan tourism is uniquely tied to heritage sites like Rosslyn Chapel and Independence Hall, as these are depicted as key sites in the fictional media as sites to unlock the mysteries of the Order of the Knights Templar. This setting is not to be confused with historical film's heritage relationship because the second aspect of the Templar quest narrative is set in modern day, but due to the follow in the Templars' footsteps narrative it also echoes the past. The relationship between fan tourism and heritage tourism and the tension created by the coexisting spaces is paramount to exploring Templar fan tourism, as the iconic historic buildings provide the protagonist with a symbolic and physical journey to the past.

Fan Pilgrimage

When examining fan tourism, the practice can be quantified as a fan pilgrimage; however, for this Templar-themed study, such language is problematic. This concept of religious travel would universally have been associated with pilgrimages to Jerusalem or the Islamic Pilgrimage to Mecca; however, this religious experience has become associated with fandom and enthusiasm for articles of popular culture. For example, despite being a popular film and heritage tourist site, Rosslyn Chapel has initially been and still is a place of Christian worship, which naturally incorporates notions of the religious pilgrimage. However, the fan tourism journey taken by fans to visit a site of textual significance can be articulated in terms of a fan pilgrimage. This type of fan activity, Reijnders explains, citing Couldry, "should be defined as 'media pilgrimages,' which are comparable to traditional, religious pilgrimages" (2010, p. 370). Urry and Larson highlight the similarity between the tourist and the pilgrim, noting, "Like the pilgrim, the tourist moves from a familiar place to a far place and then returns to the familiar place. At the far place both the pilgrim and the tourist 'worship' shrines which are sacred, albeit in different ways, and as a result gain some kind of uplifting experience" (2011, p. 12).

Despite the similarities Urry and Larson allude to above, for academic fan studies this comparison of the activity as a pilgrimage is quite problematic. Duffett explains, "Much of the discussion of fan tourism is framed by the metaphor of 'pilgrimage,' a term that relates fandom to both religiosity but also attempts to capture the emotional value of visiting places of magical interest" (2013, p. 227). The associated religiosity encompassing the term *pilgrimage* can be misleading of the interests of the Templar-themed tourist seeking to experience a closeness to an item of popular culture. Although not the focus of this book, the Knights Templar have been subsumed into New Age Christian religious groups who would associate such ventures to significant sites as an act of worship. Although the term is used in academia to symbolize fan tourism and implies religious associations, Hills perceives "Fandom both is and is not like religion, existing between 'cult' and 'culture.' 'Cult' discourses are thus not entirely hollow and empty, but neither do these discourses quite 'fit' fan cultures" (2002, p. 118). There is a contradiction in using the term pilgrimage, as parallels with fan tourism are there, but this book is examining the Templars as a subject of popular culture and not as a religious practice. Although focused on popular culture, the Christian Templar connotations are unavoidable as the medieval order was an organization of devout Christian monks, and many of the sites of Templar interest are firstly Christian holy places.

However, if the religious connotations are removed from the term pilgrimage, as Reijnders does when he cites from "Victor and Edith Turner's classic statement that a pilgrimage is more than just a physical journey: it is also a symbolic journey towards certain central values of society," (2010, p. 370) then it is justified in relation to fandom. This justification for using the term *pilgrimage* is mirrored in Duffet's evaluation of the relationship between the language of religion and fandom, writing, "spiritual metaphors are more useful as they capture the emotional transcendence of fan experience. Fans often refer to a live rock show as a religious or spiritual experience. They report being filled with the spirit or feeling a sense of closeness to their star" (2013, p. 144). It is in keeping with Duffet's notion of a spiritual experience that the fan travels to the location of the chosen text to participate, and the quest to follow in the footsteps of Templars can be arguably termed a pilgrimage in that the fans seek an emotional or spiritual closeness to the text. However, this chapter will be addressing the practice in terms of cultural tourism, which Urry and Larson explain is linked with the cultural shift to a postmodernist view where "there is a breakdown in the distinctiveness of each of these spheres of activities, especially the cultural. Each implodes into the other, and most involve visual spectacle and play" (2011, p. 98). This idea of a lack of distinctiveness between spheres of activity encapsulates the difficulty in defining the Knights Templar as a singular uncontradictory entity, as what coincides with the historical Templar does not conform to the perceptions of the Order published in Templar myth. The mythical Templar has further separated into various archetypes and roles within literature and film; thus, the real-world locations have absorbed this new Templar cultural identity into itself. For Urry and Larson, in this postmodern culture, tourism and media are intrinsically linked as "the tourist gaze and media gaze highly overlap and reinforce each other, whether people travel corporeally or simply imaginatively through the incredible range of global images that make up everyday media cultures" (2011, p. 116).

Given the notion of the fluidity of defining aspects of current culture, and although media tourism does demonstrate general similarities to a religious pilgrimage, seeing fandom as wholly religious is undermined by postmodernist views on the difficulty of viewing culture as separately distinguishable. Although the term *pilgrimage* is incorporated into the study, this chapter is exploring the tourist experience from the perspective of cultural practice of fan tourism: how the fans of Templar-themed texts desire for authenticity to the Templar myth brings them to real-world locations, locations that have had their cultural significance adapted by the association of the thematic Templar narrative. This chapter articulates the practice in terms of fan tourism, as the focus of the project is to argue for the existence of a reoccurring Templar narrative within popular culture. This chapter focuses on the appropriation of the historical order into consumable products and how the Templars' place in popular culture evolves through consumers' interaction.

Fan Tourism and Heritage Tourism

When studying fan tourism, it is not the buildings themselves that are the subject of this chapter but the fan experience offered through participating in the location. This chapter examines participation with the Templar narrative and how the Templar quest narrative enables a more intimate fan relationship with the Templar texts. Sandvoss explains the significance of studying these spaces, proposing that these geographical sites are more than physical locations because they "are socially constructed through symbols, discourse and representations. In this sense places, and in particular places of pleasure and affect, are always texts" (2014, p. 115). The significance of studying featured locations for the Templar quest narrative is that fans can follow in the footsteps of the Templars themselves, offering an essence of venturing into the mythical Templar past in search of knowledge of the film and like the narrative's protagonist discover a Templar revelation for themselves. These fan excursions are classed as fan tourism, a type of tourism where closeness to the original text is sought out by enthusiasts. Simon Hudson and J.R. Brent Ritchie writing for the *Journal of Travel Research* define film tourism as "tourist visits to a destination or attraction as a result of the destination being featured on television, video, or in the cinema screen" (2006, p. 387). Fan tourism enables a different level of fan experience, the notion of physical immersion within a geographical location associated with their favorite texts. These can be locations where films or television shows are shot, such as Cloverdale, which "advertises on their website that Cloverdale is the 'Home of Smallville'—a statement backed up by the road sign that welcomes drivers as they pass through" (Geraghty, 2011, p. 129), or as Duffett highlights, they can be "simply spaces themed as places that represented particular stars or narrative" (2013, p. 226). Both of these types of fan tourism are available for *Harry Potter* fans, who can visit the themed *Harry Potter* Universal Theme Parks in Florida and California, London filming locations or the Warner Brothers Studio Tour. Although different types of *Harry Potter* fan spaces, all three enable the fan to experience the *Harry Potter* narrative for themselves. On Universal Orlando's website, it markets its themed land with the following words:

> Step inside a world where magic is real. Within Universal's Islands of Adventure theme park you can visit the iconic Hogwarts castle and explore Hogsmeade village. And, at Universal Studios Florida theme park, you can enter Diagon Alley to enjoy a thrilling ride, magical experiences and more. Get ready to explore more of Harry Potter's world than ever before.

Universal theme parks offer fans a deeper level of interaction with their fandom, offering the chance to step inside the fictional world of Harry Potter. This notion of entering the world is mirrored by the website for Free Tours by Foot, which states that tour participants can "join us as we dive into the magical world of Harry Potter!" Aside from recreating the fictional world in a theme park, Harry Potter fans wishing to experience a closeness to a fan text by visiting the filming locations are also catered for, demonstrating the popularity of fan geographical sites and how they are marketed as a more intimate experience for fans.

A similar experience can be found by fans of the Templar texts, which can recreate the protagonists' journey into the past via a geographical site of historical significance. The historical location provides a symbolic link such as Robert Langdon's traveling to Rosslyn Chapel to discover a hidden account of history, making the journey to historical sites fundamental to the theme of visiting the sensational Templar past. The Templar quest narrative facilitates an opportunity for fans to interact with the text and mimic the protagonist in physically visiting the past; therefore, the fan has the impression of being able to journey to the past in the same way as Robert Langdon at Rosslyn Chapel or Benjamin Gates at Independence Hall. The significance of the Templar quest narrative's feature of historical sites as destinations is not unlike the recreated sites, such as Diagon Alley at

Universal Studies, only that the Templar text fan crosses over with heritage tourism, giving geographical locations subjective meaning for tourists. Fans travel to these real-world locations to become closer to the world of the text, making the fantastical seem more real. For the Templar fan, these sites give a sense of legitimacy to the Templar conspiracy theme featured in the fictional story, with the Templar myth seeming more real in the context of an actual Templar-associated historical site.

The Templar texts are not unique in the overlapping of fan tourism and heritage tourism, as Martin Jones explains, "Film tourism can thus be understood to be a facet of heritage tourism, as the nation is promoted internationally to identified target markets" (2014, p. 157). This overlapping of fan tourism provides substantial benefits for heritage tourism and can boost countries' economies. Martin Jones highlights the impact of film tourism in Britain; he writes, "The Economic Impact of the UK Film Industry dedicates around 10% of the report to film tourism, noting that an estimated £1.8 billion of visitor spend might be due to UK films alone" (2014, p. 160). While Martin Jones asserts that Scotland has long had prominent levels of heritage tourism, he argues that film tourism can significantly increase it. He cites from the Hydra Report to show the impact that the film *Braveheart* had on Scottish heritage tourism. He argues: "The Wallace Monument, for example, saw a rise in visitors in 1995 of over 50% on the previous year, and of the visitors surveyed overall, 49% had seen *Braveheart* (a higher figure than would be expected of the general population)" (2014, p. 162). Although the majority of *Braveheart* was filmed in Ireland instead of Scotland, the film's popularity created an increase in tourism for the Wallace Monument, suggesting a desire of *Braveheart* enthusiasts to get closer to the film's protagonist. The Scottish heritage site still caters to *Braveheart* enthusiasts via the gift shop, where visitors can purchase William Wallace–like teddy bears, complete with blue face, a kilt and a claymore, the historically inaccurate look designed for Mel Gibson's portrayal of the Scottish hero.

Sweden attempted to promote heritage tourism using the popularity of the *Arn: The Knight Templar* film series by promoting medieval historical sites featured in the novel and film. Hedling cites from Helltén to highlight the Swedish tourism marketing around Arn. He writes:

> In the 2008 tourist brochure for the western Gothian cites of Skövde, Skara and Falköping, much space is devoted to Arn tourism. Regarding Skara, for instance, the text in English reads: "Skara is a medieval town with monasteries, churches and even film history—through the tale of Arn" [2008, p. 66].

Martin Jones argues that for Scotland, film tourism is "the latest in a long line of shop windows for the nation" (2014, p. 164), which corresponds with

Sweden's summer tourism marketing following the popularity of *Arn: The Knight Templar*.

Although the example above evokes a reactive approach to film tourism, Hudson and Ritchie explain, "Destination marketing organizations (DMOs) can engage in a variety of marketing activities both before and after the release of a film ... but some are becoming active in encouraging producers to make films in their region to benefit from long-term tourism impacts" (2006, p. 389). Hudson and Ritchie use the collaboration between New Zealand and *The Lord of the Rings* production to highlight the planned tourism boost, writing, "During the filming of *The Lord of The Rings*, for example, media clippings mentioned that film was being shot in New Zealand, providing important early linkage between the film and the location" (2006, p. 391). Moreover, after nearly two decades since *The Fellowship of The Ring* (Jackson, 2001) was released, Hobbiton remains a popular tourist attraction. This example of collaboration between production and heritage tourism is seen by Scottish heritage and has used high-profile films such as *Braveheart* and *The Da Vinci Code* to promote tourism. This link between film tourism and heritage tourism by the collaboration of the Scottish Tourist Board and Twentieth-Century Fox aims "to market Stirling as 'Braveheart Country'" (Martin Jones, 2014, p. 166). Martin Jones draws particular attention to marketing around the release of the film, which "included bringing the premiere of the film to Stirling which, along with various competitions and a cinema commercial, was estimated to have achieved a return on an overall investment of around £254,000 worth £480,000 in hotel bookings alone" (2014, p. 166). Due to the romantic historical associations Scotland has with William Wallace, *Braveheart* shows that geographical space can have multiple associations, one with the fictional Wallace played by Mel Gibson and with the historical Scottish soldier who led the Scots to victory at the Battle of Stirling Bridge.

To address the shared experience found within a single location, this chapter draws upon Foucault's concept of heterotopia. Foucault explains that heterotopia is:

> a kind of effectively enacted utopia in which the real sites, all the other real sites that can be found within the culture, are simultaneously represented, contested, and inverted. Places of this kind are outside of all places, even though it may be possible to indicate their location in reality [1986, p. 24].

Geraghty introduces Foucault's work of heterotopia to define the ring fence of *Smallville* fan tourism within Vancouver (2011, p. 146), where the streets represent both the mundane geographical reality and the associated reality of the television show. Foucault's concept of heterotopia provides an approach to addressing how one site can contain several different associational perspectives because "The heterotopia is capable of juxtaposing in a single real place several spaces, several sites that are in themselves incompatible" (1986, p. 25). For example, the Wallace Monument provides an example as the space represents both the Mel Gibson cinematic version and historical reality as standing atop the Victorian-built tower enables visitors to view the actual battle site (a bridge) and recall the battle's location depicted in the film (a field). For the Templar-associated heritage site, Foucault's concept of singular spaces representing alternative culture can be attributed to fictional relevance and the historical significance of the heritage sites of Independence Hall and Old Pine Church Graveyard (a burial site for heroes of the War of Independence) in Philadelphia and the Rosslyn Chapel in Scotland. These sites are substantial to historical memory but also juxtapositioned as spaces of popular culture manifestation.

The dual relationship of these heritage sites coincides with Brooker's notion, "most geographical sites of media fandom are *multiply coded*; their fan significance is just one aspect of their identity" (2007, p. 430). Brooker explains that real-world mundane places can carry alternatively coded connotations from the perspective of fandom, and he uses *Blade Runner* film tourism in Los Angles as an example. For the experience of the *Blade Runner* fan tourist, Brooker found that it:

> "involves working with two maps, a real plan of LA and an understanding of the alternative, fantastical, impossible geography of Ridley Scott's diegesis. The two cannot be reconciled: most glaringly, the police HQ and Deckard's apartment are skyscrapers, whereas Union Station and the Ennis-Brown House are one-storey buildings" [2007, p. 430].

Given the popularity of a fan coded site, a once mundane site has its multiply coded location corporately advertised, such as the photo point at London's King's Cross station, which for *Harry Potter* fans is the entrance to platform 9¾. Warner Brothers advertises the mundane location as The Harry Potter Shop at Platform 9¾ and invites fans to "visit the famous trolley" via the website www.harrypotterplatform934.com, which also features photos of the cast members posing at the supposed entrance to platform 9¾, although the site was once mundane, more akin to Brooker's example of LA, as the railway station shared space was marked only by half a trolley fixed to the wall to simulate the entrance to the platform. This is a space that fans would search for and would appear mundane to anyone without the perspective of the *Harry Potter* fan tourist.

Even though the majority of films no longer generate the same level of tourist marketing once the initial buzz has settled, the site's cultural reality remains intact when gazing from that perspective, as with tourist sites associated with *Arn: The Knight Templar*, which now a decade on from

Arn's release are not widely published and the interactive promotional website www.arnmovie.com that Hedling cites is no longer active. However, In *Arn's Footsteps,* an illustrated 15-page brochure is available online that provides the key Arn locations and their significance to the series for a self-guided tour of Sweden. This brochure demonstrates the shared geographical space occupied by various Swedish historical sites, illustrating their role in Swedish history alongside the location's association with the *Arn: The Knight Templar* series. The brochure includes images and information about the novels and a short biography of the titular character Arn Magnusson and includes quotes from the book to illustrate the geographical site's relationship with the Arn series. The shared space of the heterotopia is made apparent with a carving at the Forshem Church, originally constructed in the 12th century. The brochure explains that another of the carvings (not featured in the photo) "is of the lord of the Aranäs castle, the one known as Arn Magnusson in the novel" (Praesto & Sjölin, n.d., p. 7). In reality though, the carving is of a historical figure, not the protagonist invented by Jan Guillou, but for fans of the series that carving connotatively represents Arn Magnusson—the heroic Templar knight. The brochure features how the carving is described in the Arn novel *The Kingdom at the End of the Road* (2000), describing:

> At the early Christmas service down at the Forshem church a confident and proud Arn has shown what he had commissioned, even pointing to his own figure in stone above the church portal as the one giving the church keys to the Lord. And above him was the cross of the Knights Templar [Praesto & Sjölin, n.d., p. 7].

For the carving described in the novel and mentioned in the brochure, there is no photo of Arn's carving in the brochure but only the carving of the supposed stone master who created the sculptures. The photo of the Arn carving, however, is available online via a photo-sharing site such as Flikr, uploaded by Silva_D., who demonstrates his fandom knowledge by proclaiming, "The book written by Guillou was fictional, but when he visited this church he found that it was adorned with carvings that seemed to depict a Knights Templar" (2010). The image of the carving matches the description from the novel and implies that there is substance in the fan's assertion about Guillou's inspiration. The Arn carving provides a clear example of the concept of heterotopia as the location exists as two realities in one space, the historic site and the site of the novel; fans can see a piece of history that represents the fictional character as well as the historical lords of Aranäs Castle. The production of the Arn tourism brochure shows how heritage and film tourism can be interlinked, with the separate sites existing in the same location, as can the image of the Lord of the castle and the Templar protagonist, Arn. The association of Arn with this heritage site demonstrates how participation with the Templar narrative further expands the Templar phenomenon within popular culture, as the tourist's experience at the site further correlates the fictional Templar archetype with medieval Sweden.

The Rosslyn Chapel can also be considered a heterotopic space due to the chapel's historical and cultural contexts. The Rosslyn Chapel brochure states, "Explore the mystery—Discover the History," and this marketing slogan demonstrates the existence of several different realities contained in one space. The chapel, first constructed in 1446 by Sir William St Clair, stands as a physical remnant of historical reality, while also the site contains conspiracy themes by identifying the chapel with Templar and Masonic connotations. The Rosslyn Chapel also blurs the line between heritage tourism and film tourism as the chapel trust promotes its association with *The Da Vinci Code,* even including on a timeline the chapel and the book's publication date. This use of cultural associations would coincide with Eric Hobsbawm and Terence Ranger's concept of invented tradition. Hobsbawm explains that the concept involves "a set of practices, normally governed by overtly or tacitly accepted rules and of a ritual or symbolic nature, which seek to inculcate certain values and norms of behaviour by repetition" (2012, p. 1). Most significantly for this case study is Hobsbawm's assertion of an attempt to establish continuity with a suitable historic past (2012, p. 1). Rosslyn's Templar association created a symbolic Templar reality that encourages practices such as fan tourism to the benefit of the Chapel Heritage Trust. This alternative reality draws comparisons to the invented traditions of freemasonry, which Hobsbawm uses as an example of "innovators generating their own invented traditions" (2012, p. 8).

The Chapel Heritage Trust promotes the quasi-historical theory due to the significant benefit that Brown's best-selling novel brought to the historical site. Olsberg demonstrates the rise in visitors, stating, "In the Wake of Brown's novel the number of tourists to the destination had all but doubled each year, from 38,000 in 2003 to 68,000 in 2004 to 120,000 in 2005" (Martin Jones, 2014, p. 167). The impact of Dan Brown's fiction was celebrated by a Rosslyn Chapel tour guide who told her audience that visitors went from 36,000 to 176,000 a year after *The Da Vinci Code* was released, making a point to thank Dan Brown for increasing visitors and income to the trust. This is a relationship the Rosslyn trust also promotes by selling copies of *The Da Vinci Code* in the gift shop along with the novel's supposed inspiration, the book *Holy Blood, Holy Grail.*

Fans visiting the chapel find themselves in *The Da Vinci Code* reality, the location where Robert Langdon found the location of the tomb of Mary Magdalene but also a location showcasing the artistry of the medieval period. These two realities coexist within the same geographical location; as the marketing tagline "Explore the Mystery—Discover the History" suggests, a building encapsulating the historic stonework is given more considerable significance by the connotative meaning. This two-part tagline separates the historical actuality from the conspiracy narrative. It further coincides with the concept of shared spaces with two overarching accounts of the site, one of which *The Da Vinci Code* fans seek to substantiate their perception of the truth behind the Templar myth. The most substantial point of the chapel where the two realities coexist would be the crypt, in the scene where Robert Langdon and Sophie Neveu descend to find the secret passage. Down in the crypt are two information signs explaining the significance of the space; one details the room's use as a workshop for the chapel's construction, while the other informs of the room's place within *The Da Vinci Code* novel and film. These separate realities are associations that the Heritage Trust is keen to promote as Brown's work has given a significant rise to interest in the site, a location that (according to Martin Jones) was promoted in marketing for *The Da Vinci Code* film as a result of VisitScotland joining "a business partnership with Sony Pictures entertainment to market the locations" (2014, p. 157), and like the dual tagline suggests, the Rosslyn Chapel still markets itself thematically with *The Da Vinci Code* alongside its Scottish heritage.

The tagline expresses that the site has coexisting realities: the separate conspiracy narrative has drawn the tourists to the space, and the shared space will expose them to the historical-cultural significance of the site. This may cause tensions between the contrasting realities in that the facts do not support the assertions of the Templar narrative of the quest. This tension between the myth and the reality is addressed by Laing and Frost's study of King Arthur and Robin Hood tourism, where they highlight that the "English heritage's brochures of Tintagel make overt reference to King Arthur" and a video focused on discrediting the associated myth, which, they state, "disappointed many of the visitors" (2018, p. 102). They also explain that a similarly disappointing experience was found at the tourist attraction *The Tales of Robin Hood* in 1989, whose "interpretation at that time firmly explained Robin never existed and that popular media repetitions were rubbish" (2018, p. 104). However, Laing and Frost cite Shackley (2001) to inform that the attraction changed focus "with the release of the Kevin Costner film" in 1991 (2018, p. 104). The tension between the coexisting spaces at Rosslyn Chapel is demonstrated by the lively exchange on the Rosslyn Chapel official Facebook page. The page usually informs of upcoming events at the chapel or updates on the chapel's conservation, such as the post on August 5, 2018, "The stained glass window in the crypt looks wonderful after being cleaned earlier," with an accompanying photo of the window. The page, however, demonstrated the tension between the shared site realities when posting a message: "Today there are many theories about what could be below, an alien space ship, the Templar treasure, the Holy Grail itself or listening to our guides all the socks that go in the washing machine and don't come out" (January 5, 2018). This tongue-in-cheek post ended with posing the question to the page's followers, "But are the vaults even there and what could they hold?" (January 5, 2018), which started an ardent exchange among the page's followers. The first comment was by Facebook user 1, who asks the question, "Has any legitimate work ever been done to see if they [sic] are indeed vaults there?" The page's admin replies, "Yes, a vault exists but it is sealed. It's the burial place of the Rosslyn Barons and as sepulchre, will not be disturbed." Facebook user 1 responds with the suspicious Fry (character from *Futurama*) meme, which suggests that Facebook user 1 did not agree with the actuality of the page's response as it diverges from the conspiracy narrative and suggesting its falsehood from a position of authority.

Further examples of tension between the shared space are shown by Facebook user 2, who is quick to rubbish the chapel's Templar associations writing, "The entire Templar crap is getting old with Roslyn [sic] stories!" Another user, Facebook user 3, suggests that all the posters are wrong and posts, "The Holy Grail, the cup of Christ is in Europe, in a glass vault underground only special people can see it." Dan Brown's novel is introduced into the debate by Facebook user 4, who posts, "The Grail isnt [sic] a cup ... didn't [sic] you read?" The posts on this thread demonstrate the tensions between the perceptions of the sites' associated realities, notably when the historical findings do not support the Templar conspiracy myth.

The tourist's perception of the site gained from literature or filmic depiction can also cause tension if the reality deviates from a preconceived understanding of the site. The tension between the fictional depiction and reality is addressed by Frost, who explains, "historic films have the potential to strongly imprint a particular historical interpretation upon the minds of potential visitors" (2006, p. 249). Frost alludes that this perception "may create tensions, if that interpretation differs markedly from those provided by the existing attraction and tour operators" (2006, p. 249). This tension is demonstrated in a review of Rosslyn Chapel on Tripadvisor, where they exclaimed their disappointment at discovering that the Templars' historical reality did not align with their perception. In this review, the Rosslyn Chapel visitor explained how the tour guide did not discuss Templar or Masonic signs and posted, "he told me that the Templars had disappeared before the chapel is built and that therefore the hypothesis was not true" (Agunsuni, 2016). The tension created by the contrast of reality and expectation is further demonstrated by the reviewer's suggestion that the chapel "stop selling Templar books in your gift shop and Templar pendants or gifts with Masonic signs" and that "neither should you refer to the book of Robert Langdon" (Agunsuni, 2016). Further tension for Templar fans visiting the heterotopic sites can be experienced by a dismissal of the site's association with the fictional reality, which is demonstrated by a tour guide who, when conversing with me on the Philadelphia walking tour that I attended to research participation with the Templar narrative, did not want to include the *National Treasure* sites on the tour as the film promotes myth instead of history.

One of the *National Treasure* sites that the tour guide diverged from is the Old Pine Church, and this multiply coded site is a graveyard that, according to the signpost, provides "a self-guided tour of Old Pine's historic graveyard." The sign states that visitors can "Walk now in the footsteps that of people who held the nation together during its formative years in the 18th & 19th centuries." This historic graveyard features the resting places of notable Americans of the War of Independence, such as the grave of William Hurry 1721–1781, as the gravestone states, "who rang the bell proclaiming the declaration of independence." This heritage site is also the location where Nicolas Cage is chased through a graveyard in *National Treasure*, which is attested to by a small sign at the spot he enters the graveyard. This heterotopic site demonstrates the tension created by one space containing two realities, the historical heritage site and the filming location for the text associated with the Templar conspiracy myth.

The difference between the expectation of the fan-associated site with the reality of its actual location provides another aspect for the tension between the realities of the shared space. This was a criticism levied at *The Best Exotic Marigold Hotel* (Madden, 2011), a film that created an idealized depiction that Kork writes is "pleasing to watch and increasing the tourist demand for India, [the film] was criticised for 'sugar-coating' the destination and inaccurately portraying certain social elements of it" (2018, p. 75). This example of the difference in the social elements of reality compared to the idealized perception can also create tension between the coexisting spaces. A tension that would be experienced by the *National Treasure* fan visiting Philadelphia, a city depicted in the film as an optimistic link to America's Founding Fathers, is, in reality, "ranked the poorest metropolitan area of the country's biggest cities" (Lozano, NBC, Sep 26, 2018). This difference between expectation and reality is an aspect of the tourist's relationship with the local population; as Urry and Larsen explain, "there are usually large inequalities between the visitors and the indigenous population, most of whom could not envisage having the income or time to be tourists themselves" (2011, p. 62). This creates further tension for the fan tourist, as the reality of the site differs from the fictional perspective they had before visiting the real-world location, an experience shared by a *Da Vinci Code* reader who explained in his Tripadvisor review that after reading *The Da Vinci Code*, he "believed that there was something mysterious about the chapel, but it was only when I visited, that I realised that there is nothing mysterious" (David P, 2015). Despite the difference between reality and fiction, the Templar tourist will also discover tension between the coexisting realities within the multiply coded space, the contrasts between both the historical reality and Templar conspiracy narrative.

The Templar quest narrative revolves around the journey into the world of the sensational to find an item of significance. This narrative has evolved to create the second aspect of the narrative, following in the Templars' footsteps, which reworks the mythical aspects of the narrative, such as the quest of the Holy Grail, most notably the cup of Christ, which essentially makes the Templar past the sensational world; the protagonist must venture to discover the Templar revelation, which has a benefit for Western society. It is this narrative function of the Templars' past that then intrinsically links Templar fan tourism with heritage tourism. The quest narrative of following in the Templars' footsteps incorporates iconic historical sites which give this journey into the past a physical presence as well as a symbolic presence. Gaining greater knowledge of the Templar myth by visiting the fan site symbolizes the Templar revelation of the narrative, as fans seek the greater truth behind the Templar myth. The myth is attributed as a perceived credibility through the associations of heritage sites such as Rosslyn Chapel.

Templar fan tourism for texts that include the quest narrative will merge into sites that possess a heterotopia of realities within one geographical location, as in the Rosslyn Chapel. This shows the potential for one site to have a separate meaning for fans of *The Da Vinci Code*. For fan tourists of these Templar-themed texts, the sites will be linked to heritage tourism through the thematic aspect of the following in the Templars' footsteps quest narrative, although these mythical Templar associations create contrasting realities and tension between perceptions of these multiply coded sites. However, the emergence of tensions through fan tourism is not unique to the Templar myth's link to heritage sites, as Williams explains that there is tension for all sites. Williams states, "This tension between commercialization and the lived experiences and practises of fans sit alongside other debates around the 'authenticity' of experiences, how fans can engage in certain practices at meaningful sites" (2018, pp. 104–105). The coexisting realities of the real and the fictional will always cause tensions, such as *The Da Vinci Code* reader David P's disappointment when visiting the real-world Rosslyn Chapel. However, the inevitable tensions with the heritage sites are due to the clash of historical and mythical perceptions. Fans of these Templar-themed texts will encounter these while investigating the site and feeling closer to the perceived truth behind the Templar myth, just like the protagonists in the Templar quest narrative.

Immersion Through Tourism

Chapter 2 explored how fans immerse themselves into the story world through play and performance by controlling and interacting with the Templar knight narrative and how game producers influence those experiences by incorporating established aspects of the Templar knight narrative to facilitate this immersion. While Chapter 2 explored fan immersion in a digital sense, with computer games and fan film, this chapter argues that fan tourism enables a physically immersive experience that facilitates fan interaction with the Templar narrative. Fan tourism is more than just visiting filming locations in person; it allows fans to immerse themselves within the narrative in a kinetic and symbolic way. The importance of symbolic immersion is highlighted by Reijnders, who explains, "media pilgrimages are not only a physical journey to a location that is important in the context of a particular media story, but also represent a symbolic journey, during which the distance between the 'ordinary world' and the 'media world' is collapsed" (2010, p. 370). This notion of the fusion of the physical and symbolic is explored by Hills, where he explains, "Through visiting cult geographies, the cult fan is able to extend an engagement with a text or icon by extratextually 'inhabiting the world,' in a restricted or imaginary sense, of the media cult" (2002, p. 145). This participation is both physical and symbolic in that fans travel to real locations that have symbolic meaning to them but appear mundane to those uninitiated to the Templar-themed text.

Brooker explores the concept of the closeness fans feel to shooting locations, explaining, "On our journey to 'the promised land,' where we lose ourselves and become immersed in the favoured text or site, we are in a stage of inbetweenness" (2005, p. 12). Using a still image of the film text to compare to a real-world geographical location is a common way for fans to experience an immersion with the text, a practice carried out by tour guides at the Old Pine Church. A tour company manager described in an email that the tour guide displays a still from the chase scene in *National Treasure* at the spot where the scene was filmed. Showcasing the closeness of the real-world location to the fictional world through the fan tourist practice of comparing a still from the film to the real location enables a deeper connection to the world of fandom, but unfortunately for fans, the reality is still outside the fictional world. To address the attempt to experience the cultural perception of the space, Brooker turns to Turner's concept of "the liminal, from the Latin 'limen' or threshold" (2005, p. 12) to address the limitations of fans' closeness to the fictional world of *Blade Runner*.

Turner defines *liminal*, writing, "The passage from one social status to another is often accompanied by a parallel passage in space, a geographical movement from one place to another" (1974, p. 58). This concept is addressed by Brooker to examine the notion of the state of inbetweenness. The liminal, according to Turner, "may take the form of a mere opening of doors or the literal crossing of a threshold which separates two distinct areas, one associated with the subject's pre-ritual or preliminal status, and the other with his post-ritual or postliminal status" (1974, p. 58). The notion of a threshold between two realities encompasses the duplicity of the realities within the space of the Templar-associated heritage sites. The notion of the threshold to the fictional world is also addressed by Reijnders, who cites Turner and Turner to explain this concept in the context of fan tourists touching the fictional world, writing, "this quest is part and parcel of all media pilgrimages. In the words of Turner and Turner, every pilgrim goes through a 'pre-liminal phase' in which he/she steps out of his/her everyday life and gains access to holy or magical locations" (2010, pp. 371–372). This comparison of the fan objective to access fantastical locations draws a comparison with the Templar quest narrative of the journey to the Templar mythical past from the story's modern-day setting. Reijnders highlights the fan's quest to access the fictional world, in one case through the location of a door on Westminster Bridge, which is used in the James Bond film *Die Another Day* (Tamahori, 2002) as a secret entrance to MI6 headquarters. Reijnders evidences this through an interview with a fan, underlining, "The fact that the door can be seen and touched is enough to justify the journey to Westminster Bridge. As Delmo said in his interview, actually touching this door and taking a picture of it, allowed him to make Bond's world 'more realistic' and tangible" (2010, p. 371). For the uninitiated, the door appears mundane and perhaps hidden in plain sight, but for the James Bond fan it provides a symbolic point of immersion, standing as a literal threshold and a symbolic one.

This experience of closeness for the James Bond fan by viewing the threshold of the fictional world could be shared by the *National Treasure* fan when visiting Independence Hall. In the film, while hunting down the next treasure clue, Ben Gates and his companions sneak away from a guided tour inside and jump over a roped staircase to ascend into the hall's tower. Similar to the fan's relationship with the door on Westminster Bridge, the roped staircase represents the threshold to the reality of *National Treasure*, as fans can copy the protagonists and take the tour. However, jumping over the rope, like the characters, would not lead to adventure but would get the fan in trouble with the park rangers. The roped staircase, like the bridge door, represents the state of inbetweenness, where the fictional text and real world meet to create an impassable threshold, which for fans, Brooker explains, means "they never reach the peak of intense connection with the 'promised land'" (2005, p. 13).

This sense of liminal inbetweenness felt by fans is openly promoted by Rosslyn Chapel. This chapter has already explored how the heritage site markets itself as a *Da Vinci Code* fan tourist site, but this location asserts its appearance in the film by referring to the exact place the actors stood. Specifically, down in the chapel crypt is a sign that shows a film still of Robert Langdon and Sophie Neveu entering the crypt: the location of the characters' entrance is to the right of the sign. This sign provides a focal point where the texts merge with reality and enable the fan to visualize the fictional world, which enables the fan to bridge the gap between reality and fiction. Although the Templar quest narrative promotes fans using their knowledge of the text to complete the quest like the protagonists, in the chapel the fan does not need to rely on fan knowledge as the Rosslyn Chapel enables fans to experience the threshold of the fantasy world. When explaining how fans deal with the visual difference between the real LA location and the futurist LA in *Blade Runner*, Brooker explains that fans can "bridge the gap between real and fictional through photoshop, carefully-angled pictures, graphic effects and editing" (2005, p. 26); this bridging is provided for the visiting *Da Vinci Code* fans by the Rosslyn Chapel. The sign in the crypt ties in to the Templar quest narrative as it points the reader to the end of the quest, the room that Langdon and Sophie enter to find the secret grail entrance. It states, "This still from the film shows the characters discovering a secret door in the floor of the vestry which leads into an underground chamber. This vault does not exist in the chapel or if it does, it has yet to be found." This points towards the connected narrative of the film and the geographical location edited together within this signpost. Unfortunately for *Da Vinci Code* fans, the room off the crypt does not lead to the same one entered by the fictional characters and does not have a secret entrance to the grail. This reality means the fan can no longer follow in the protagonist's footsteps as the lack of a secret entrance provides a symbolically blocked threshold to the fantasy world.

In his work on *The X-Files* fan tourism, Hills notes that the tourist experience is not officially offered to fans. They must rely on their own research using blogs or forums to discover key locations and then having to resort to comparing the mundane real world to a screenshot of the fan text. As this chapter has identified, the Rosslyn Chapel openly promotes the site's relationship with *The Da Vinci Code*, which means it does not coincide with the experience of *The X-Files* fan tourist. However, what is significant is how the fans desire to replicate the series characters by "The 'tracking down' of sites, hence replicates the narrative structure of the programme" (2002, p. 114), a character emulation that is sought out and marketed to fans of *National Treasure* and *The Da Vinci Code*. The opportunity for fans to emulate the traits of the protagonists is featured within the *National Treasure* DVD, which encourages fans to solve a puzzle to unlock hidden bonus features, getting clues from the available bonus features. The interactive menu on the DVD encourages the consumers to replicate the actions of Ben Gates but from the comfort of your own home. A physical quest was used for marketing the film around its release with Disney producing tourist maps of Philadelphia and Washington, D.C., both significant locations of the film setting. This marketing strategy was explored in an article on the website TripSavvy. The article is titled, "National Treasure: Hollywood Film Sparks Real-Life Adventure," a title which ties into The Washington, D.C. Convention & Tourism Corporation (WCTC) and the Greater Philadelphia Tourism Marketing Corporation's (GPTMC) use of the film's popularity trope to market heritage tourism. The article explains, "Using images and clues from the film, the tour leads visitors on a multi-day, two-city tour of National Treasure's key locations. The WCTC and the GPTMC have outlined the tour in a 10-panel, four-color brochure, illustrated with photos from the film, which points visitors to both historic and contemporary stops" (Fischer, 2017, May). These cities' tourism boards are encouraging fans to play at following in the historic footsteps by participating with the film's shooting locations. Thus, the organizers of the tour are using the Templar quest narrative of the film to enable participation with the text but also with the geographical location they are seeking to promote. For *The Da Vinci Code* film, a similar marketing approach was used called The Da Vinci Code Adventure. Martin Jones explains that the campaign "provided an opportunity for winning teams from various countries (including Australia and the USA) to visit locations featured in the film, and to learn about their history by solving clues and completing tasks there" (2014, p. 167). This marketing venture highlights the attractiveness of visiting the geographical locations associated for fans and the desire to boost the immersive experience through carrying out activities that emulate those of the protagonists. The functionality of the quest narrative, as a story tool, is replicated as a viable way to produce fan experiences, as it enables that desired deeper sense of integration through place and participation.

While visiting the fan location enables connection, participation on location provides the possibility of a more profound sense of immersion through recreating the characters' activities. As mentioned in The Da Vinci Code Adventure, the prize is not only the chance to visit the locations but also mentions activities that are the essence of the protagonist's behavior. The protagonists of the Templar-themed text rely on their knowledge of history/symbolism to solve the puzzles that enable them to continue their quest, which is a feature of fan tourism, as fans rely on their knowledge of the text to give purpose and propulsion for their fandom quest. In competing in The Da Vinci Code Adventure, fans can play at being their favorite characters by taking part in a competition that involves carrying out tasks that simulate the actions of their fandom texts, while to a lesser degree fans visiting the Rosslyn Chapel are encouraged to decipher the meaning behind the chapel's carvings, such as the carving of "Indian Corn" located in the south aisle. The Rosslyn Chapel website explains that the chapel was built before 1492 and asks, "could these carvings of Indian corn be proof that Scottish knights reached America first?" In examining such symbolism in the chapel's carvings fans can become a symbologist like Robert Langdon, and like the puzzle-solving of The Da Vinci Code Adventure, this interaction enables a deeper sense of immersion.

Rosslyn Chapel promotes itself as a place of mystery, demonstrated by the chapel's brochure tagline "Explore the Mystery—Discover the History." However, long before the chapel agreed on a partnership deal with Sony to market the location, the unique chapel has been associated with themes of conspiracy and shadowy groups. Despite the wonder of the chapel's architecture, there are notions that the Rosslyn Chapel has a deeper significance. In his book of the Templar sites of Britain, Simon Brighton addresses the cultural associations of the chapel's architecture, explaining, the "symbolism is recorded: a codex for the modern researcher to decipher, trying to get close to the medieval mind of William St Clair and the vision of the Knights Templar" (2006, p. 241). The perceived Templar symbolism is identified for visitors by signs such as the burial stone of William de Sinncler, which explains that the "slabs bears a floriated cross often associated with the Knights Templar" and engraved underneath is "WILLIAM DE SINN-CLER KNIGHT TEMPLAR."

The other key Templar symbol promoted by the site is the Lamb of God, which the Rosslyn Chapel visitor brochure states, "As well as being a reference to Christ, the Lamb of God was a symbol of the Knights Templar, whose aim was to protect pilgrims travelling to the Holy Land during the Crusades." The brochure is more ambiguous about the meaning, but the information sign for the carving at the site caters more to the Templar mythical narrative with an additional sentence of "Many stories surround the Knights and their quest to find and protect the treasures of the ruined Temple of Solomon in Jerusalem." This line directly conforms to the Templar quest narrative referring to the perceived location of both the physical Holy Grail and its reimagining as the tomb of Mary Magdalene in *The Da*

Vinci Code. This additional sentence offers fans seeking truth to the Templar myth a sense of legitimacy, as this historically false narrative is provided in the context of a historic heritage giving validity to the mythical Templar theme associated with the site. The concept of solving the secret symbolism is further thematically promoted within the chapel; for example, on one of the signs explaining the significance of the carved cubes in the Lady Chapel section, it states, "Each one is carved with individual symbols. Various theories suggest that these represent musical notes or keys to a secret code." This theme of solving chapel mysteries encourages participation with the site, offering the visitors the illusion of opportunity to uncover secrets of their own.

The thematic marketing of the chapel is further embedded through the information talks carried out by staff; RosslynChapel.com states, "cover some of the Chapel's history, the family's story and highlight some of the key carvings." The Rosslyn information talks by the tour guide ended with the questions, "Will you find the treasures of the Knights Templar? Will you find the Holy Grail?" These talks leave the theme of fantastical mystery as the conclusion of the talk, which is given an added weight of authority by an official member of staff. This is the weight that fictional characters Langdon and Teabing's academic credentials give to the fantastical conspiracy revelations when educating Neveu (and the reader) in Brown's work. The chapel's information talks further blur the line between the coexisting realities, catering for both the interest around the heritage site's historical context and the mythical Templar associations. This interests *The Da Vinci Code* fans seeking a greater understanding of the truth behind the Templar myth. This theme of uncovering hidden revelations is further enshrined in the visitor experience by the chance to purchase books such as *Holy Blood, Holy Grail*, *The Sion Revelation* (Pickett & Prince, 2006) and *Rosslyn and the Grail* (2005, Oxbrow & Robertson), quasi-historical books that detail the site's mythical association.

The encouragement for visitors to participate with the site to experience the secrecy theme is celebrated by *The Da Vinci Code* fans in reviews on Tripadvisor. A Tripadvisor review by 84u2c titled, "Be [*sic*] your own professor Langdon of the Da Vinci Code!" explains how they "got to play Da Vinci code all on my own. Absolutely fascinating and thoroughly enjoyable for the explorer and code solver in all of us" (March 2017). Another review of Rosslyn Chapel by Grigs27 is titled, "felt like professor Langdon" (August 2014). These reviews demonstrate that the thematic experience the site is promoting is one that *The Da Vinci Code* fans are not just seeking but identifying with as a unique way of interacting with the narrative made possible through fan tourism to the Rosslyn Chapel. The Templar quest narrative following in the Templars' footsteps is the protagonist's physical and metaphorical journey to the past to learn a Templar revelation. The Rosslyn Chapel provides a sense of this experience for fans wishing to engage with the text's narrative on a kinetic level and encourages fans to become, in effect, active researchers. With the act of visiting the geographical location where the text is set, fans can interact physically by standing where the characters stood and interact symbolically by engaging with the thematic mystery associated with the site, which further embeds their perception of the Templar Phenomenon in popular culture.

Play and Performance

The significance of fan tourism to the Templar narrative is more than using it as an example of fan interaction but how this interaction expands the Templar narrative through Jenkins' concept of textual poaching. Sandvoss explains that for fan tourism, "Fans are in this sense engaged not so much in textual poaching as in textual roaming" (2005, p. 54), a practice where participating fans create a sense of ownership and potential new narratives. Alderman emphasized this aspect of fan tourism in his arguments around practices of Elvis fans visiting Graceland, which he claims are "authoring." Duffett cites Alderman to explain that he "has argued that such visitors are not just consumers shuttled round the mansion, but they are also, in effect, participating by 'authoring' their own involvement" (2013, p. 231). This premise suggests that fan tourism is an act of authorship and that fans create their own experience through physical interaction. However, this implies an individually unique experience for individual fans, which Duffett argues is problematic as "why so many people desire to experience something so similar and whether they all leave with same experiences" (2013, p. 231).

What enables the perception of a unique fan experience is the physical participation enacted by fans, which Sandvoss examines by drawing from Aden's concept of purposeful play, which he explains "can be envisioned as a purposeful play in which we symbolically move from the material world to an imaginative world that is in many ways a response to the material" (2005, p. 54). The importance of the interactive nature within fan tourism is explained by Sandvoss, who states that places "are socially constructed through symbols, discourses and representations" (2014, p. 115). The Washington, D.C. Convention & Tourism Corporation (WCTC) and the Greater Philadelphia Tourism Marketing Corporation (GPTMC) mass-produced an identical brochure for fans to market the city around *National Treasure's* release. However, in interacting with the world of the text, fans are able to participate with the text and have their own unique *National Treasure* experience. This suggests that the mass production of brochures does not equate to a mass ritual experience, and therefore, there is an element of Jenkins' poaching concept in the personalization of the text.

The personalization of the text is a sentiment explored by Brooker, who analyzes *Blade Runner* fan pilgrimage, writing, "the Blade Runner pilgrimage experience has to be carved out for oneself, 'poached' (following Jenkins 1992) from a range of other possible meanings and constructed by the individual through a committed act of investment and imagination" (2005, p. 24). This unique experience will affect the relationship fans have with the text, which Brooker perceives, "The memory of having occupied the space where the film was shot … provides a link between the viewer and the screen text" (2005, p. 27). The fan pilgrimage enables fans to participate with the fantasy location of their chosen text; fans of the Templar film case studies can physically interact with the Templar quest narrative through play, and much like the text's protagonist, the fans can follow in the footsteps of the Templar. This participation with the quest narrative emulates the protagonist's new knowledge gained through the Templar revelation feature (see chapter 3) in that the experience of interacting with the geographical relationship gives fans a newer, more intimate relationship with the text. This intimate understanding is the revelation or symbolic grail that fans achieve at the end of their quest, which is an experience only achieved via participating with the text's geographical location.

The official brochure that enabled convenience for *National Treasure* fans wanting to explore the film location has since been discontinued, as the film was released well over a decade ago and is no longer used by the cities to market for tourism. *National Treasure* fans will have to rely on their own research skills and expert knowledge. The emulation of the skills of fictional fan favorites at locations associated with the text can enable fans to feel a more profound sense of closeness with their beloved text, such as throwing a pitch at the *Field of Dreams* (Robinson, 1989) farm in Iowa. The increase to the immersive experience is explored by Reijnders analyzing James Bond fandom. Reijnders asserts, "This feeling is intensified by performing certain routines at the location. Most of the respondents said that while at the location they assume a Bond pose, with their index fingers representing pistols" (2010, p. 373). Such actions by fans at important locations are mentioned in Hills' account of *X-Files* fandom, where he cites from *Focus* (1997) to highlight fan recreation on location of Scully's kidnap. Hills cites: "To recreate the scene she tied up her young son and placed him in the boot of their rental car and then photographed him there" (2002, p. 149). These fan actions of throwing a baseball, posing as James Bond using your finger as a rudimentary gun, or as I did in Philadelphia, posing beneath the Rocky statue and recreating the Apollo Rocky punch from the end of *Rocky III* (Stallone, 1982) bear a resemblance to Lancaster's approach of performance fandom defined in Chapter 2.

Although not as well marketed as the *National Treasure* tours were around the release, fans can take part in more general Philadelphia tours, which cater a small portion of the tour to filming locations including *National Treasure*. For example, the city of Philadelphia actively promotes its setting in fictional films as soon as tourists depart the plane, where movie posters of films including *Rocky* (Avildsen, 1976), *The Village* (Shyamalan, 2004) and *National Treasure* line the walls as you travel along the airport's travelator. Tours that still cater to *National Treasure* fan interest include the walking tour, Real Philadelphia Tour (Insider's Guide to Philly), which makes the Old Pine Church and setting of a chase from *National Treasure* part of its four-hour tour. Once on location, the tour guide would show a still of the chase scene in the film to show the location's role to the tour group. The use of a film still on a tour is an approach, as with the film still displayed at the Rosslyn Chapel crypt, which enables the bridging of the gap between worlds such as explained by Brooker's analysis of *Blade Runner* tourism.

Fan performance at significant, textual geographical locations enables a deeper sense of immersion, which is not exclusive to fan tourism as the concept of immersion through performance was analyzed alongside fan film depicting the Templar knight narrative in Chapter 2. However, the act of performance and its potential enhancement of immersion demonstrate cohesiveness of performance with fan tourism. Lancaster defines immersion as "the process by which participants break the frame of their actual 'everyday' world, allowing them to interact in some way within the fantasy environment" (2001, p. 31). This desire of immersion with the fantasy world is apparent within the desire of the fan to walk where their favorite characters have walked. However, as Brooker has explored in his study of fan pilgrimage, the desired feeling of closeness falls short, which creates the in-between liminal state. Fan poses or recreations can help deepen the sense of immersion within the story world through the act of performance. The concept of the active performer attempting to transcend from their reality into the world of the fandom coincides with the immersive desire of fan tourism that ultimately leaves fans on the threshold of the fandom world; they are in a sense stuck between worlds. This idea of fan immersion through performance coincides with the symbolic actions of fans at important locations, such as an *The X-Files* kidnapping scene recreation cited by Hills, which heavily indicates a performance by fans (2002, p. 149). What constitutes a performance can be subjective, but that is not to say that the fan posing as Bond or a *National Treasure* fan posing at the Old Pine Church gate to represent the film's chase scene is not a performance.

Lancaster's concept of fandom performance is not purely for theatrical presentations, as Sandvoss explains, "Lancaster's account is based on the insider perspective that arises from his own regular participation in the viewing of the programme [Babylon 5], web-based discussion groups, role-playing, card games and multi-user domains" (2005, p. 45). Lancaster's wide-ranging bracket for fan activities moves his approach beyond the simplistic theatrical connotations of performance, which suggests that immersive behaviors carried out by fans can be considered performances. Such performances by fans of these Templar texts are demonstrated by a photo of a woman recreating the scene from *National Treasure*, where Ben Gates and his companions venture over the rope barrier to ascend the tower in search of the next clue. The photo's caption states, "Just doing my best National Treasure Ben Gates climbing over a restricted rope blocking off a staircase at Independence Hall impression." To coincide with the recreational pose, the caption of the photo showcases the person's fandom by informing of the cultural relevance of the site, posting, "'Excuse me! Will we be going up to the roof today to see where Nicolas Cage discovered Ben Franklin's ocular device behind the brick?'" (Hall of Independence visitor 1, Facebook, 2015).

The difference between play and performance concerning fan tourism is often not fixed as the terms are used interchangeably, as play and performance both require fixed boundaries to exist, in both a physical sense, such as space or in a symbolic sense as rules to hold the fan practice. Of course, fan tourism also requires a location to be a destination of the text's dual reality, so the three are intricately linked, which means the boundaries between play and performance often blur and merge. The concept of play within pilgrimage is analyzed through Geraghty's study of *Smallville* fan tourism, where he cites Hills to associate "the movement and practices of fans in geographical spaces within notions of 'affective play' and social interaction" (2011, p. 137). Hills' concept of affective play reasons, "it deals with the emotional attachment of the fan," and "it suggests that play is not always caught up in a pre-established 'boundedness' or set of cultural boundaries" (2002, p. 112), which Lancaster explains as vital to be defined as fan performance. However, the language of performance is used by Reijnders when examining James Bond fan testimonies around their behavior at Bond film sites. He asserts, "By performing Bond, these fans perform and thereby reconstruct a specific masculinity" (2010, p. 374). Reijnders describes the activities of James Bond fans ranging from posing at sites to renting an Aston Martin to "retrace the route that Bond drove in one of the films or novels" (2010, p. 373). What sets this fan tourism study apart from notions of play is the transformative, psychological experience recorded by Bond fans. Reijnders asserts that Bond locations are "material symbolic sources of masculinity, where the individual's sexual identity can be rediscovered, delineated and reinforced" (2010, p. 374). These practices described by Bond fans demonstrate the desire of fans to be close to the fictional world but also how performance at these sites enables fans to identify with Bond and the associated character aspects. The relationship of fandom with performance, Sandvoss explains, is more than construction identification with the text: "Places of fandom thus take on a dual meaning. On the one hand, they incorporate tendencies to placelessness for their other-directedness with respect to the fan text; on the other hand, they are transformed into the territorial focus of individual and group identities" (2005, p. 66). The concept of the transformative role in fan performance is due to the focus and behavior of the fan, but this is in relation to the text as the location. For example, the James Bond locations in London will appear mundane to those not antiquating the location with the Bond text.

Where the concepts of fan pilgrimage and fan performance merge is that they are focused around created sites. Whether this is the Harry Potter studios, the streets of Los Angeles or the character sheets within a published role-playing game, they have been purposefully constructed to create an immersive experience, either as locations for a spectatorship narrative or to participate with through play and performance. Participation with the fantasy world through play was explored in Chapter 2, where players can play with the historical Templar world and interact with an environment that could only be viewed through fictional film. Playful interaction with the associated environment of the text is demonstrated by the video uploaded to YouTube by Tripfilms (11 July 2008) titled, *A Da Vinci Code Tour of Paris*. In the video, Hillary, the virtual tour guide, dresses in an outfit of a coat, shirt and skirt and hairstyle that matches the character, Sophie Neveu. *The Da Vinci Code* tour starts in the Louvre where Hillary then playfully interacts with the environment, winking when standing in front of Da Vinci's painting *the Virgin on the Rocks,* which *The Da Vinci Code* fans would know holds a clue to the quest for the Holy Grail.

The video also holds performance aspects as when Hillary walks through the famous heritage site of the church of Saint-Sulpice, her voice-over dramatically states, "Ok, this place is seriously creepy. It's huge, it's dark and there aren't many people around" (2008), with the camera zooming to a close-up of her looking apprehensive. Although other tourists are visible behind her, the video here tries to recreate *The Da Vinci Code's* theme of mystery and suspense. Hillary's performance continues as she emulates the clue spotting and puzzle-solving of Dan Brown's protagonists, as she examines a carving, stating, "check this out. Opus D! Followed by who knows, they've scratched it out." With some ominous background music, Hillary takes the carving of Opus DOM Sacrum out of context and playfully suggests it relates to the Opus Dei order featured as antagonists in Brown's story. Through this participation, Hillary can immerse herself within the fictional world of *The Da Vinci Code*, by visiting the geographical sites and interacting with them through acts of play and performance.

Regarding fan pilgrimage, the concepts of play and performance start to blur, as Chapter 2 argued, the act of play creates boundaries that play is facilitated within. However, Lancaster's notion of performance decrees, "the various sites of the imaginary entertainment environment … can be perceived as sites of performances" (2001, xxviii). Lancaster defines these sites, not in the traditional theatrical sense of a stage or set but as immersive mechanisms such as online forums and role-playing games. For example, Lancaster defines the site of performance as the character record sheet of the *Babylon 5* role-playing game, arguing, "The character record sheet becomes the site, the interface, for transforming this fantasy into reality" (2001, p. 63). This suggests that as fan pilgrimage is the fan's quest to visit sites of symbolic importance to feel close to the fictional world and then to pose or recreate themes identifying with their fandom, these become sites of performance to enable deeper immersion within the fictional world. However, this comparison is simplistic in its assumptions that text-related acts are acts of fandom. Sandvoss argues that Lancaster's notion of performance is problematic, highlighting, "not all fans engage in performances of game-play, and not all performers in role-play or fantasy games are fans" (2005, p. 46). This would underline that not all visitors to popular culture sites such as the Harry Potter-themed rides in Universal Studios are Harry Potter fans, and therefore defining photo poses as performances is too encompassing. Although the performance made by Hall of Independence visitor 1 and Hillary can be assessed as fans due to the post's display of knowledge of the text, not all performances of these Templar texts can be attributed as fans, such as the short film *National Treasure* (2-minute theater) (May 6, 2015) uploaded by Cara Thompson. Although the short film features the lead actor performing like Ben Gates with his hair styled to match, this video is one of dozens of short filmic recreations the user has uploaded to YouTube. Although the short film is not filmed on location, the film underlines Sandvoss's notion that labeling all performers as fans is problematic.

Determining whether posing at a fan site is an act of play or performance can only be assessed based on the individual cases, but what is comparable is the pretense of transforming reality through the action. Fortunately, fan tourism does provide evidence of these acts of play and performance due to the importance of capturing images of oneself to prove your journey to the site and showcase your knowledge of the site's importance. Geraghty explains that proving you have been to the sites is part of creating the fan sense of belonging, and in regard to Smallville fandom, he writes, "Meaning, attachment, and a sense of belonging are created through physically being in the city where a television series is filmed, recreating moments of viewing and sharing the experience with others after the event" (2011, p. 137). Sharing the experience can be seen in a photo uploaded to Facebook by a *Da Vinci Code* fan, which shows her sitting in front of Arago medallions on the floor of the Louvre in France, which *Da Vinci Code* fans know indicate the rose line for Robert Langdon to find the grail's resting place at the Louvre. Sharing these photos not only showcases the uploader's knowledge of *The Da Vinci Code* but also demonstrates their attachment to the text. Capturing photos at culturally significant sites is part of creating the unique fan experience and the sense of authoring proposed by Duffet. The uniqueness of the experience is further amplified by the acts of recreation by fans which, once home, they can post online to demonstrate they were there and change their perception when again viewing the text, having visited the location in real life.

The importance of sharing the experience when the fan is back home is demonstrated through Aden's concept of the return home, which Brooker cites as "leaving the liminal, coming back to normal life-ideally, on new terms-and gaining a new and enhanced, albeit temporary, perspective on the everyday" (2005, p. 27). This concept of the return home uses the language of a journey and coincides with the classical mythic story structure defined by Joseph Campbell. This is in part inspired by the Arthurian myth, which is the origin of the Templar quest narrative. In effect, the fan Templar quest follows the narrative thread of the mythical quest that it is replicating, and therefore the fans can follow in the Templars' footsteps via sharing their fan tourism experience. This sharing unconsciously completes recreating the Templar quest upon their return home. The quest's completion upon the fans' return is demonstrated by the video National Treasure Philly Walking Tour (March 4, 2018) uploaded to YouTube by Joseph Naylor, where the uploader explains while at the heritage site Independence Hall what scenes of the film were shot there intercut with clips from the *National Treasure* film. The video explains how they asked the tour guide where the film was filmed and how the tour guide explained to them, "the only parts that were filmed here were when they're up in the tower. On the roof. When they leave, we didn't actually let them tear out a brick" (2018). This video allows the *National Treasure* fan to share his new knowledge online by sharing the video that is intercut with scenes from the film to show the legitimacy of the new knowledge.

To explain the importance of capturing photos on site, Hills cites Sontag, who argues that fans need "to have reality confirmed and experience enhanced by photographs is an aesthetic consumerism" (2002, p. 150). Of course, for holiday photos "the scale of this practise is significantly larger now than ever" (2017, p. 116); according to Linden and Linden, advances in digital photography and use of social media sites like Instagram and Twitter have heightened its significance. Linden and Linden make clear that when examining the role of photographs, there is also an aspect of narcissism in the importance of sharing these images. They suggest that images of oneself and especially the "selfie" photo is more than "The importance of being seen as somebody who is creative and does interesting things can not be completely separated from the need for communicating and sharing experiences with friends and family" (2017, p. 117). However, in the context of fan tourism, these photos share the fan's experiences and preserve the memory of fan immersion within the fictional world of their favored text and the sharing of these images in part adds to the fan's sense of ownership of the text.

The keeping of records of fans' journeys is more than a habit of narcissism but provides fans with a reference point to remember their journey to the threshold of the favorite text. Brooker demonstrates the importance of recording the liminal experience upon the return, as recalling the shared space creates a deeper sense of belonging between fan and text. He explains, "The memory of having occupied the space where the film was shot, of standing in a place that, while grounded in the everyday, was nevertheless the parallel-world neighbour of a site Rick Deckard had walked or driven through, provides a link between the viewer and the screen text" (2005, p. 27). This recollection of the closeness felt by the fans standing on the threshold of the story world creates deeper integration when interacting with the text's narrative. In posting the images of their fandom, fans "are getting closer still to both the text and physical space they once occupied—returning to a place to which they now feel they really belong" (Geraghty, 2011, p. 136). The photo serves as a reminder for when the fan shared the heterotopic space of both geographical and symbolic. In regard to the Templar fan tourist, the photo and video show the point where history and popular culture meet in the same space, such as the photo of Hall of Independence visitor 1 who posed at the rope barrier on the staircase, mimicking Ben Gates.

The significance of immersion through fan action is further supported through examining fan photos from *National Treasure* and the *Da Vinci Code* filming locations, which show a repetition of the meaning within the text and similar playful acts of fandom. Searching for *The Da Vinci Code* on Facebook in the photo category will bring up multiple photo repeats of the same location and near-identical photos of poses in front of the bottom of the pyramid in the Louvre. In the film and novel, the Louvre is a significant location as it is the resting place of Mary Magdalene who, according to Brown, is symbolized as the Holy Grail. These photos uploaded to Facebook also include captions which indicate the fans' acts of play, such as "is the grail really there? #TheDaVinciCode" (Louvre visitor 1, 2016) or "Looking for the Da Vinci Code" (Louvre visitor 2, 2009). A *National Treasure* fan demonstrates her knowledge of the film with a photo, posing next to the Liberty Bell with the caption, "Liberty Bell #nationaltreasure #where is the next clue" (Liberty Bell visitor 1, 2016, Facebook), which demonstrates knowledge of the site's significance to the film text but also shows a sense of playful immersion through the photo caption. These photos demonstrate how the malleability of the Templar narrative has blurred real history, Templar conspiracy myth and the film merged together into one geographical location, which coincides with Brooker's concept of multiply coded places. Although Aden explains the personal significance of the return home to the fan (Brooker, 2005, p. 27), it also provides the opportunity to examine the evidence of Templar fan tourism. Moreover, this evidence demonstrates how these acts of fandom have further evolved the Templar quest narrative within popular culture, not only through the text's association with landmarks but also provide a platform for showcasing the fan's tourist experience through individual acts of play and performance.

Conclusion

Fan tourism demonstrates how fans engage with the narrative of their favored texts beyond the viewing format which was initially provided. This chapter analyzed how fans seek to engage kinetically with the textual narrative to form a new relationship, one that they perhaps could not achieve with the conventional, more passive engagement of viewing the screen narrative. Analyzing fan tourism, alongside the reoccurring Templar narrative of the quest, showcases how my concept of the Templar urtext further evolves in recent popular culture due to fan interaction. The practice of fan tourism influenced by the Templar narrative underlines the significance of the malleability of the Templar narrative as fan tourism enables fans to gain a deeper understanding or relationship with the text. The fan of the Templar text is seeking to find, seeking to impose their own subjective truth onto a multifaceted narrative of the ultimately contradictory Templar urtext.

The lack of a single, definitive version of the Templar's legacy, due to their Order's extinction in the 14th century, has enabled the narrative's evolution to take on new forms. Due to the Templar narrative's malleability, fans can create their own personalized narratives through their own quest to these sites of textual importance and then share these new narratives via photos and posts, documenting the experience, which enables the Templar phenomenon to further expand across mediums in popular culture. In examining fan activity with the Templar narrative, the study demonstrates how the Templar quest narrative has further evolved beyond a phenomenon that fans endeavor to experience and expand the narrative themselves.

The second aspect of the Templar quest narrative, following in the Templar's footsteps, depicts the protagonists' venture into the past to learn of the beneficial Templar revelation. Fans replicate this journey taken by the text's protagonist through the act of fan tourism. The Templar revelation discovered by the texts' protagonist is echoed by the fans' greater understanding and deeper relationship with the text and the truth to the Templar myth. With fan tourism, fans are able to recreate the journey of the protagonist and have their own quest to follow in the Templars' footsteps into the past, in both a symbolic and physical sense. Although full immersion into the fictional world is impossible, the fan undertakes a physical venture to the past as the Templar quest narrative is intricately linked to iconic historical sites.

This use of iconic historical sites by the text brings Templar fan tourism into contact with heritage tourism, as the sites demonstrate the symbolic journey to the past and a physical journey due to the history of the location. Film tourism and heritage tourism are known to overlap, but the significance of the relationship with Templar tourism is that these quest narratives are set in the modern day and that these sites provide the link for the protagonist and therefore the audience to the past. This relationship between Templar and heritage tourism coincides with the concept of heterotopia, for which two different realities coexist within the same geographical space, that of historical-cultural memory and the fantastical Templar narrative. This shared space of heritage and film tourism is often promoted from the venue itself, with Rosslyn Chapel selling books such as *The Da Vinci Code* and *Holy Blood, Holy Grail*. The chapel trust incorporates this shared interest in the spaces with its marketing tagline "Explore the Mystery—Discover the History," which caters to the crossover of site interest in both Templar tourism and heritage tourism.

Templar tourism is ultimately linked to heritage tourism due to the historic nature of the Templars' presence, but it is the modern-day setting of the Templar quest narrative that makes this link significant. Templar tourism enables fans to mimic the quest of the text's protagonist, which leads them to iconic, historic sites in their search of the Templar past. This reliance on iconic architecture to depict this journey to the past fuses together Templar and heritage tourism; however, the fans desire to visit significant Templar sites will undoubtedly boost trade for the heritage site, be it temporarily as in the case of Philadelphia's historic sites or in a more long-lasting way as with Templar interest at Rosslyn Chapel.

Visiting a geographical site, be it a manufactured one like Universal Studios theme park or a filming location, enables the fans to gain a sense of immersion within the fictional world of their fandom. A full immersion into the fantastical world for the fan is, of course, impossible, which leaves the fans who engage in fan tourism on the threshold of the fictional world. This level of immersion is defined as the liminal state of inbetweenness, where the fan finds themselves between the real world and the fictional world. This desire of immersion is acted out by the fan's physical engagement with the site's location and physically walking where the characters have walked, which coincides with the fans personally engaging with the Templar quest aspect of following in the Templars' footsteps.

The significance of Templar fan tourism is more than the possibility of fan emulation through a quest of their own, but it is the personalization of this immersive experience through the concept of fans' authoring their experience that further embeds and expands the Templar phenomenon within popular culture. Despite the singular experience marketed by Templar-associated sites, fans can achieve a more profound sense of integration through acts of play and performance with the Templar quest narrative. The deeper sense of integration gained through acts of play is evidenced through tourist reviews, who claimed to emotionally connect to the text's protagonist, as well as the captions promoting related activities such as "seeking the grail," alongside photos uploaded to social media. For fans visiting heritage sites associated with the Templar texts, it is a blurring of realities but also a blurring of history and myth, which provides historical legitimacy to the truth behind the Templar myth that the fan hopes to gain a deeper relationship with through this act of immersion. For fan tourists, this liminal experience is further acquired through acts of performance and play, which are utilized by the heritage sites seeking to promote themselves, such as Rosslyn Chapel encouraging visitors to attempt to find the Holy Grail or the Philadelphia Tourist Board publishing a *National Treasure*-themed brochure that encourages visitors to engage with the city using the skills and knowledge possessed by the film's protagonist.

The final aspect of fan tourism is the return home, and like the concept proposed by Joseph Campbell, the fan now has a new understanding of the text, be it a geographical reality or a new empathic relationship gained through immersion within the world of the text. The return home provides a similarity to the new equilibrium achieved by a text's protagonist's discovery of the Holy Grail or symbolic grail in the guise of a Templar revelation that provides a benefit for the wider population, be it physical like the first quest aspect or a cultural value like the second aspect. The act of fans sharing their immersive experience of their acts of play and performance online, in a sense, emulates the quest's sharing of the grail benefits, as fans are contributing to the further evolution of the reoccurring Templar narrative.

Conclusion

Knightfall *and the Templar Narrative*

For the introduction, I set out to link the historical Knights Templar and their myth to their depiction in popular culture. This study has addressed the gap in Templar academia by examining high-profile Templar-themed texts dating from the 12th century, such as *Parzival* right up to *The Da Vinci Code* in the 21st century. The book first established the fundamental Templar archetypes in fiction, drawing upon contradictory themes of white nationalism, multiculturalism, Arthurian myth and conspiracy; this I surmised as the Templar narrative. The second was to investigate how this narrative has evolved over the century with multiple depictions in popular culture and explain why this medieval order of knights is still so prominent in the 21st century.

In examining the evolution of the Templars' depictions in popular culture, this book has shown that the Templars became a malleable concept due to a lack of ownership over their legacy following their abolition in 1312. The Order's sudden demise enabled the Templars to hold several contradictory aspects. The thematic structure approach demonstrated how the multifaceted Templar narrative attained themes of chivalry, colonialism, multicultural nationalism and a typological link to the modern West. This study of the Templar urtext has updated the study of the Knights Templar to provide the link between the Templar myths of cruel, fanatical warriors, the grail and freemasonry to modern fiction through various media formats such as literature, film, video games and tourism.

The Templar narrative would further expand through *Knightfall* (Handfield & Rayner, 2017–2019), a new drama series from History (formerly The History Channel from 1995 to 2008), whose previous historical drama, *Vikings* (Hirst, 2013+), *Variety* describes as "one of the most subversive and beautifully shot sword epics around" (Ryan, 2017 December 6). *Knightfall* is set at the end of the 13th century and dramatized the Knights Templars' final years, the politics around their demise and the search for the

Holy Grail. The show's protagonist is a fictional Templar knight, Landry de Luzan (Tom Cullen), who becomes Master of the Paris Temple and is charged with finding the Holy Grail while hiding his affair with Queen Joan (Olivia Ross) from the King of France, Phillip IV (Ed Stoppard) and navigating machinations of his advisor William de Nogaret (Julian Ovenden).

The ten-episode television series debuted in 2017 to disappointing reviews, with *Variety*'s backhanded compliment, "If you set your expectations low, and just want something fairly mindless with acceptable swordplay and a couple of decent performances, you'll be fine" (Ryan, 2017, December 6). Lowry, writing for CNN, also reviewed the show negatively, writing, "On paper, History's 'Knightfall' sounds like a great idea. However, 'Knightfall' proves that it's possible to come equipped with all the right accessories and still produce a show that winds up looking underdressed for a knight on the town" (2017, December 6). Despite the negative reviews, in the summer of 2018 it was announced the Templar series would be picked up for a second season (Sandwell, August 21, 2018).

The significance of the series *Knightfall* is that it provides a clear example of how the Templar narrative continues to evolve as this Templar story amalgamates the quest narrative into the Templar knight narrative. This Templar series takes inspiration from the medieval Templar dramas before it by including the heroic Templar aspect in the form of Landry. Landry is the polar opposite of the series Templar villain, Gawain (Pádraic Delaney), who is corrupted by the grail and betrays Landry. Like with the previous case studies of *Kingdom of Heaven, Arn: The Knight Templar* and *Ironclad*, the first instance of violence showcases the Templars' moral compass with a speech delivered by the Templar Master, Godfrey (Sam Hazeldine), when the Templars are under siege at Acre:

> Nearly two hundred years ago, nine knights founded our Order to protect pilgrims on the road to Jerusalem. Today Acre is our stronghold in the Holy Land, and we will never relinquish it. We fight for more than just this city, more than just the men and women who will die if it falls; today, we fight for the grail. Take every life you must take, but take no more and remember that we answer to God just as we fight for God, and we win by the grace of God [Handfield & Rayner, 2017–2019].

This speech informs the audience that the Templars are on the defense, defending their home, the people, and the grail. Their actions are further justified to the audience by the reminder that the Templars must only harm those they must in order to defend the city, people, and the holy relic. This introduction through justifiable violence is similar to other heroic Templars, such as Arn Magnusson's defending a woman from a group of drunken men and Thomas Marshall's skirmish against King John's men to protect the elderly abbot. It is also the polar opposite of the villainous Templar knight whose first use of violence is oppression, such as the robbery and slaughter of Muslim merchants by the Templars in *Kingdom of Heaven*. Landry follows in line with previous Templar heroes in that he uses his martial abilities to protect the helpless, which he demonstrates in his second incident of violence when he leads the Templars from the Paris Temple to defend the Parish Jewish community from attack by de Nogaret's men.

Landry shares many character similarities to the previous heroic Templars, Arn and Marshall, as, like them, despite being a Templar, he is an outsider to the church hierarchy and the broader Templar Order. The heroic Templar weakness of succumbing to the charms of women is Landry's greatest obstacle as his affair with Queen Joan has disastrous consequences for himself, Joan and the Templar Order. Aside from sharing the heroic Templar's archetypal weakness, Landry also demonstrates the same respect for other cultures and races shown by Arn Magnusson. Co-Creator Richard Rayner explained in an interview with *The Hollywood Reporter* that they did not want the show to be about the factional conflicts of the Crusades, not wanting to create a show focusing on "200 years of Christians fighting Muslims" (Roxborough, 2017, April 5). The protagonist in the show is a multicultural Templar knight who, like Arn's friendship with Saladin, earns the respect of Rashid (Akin Gazi), a Saracen and leader of the Brotherhood of Light, a multiracial and multi-faith Assassin-esque organization. Landry and Rashid become allies, and they fight side by side, attempting to recover the grail.

Landry also stands up for the persecuted Jewish community in Paris and passionately pleads to all his Templar brothers to intervene. During a meeting at the Paris Temple, Landry says, "We are Templars. We are warriors. We're supposed to fight for the Holy Land. Safe passage for pilgrims. Instead, we dole out a few loaves of bread, so nobody notices we are hoarding our wealth, we ignore the treatment of the Jews of our own city." Landry's empathy with other faiths is not shared by fellow Templar knight Gawain, who says coldly, "The Jews are not our problem" (Handfield & Rayner, 2017–2019). If not for the intervention of the multicultural Templar hero Landry, then the Jewish community would have been helpless.

Knightfall demonstrates the amalgamation of the Templar narrative as it also includes the quest narrative within its medieval setting. Aside from the heroic Templar Landry's skirmishes protecting the innocent, the quest to find the Holy Grail is the show's main story. Rayner discussed in an interview his interest in the Templar myth when discussing the Templars' abolition. In an interview published in *Exposition Review*, he said, "no one knows what happened to all the various treasures—potentially even the spirit of destiny, the holy grail—they'd accumulated during the Crusades, and a thousand conspiracy theories flow from that moment" (2016, p. 46). In *Knightfall*, the grail is depicted as a simple wooden cup, similar to the grail in *Indiana Jones and the Last Crusade* and is said to hold the power of healing. The series includes archetypal Arthurian characters in the form of Gawain, who is corrupted by the grail's powers and betrays Landry in an attempt to seize the grail for himself. Parzival's character is also featured in the series, who in this Templar story is called Parsifal. Like Wolfram von Eschenbach's Parzival, Parsifal is a naïve outsider who becomes embodied in the knightly quest for the grail. Apart from Arthurian tropes, the most significant inclusion of the quest narrative aside from the grail as a physical MacGuffin is that Landry must revisit his past to find the grail. Like the aspect of following in the Templars' footsteps, Landry must venture into the past to find the grail; however, it is his past he must revisit in his quest for the grail.

The series mixes dramatized history with myth as it does feature historical characters and depicts actual events of that time, but these interslice with fictional characters and with the mythical Templar grail associations. Of course, historical accuracy in a fictional drama would be impossible, but the series benefits from a sense of historical authenticity due to its distribution by History, medieval visual tropes and endorsement from TV historian Dan Jones. Dan Jones acted as a consultant and said *Knightfall* "shows both the history and the legend of the Templars" (Roxborough, 2017, April 5). This sense of legitimacy is encapsulated in the opening credits, as it states, "History presents," implying a truth to the Templar grail myth and an element of historical legitimacy to this fantastical Templar television series. The 21st-century depictions of the Templars are contradictory, as are the centuries of myth following the Order's demise. The 14th-century end to any Templar authority supports the malleable consistency of the Templar legacy that created flexibility to evolve the Templars when represented in new media formats. *Knightfall* shows the continual evolution of the narrative through its amalgamation of the contrasting aspects, which further gives legitimacy and embeds the Templar myth into popular culture. The variety of the Templars' depiction in new media highlights the relevance and importance of this study. Although it provides an original investigation that addresses a gap in Templar research, the continual evolution of Templar depictions means that the newest forms will need further analysis.

The Templars in Popular Culture

This book aimed to address the gap in Templar academia by investigating why the Templar myth became so widespread across multiple media platforms and to define the reoccurring Templar archetypes into what I call the thematic Templar narrative. This book identified the two most significant depictions of the Knights Templar in popular culture: the Order as guardians of the grail in medieval Arthurian literature and as the evil knights in the 19th-century works of Sir Walter Scott. These two different Templar incarnations provided a framework for investigating how the Templar urtext expanded through representations in significant literature, film, computer games, and fan participation, such as fan performance and play within cosplay, fan videos, and tourism. Although a significant amount of the book focused on fictional Templar stories, to further determine the narrative's evolution, it also needed to examine the dilution of historical actuality by fan interaction and the authoring of new fan texts. From examining kinetic levels of audience engagement, fans of Templar-themed texts use acts of play and performance to further immerse themselves interactively within the fictional reality of the Templar myth, acts that further cement connotative Templar perceptions and expand the malleable Templar narrative into new texts. The approach provided an original method to analyze the Templars as a widespread cultural phenomenon as their multifaceted perception has evolved through various types of media which address how Templar myth influences popular perceptions.

The Knights Templar have been featured in works of fiction for centuries, with further Templar texts being released during the writing of this book. The case studies chosen were the most culturally significant and financially successful texts, which would clarify the level of exposure and relevance these examples held in popular culture. The validity of the case studies' notoriety was instrumental in identifying key examples for participatory texts such as computer games, fan film and tourism sites as the case studies needed to show significant cultural presence and be more than a niche practice. Therefore, this book used an internationally successful game franchise, a prevalently well-viewed fan film and iconic heritage sites as the central case studies to analyze the evolutionary effect their participatory media has on the thematic Templar narrative in popular culture.

The Templars' arrest and then their abolition in 1312 sent shock waves throughout medieval Europe, tarnishing their reputation. With the abolition and execution of the Order's leaders, there could be no authority over the Templars' legacy, leaving the accusation of heresy, among other things, forever associated with the Templars. Contradictory myths and unfounded associations such as those levied by Phillip IV of France influenced the popular perception of the Knights Templar to this day, attributing a malleable quality to the Order. This malleability contributed to the transformation of the Templars' story into the multi-strand Templar narrative that has evolved and expanded throughout the centuries via new literature and film and participatory media such as fan videos to computer games and fan tours. The Templar narrative incorporates contradictory aspects that have flourished in popular culture due to the Order's sudden demise and loss of control over their heritage. It is because of this lack of authority over their legacy that the Templar narrative has expanded and shaped the popular perception of the infamous Order of the Poor Fellow-Soldiers of Christ and of the Temple of Solomon, known commonly as the Templars.

Appendix:
Knights Templar Films,
Television and Video Games

Ivanhoe 1913—British (Film)

This British production is the first film adaptation of Sir Walter Scott's novel and was released in July. This silent film is directed by Leedham Bantock and stars Lauderdale Maitland as Ivanhoe, with Ethel Bracewell as Rebecca and Nancy Bevington as Lady Rowena. The role of the villainous Templar, Brian de Bois-Guilbert, is played by Harry Lonsdale.

Ivanhoe 1913—American (Film)

This American adaptation was released in September, a few months after the release of the British version. This silent film is directed by Herbert Brenon and stars King Baggot as Ivanhoe, with Leah Baird as Rebecca and Evelyn Hope as Lady Rowena. The villainous Brian de Bois-Guilbert is played by Wallace Widdicombe.

Ivanhoe 1952 (Film)

Directed by Richard Thorpe, this MGM production is in color and sports a star-studded cast of Robert Taylor as Ivanhoe, Elizabeth Taylor as Rebecca and Joan Fontaine as Rowena. In this adaptation the role of de Bois-Guilbert is played by George Sanders.

Ivanhoe 1958–1959 (TV Series)

This British production from Screen Gems Television and Sydney Box Productions ran for one season of 39 episodes. The series stars Roger Moore as Ivanhoe and Robert Brown as Gurth and Andrew Keir as Prince John. The series is based loosely on Sir Walter Scott's novel.

The Revenge of Ivanhoe/La rivincita di Ivanhoe 1965 (Film)

This Italian film is the first non–English-speaking film adaptation of *Ivanhoe* and is directed by Tanio Boccia. The film stars Clyde Rogers as Ivanhoe, with Gilda Lousek as Rowena of Hastings and Audrea Aureli as the villainous knight Bertrand of Hastings. This adaptation differs from Sir Walter Scott's original novel with changes to many of the character names and removal of key characters from the novel. Most significantly, the film removes the character of Rebecca and has Rowena on trial in her place.

Ivanhoe 1970 (Miniseries)

The BBC adapted Sir Walter Scott's novel into a ten-episode miniseries directed by David Maloney. The miniseries stars Eric Flynn as Ivanhoe and Anthony Bate as Sir Brian de Bois-Guilbert. Vivian Brooks plays Rebecca, while Rowena is played by Clare Jenkins.

Tombs of the Blind Dead 1972 (Film)

Amando de Ossorio directs this Spanish/Portuguese horror film, which unleashes evil, undead Templar knights upon terrified teenagers. These undead knights are blind and wear the iconic white surcoat and red cross (although a variation on the original) and are called Knights from the East in the original version. However, they are referred to as Templars in the English-dubbed version. These knights may be blind and slow but are still accomplished horse riders, and when Virginia White (María Elena Arpón) unknowingly camps near their tombs, these evil knights ride after her and feed on her.

Ivanhoe 1982 (TV Movie)

This American production is the first English language feature-length adaptation of Sir Walter Scott's novel since Thorpe's 1952 Hollywood feature film. This version from Rosemont Productions and Columbia Pictures is directed by Douglas Camfield and stars Anthony Andrews as Ivanhoe and Sam Neill as Brian de Bois-Guilbert. Rebecca is played by Olivia Hussey with Lysette Anthony as Lady Rowena.

The Ballad of the Valiant Knight Ivanhoe/Ballada o doblestnom rytsare Ayvengo 1983 (Film)

This Soviet production is the second non–English major production of *Ivanhoe* released (not including the 1971 Italian film *Ivanhoe, the Norman Swordsman/La Spada Normanna*, which features a character called Ivanhoe as the titular character but has an entirely separate story set in a separate time period). The Russian-language film is directed by Sergey Tarasov and starred Peter Gaudins as Ivanhoe, Tamara Akulova as Lady Rowena, with Boris Khimichev as Brian de Bois-Guilbert.

Indiana Jones and the Last Crusade 1989 (Film)

Harrison Ford returns as Indiana Jones in Steven Spielberg's third film in the series. Although the story features the ultimate MacGuffin, the Holy Grail, Indy is searching for his father, Henry Jones (Sean Connery), who has gone missing during his quest for the grail. Aside from dealing with villainous Nazi soldiers, Indiana must contend with the Brotherhood of the Cruciform Sword, a Templar in all but name order, whose purpose is to protect the grail at all costs. After three trials, Indiana comes face to face with the last surviving Knight of the Cruciform Sword (Robert Eddison), one of three brothers who found the grail during the Crusades. Although the knight's garb includes grail imagery, the knight is dressed with the iconic white tabard and red cross.

Ivanhoe 1997 (TV Miniseries)

This adaptation of Ivanhoe is an American and British joint production from A+E Networks and the BBC and spanned six episodes. Directed by Stuart Orme and starring Steven Waddington as Ivanhoe, Susan Lynch as Rebecca, Victoria Smurfit as Lady Rowena and Ciarán Hinds as Brian de Bois-Guilbert. Steven Waddington would go on to play the Templar Grand Master Torroja in *Arn: The Knight Templar* (2007).

The Minion 1998 (Film)

Dolph Lundgren stars as Lukas Sadorov, a Templar knight who has been sent by the Order to find a lost key that will open the gates of hell. In 1999 this key is discovered in New York City and is also sought by The Minion, a servant of the Antichrist who can possess and take control of human bodies, meaning The Minion could be anyone. Wielding a spiked gauntlet, Lukas must prevent the Minion from opening the gates of hell and unleashing the Antichrist upon the earth. The film currently has an audience score of 16 percent on Rotten Tomatoes.

The Dark Knight 2000 (TV Series)

In this New Zealand/British joint production adaptation of Sir Walter Scott's book, Ivanhoe is a returning Crusader dressed in full Templar garb. This TV series reimagines *Ivanhoe* to include fantasy elements. Templar Ivanhoe played by Ben Pullen must fight the tyrannical Prince John's soldiers and battle against John's magic-wielding servant Mordovr (Jeffrey Thomas), who can use his powers to reanimate the dead as monsters.

National Treasure 2001 (Film)

Nicolas Cage stars as Benjamin Gates, born into a family of treasure hunters who have for generations searched for the lost treasure of the Knights Templar. Gates must follow a series of cryptic clues that lead him to American Independence heritage sites and even steal the Declaration of Independence. Gates must find the

Templar treasure before fellow treasure hunter and criminal Ian Howe (Sean Bean) while dodging the American authorities.

Revelation 2001 (Film)

A British film by Stuart Urban delves into the Templar myth by introducing their modern-day successors called the Order. The Order is searching for the relic known as Loculus, which has been hidden from this evil, shadowy group by Magnus (Terence Stamp), who before his death at the hands of the Order tasks his codebreaker son, Jake (James D'Arcy), and Occultist Mera to find the Loculus before the Order. The Loculus contains Christ's DNA, which the Order will use to clone Christ, but which the Order can control through splicing Christ's DNA with that of the grand master (Udo Kier).

Kingdom of Heaven 2005 (Film)

Ridley Scott's Crusades epic depicts the loss of Jerusalem to Saladin, a crisis that launched the Third Crusade. This historical epic stars Orlando Bloom as Balian of Ibelin, an agnostic Crusader, and Ghassan Massaoud as Saladin, the Sultan of Egypt; both these men lead opposing forces during the siege of Jerusalem. However, before the climactic battle, they must contend with Guy de Lusignan's machinations (Marton Csokas) and Raynald of Châtillon (Brendan Gleeson), whom Scott has reimagined as fanatical racist Templars who are determined to start a war with Saladin.

The Da Vinci Code 2006 (Film)

The best-selling Dan Brown novel is brought to the silver screen by director Ron Howard and stars Tom Hanks as the clue-finding Harvard professor of symbology, Robert Langdon. When Langdon is falsely suspected of murdering Louvre curator Jacques Saunière (Jean-Pierre Marielle), he and police Cryptographer Sophie Neveu (Audrey Tautou), who is also Saunière's granddaughter, must flee from the authorities and the fanatical Opus Dei. With the help of grail historian Sir Leigh Teabing (Ian McKellen), Langdon and Neveu follow the clues to find the resting place of the Holy Grail, which is revealed to be Christ's lineage on earth, a secret which brought down the Knights Templar and was kept hidden by secret society the Priory of Sion.

Assassin's Creed 2007 (Video Game)

This game is the first in Ubisoft's series of a globally popular game series, which contains two narratives, one of bartender Desmond Miles and his ancestor Altaïr Ibn-La'Ahad. In the modern day, Desmond is kidnapped and forced to relive his ancestor's memories through the animus machine. The majority of the game is set in the Holy Land during the Third Crusade, where this open-world, action-adventure, stealth game sets the players against the Knights Templar as a member of the Assassins. The player takes on the role of Altaïr, who must assassinate nine members of the Templar Order. During these assassinations, Altaïr learns that the Templars are searching for a relic called The Apple of Eden, which belonged to a forgotten civilization.

The Last Templar 2009 (TV Series)

The race to find the Templars' lost treasure begins when four men on horseback dressed as Knights Templar steal a Templar decoder from the Metropolitan Museum of Art. This attack sets Archaeologist Tess Chaykin (Mira Sorvino), who is half Indiana Jones and half Robert Langdon, off on a quest to retrace the steps of the Last Templar and find the Templars' lost treasure. Like *The Da Vinci Code*, the treasure turns out to be a revelation that would shake modern Christendom to the core. Based on the best-selling book by Raymond Khoury, *The Last Templar* is a Canadian two-part mini television series.

Arn: The Knight Templar 2007 (Film) and *Arn: The Kingdom at the End of the Road* 2008 (Film)

These two films tell the story of Arn Magnusson (Joakim Nätterqvist), a Folkung nobleman who is banished to the Holy Land for 20 years by the church for having premarital relations with his lover, Cecilia Algotsdotter (Sofia Helin). Both are forced to take 20 years' penance, Cecilia in a convent and Arn as a Templar knight in the Holy Land. In the Holy Land, Arn battles against Saladin's (Milind Soman) forces and gains the Sultan's respect and support when gravely needed. After the devastation at the Battle of Hattin, Arn returns to Sweden as a battle-hardened Templar, having served the 20-year penance, and is reunited with Cecilia and meets his son Magnus (Martin Wallström). Arn must use his martial abilities he honed as a Templar knight to lead the Folkung soldiers in a battle against a Sverker/Danish invasion.

The First Templar 2011 (Video Game)

This action-adventure game developed by Haemimont Games lets the player play as Celian d'Arestide, a Templar knight searching for the Holy Grail but has lost his memory of who he is. There are other playable characters, but Celian is the game's main protagonist. The game is set at the turn of the 14th century and the Templars' downfall, featuring levels where the player must escape the siege of Acre and King Phillip IV's forces. Celian learns that he is, in fact, the first grand master of the Templars, Hugh de Payns, and had used the grail to prolong his life. Celian had hidden the grail as its power was too great and must fight against the Templars to stop them from finding the grail.

The Cursed Crusade 2011 (Video Game)

The Cursed Crusade is an Xbox 360 co-op, action-adventure game set during the Fourth Crusade by Kylotonn, where the player can play as Denz de Bayle, a Templar who can use demonic curse powers to boost his combat abilities, who is searching for his father. Like *The First Templar*, this game is nothing on the Ubisoft predecessor; IGN gave this game a negative review and a score of four out of ten.

Ironclad 2011 (Film)

James Purefoy stars as Templar Knight Thomas Marshall, who must fight against overwhelming odds to hold Rochester Castle against King John (Paul Giamatti) and his mercenaries. Marshall and a small group of defenders must hold out against hunger and repeated attacks by King John's forces until a relief force from France can arrive.

Dracula Untold 2014 (Film)

This Dracula origin film stars Luke Evans as Prince Vlad, who gains supernatural powers to fight the Turkish Empire, thus becoming the infamous vampire Dracula. The Templars feature in a montage of images showing Vlad the Impaler defeating the Turkish Empire's enemies. However, the film opens with a voice-over telling the setting of the year 1442, which is over 100 years since the Knights Templar were abolished.

Assassin's Creed 2016 (Film)

Michael Fassbender stars as Callum Lynch/Aguilar de Nerha in the live-action *Assassin's Creed* film adaption, directed by Justin Kurzel. Although the past narrative is set in the year 1492 in Spain, it follows the same story direction as the original game, stopping the Templars from getting the Apple. Aside from the change to the protagonist and his ancestor's name, the significant difference from the game's story is that the majority of it is set in the modern day. The film adaptation is the opposite of the hugely successful game and focuses far more on Callum's incarceration by the Templars than on the historical Assassin action that the franchise is famous for.

The Mummy 2017 (Film)

The latest remake of the horror classic directed by Alex Kurtzman includes zombie Templars. These undead knights are risen from their graves by the film's mummy monster Ahmanet (Sofia Boutella) to act as her minions. Ahmanet is hunting Nick Morton (Tom Cruise), whom she wants to use as a vessel to summon the deity Set. The Templars are featured in this ancient Egyptian horror action film as the Templar tomb contains a red jewel that Ahmanet needs to acquire to summon Set.

Knightfall 2017–2019 (TV Series)

This television series depicts the final years of the Knights Templar and the quest of the Master of the Paris Temple, Landry de Lauzon (Tom Cullen), to find the Holy Grail. Aside from Landry's quest, the Templars face hostility from the

French monarchy when King Phillip IV (Ed Stoppard) begins to see the Templars as a potential threat to his sovereignty over France. The political fallout is put into further crisis when the king discovers Landry has been having an affair with his wife, Queen Joan (Olivia Ross), and she is expecting Landry's child.

Robin Hood 2018 (Film)

Taron Egerton stars as Robin Hood in this Iraq War commentary adaptation. The film starts with Robin of Lockley's anguish at being called up to fight in the Third Crusade, where he and a group of soldiers patrol a ruined city in the Holy Land. The revisioning of medieval warfare includes the Crusaders using their longbows as if they were rifles and taking cover behind walls from the Saracen's guerrilla warfare-style attacks with rapid-fire crossbows. If the comparison was not clear enough, the Crusaders call for artillery support via flags for catapults to rain debris down on the Saracen troops within the city. Robin is discharged from the Crusades when he tries to prevent the Crusaders, led by Guy of Gisborne, from executing Saracen prisoners tortured for information. The Crusaders' base is decorated with Templar flags, implying that these Crusaders are part of the Knights Templar.

Bibliography

Aberth, J. (2003). *A Knight at the Movies: Medieval History on Film*. London: Routledge.

Adamson, A. & Jenson, V. (Dirs.). (2001). *Shrek* [Motion picture]. United States: Dream-Works Animation, DreamWorks, Pacific Data Images (PDI), Vanguard Films.

Al-thīr, Ibn. (1969). "The Battle of Hittīn." In F. Gabrieli (Ed.), *Arab Historians of the Crusades* (pp. 119–125). London, Routledge.

Altman, R. *Film/Genre*. London: BFI, 1999.

antec12gtx260. (2011). "Re 'The First Templar' Trailer" [Video file]. Retrieved from https://www.youtube.com/watch?v=l1H82lij__c.

Arion Communications Ltd., Dagsljus Filmequipment, Danmarks Radio (DR), Europa Film Sound Production, Film i Väst, Juonifilmi, Molinare Studio, SF Norge A/S, Sandline Production, Sheba Films.

Arion Communications Ltd., Dagsljus Filmequipment, Danmarks Radio (DR), Europa Film Sound Production, Film i Väst, Juonifilmi, Molinare Studio, SF Norge A/S, Sandline Production, Sheba Films.

Aronstein, A. (2015). "'The Da Vinci Code' and the Myth of History." In K.J. Harty (Ed.), *The Holy Grail on Film: Essays on the Cinematic Quest* (pp. 112–127). Jefferson, NC: McFarland.

Aronstein, S. (1995). "'Not Exactly a Knight': Arthurian Narrative and Recuperative Politics in the Indiana Jones Trilogy." *Cinema Journal*, 34:4, 3–30.

Aronstein, S. & Torry, R. (2009). "Chivalric Conspiracies: Hollywood's Templar Legacy." In N. Haydock (Ed.), *Hollywood in the Holy Land* (pp. 225–245). Jefferson, NC: McFarland.

Asbridge, T. (2012). *The Crusades: The War for the Holy Land*. London: Simon & Schuster.

"'Assassin's Creed' Achievements." (n.d.). Retrieved from https://www.xboxachievements.com/game/assassins-creed/achievement/10454-Personal-Vendetta.html.

Avildsen, J. (Dir.). (1976). *Rocky* [Motion picture]. United States: Chartoff-Winkler Productions.

Baigent, M., Leigh, R. & Lincoln, H. (1982). *The Holy Blood and the Holy Grail*. New York: Dell.

Bergman, I. (Dir.). (1957). *The Seventh Seal* [Motion picture]. Sweden: Svensk Filmindustri.

Boam, J. (Writer). (1988). *Indiana Jones and the Last Crusade* [Screenplay]. United States: Paramount Pictures, Lucasfilm.

Booker, C. (2011). *The Seven Basic Plots: Why We Tell Stories*. London: Continuum International.

Boorman, J. (Dir.). (1981). *Excalibur* [Motion picture]. United States: Orion Pictures.

Booth, P. (2010). *Digital Fandom: New Media Studies*. New York: Peter Lang.

Booth, P. (2015). *Game Play: Paratextuality in Contemporary Board Games*. London: Bloomsbury Academic.

Booth, P. (2015). *Playing Fans: Negotiating Fandom and Media in The Digital Age*. Iowa City: University of Iowa Press.

"'Breivik manifesto' details chilling attack preparation." (2011, July 24). *BBC News*. Retrieved from https://www.bbc.co.uk/news/world-europe-14267007.

Brett, A. (2014, September 24). "Ridley Scott: *Kingdom of Heaven*." *BBC*. Retrieved from http://www.bbc.co.uk/films/2005/05/04/ridley_scott_kingdom_of_heaven_interview.shtml.

Brighton, S. (2006). *In Search of the Knights Templar: A Guide to the Sites of Britain*: London: Phoenix Illustrated.

Brooker, W. (2002). *Using the Force*. London: Continuum International.

Brooker, W. (2005). "The Blade Runner Experience: Pilgrimage and Liminal Space." In W. Brooker (Ed.), *The Blade Runner Experience: The Legacy of a Science Fiction Classic* (pp. 11–30). London: Wallflower Press.

Brooker, W. (2007). "Everywhere and Nowhere: Vancouver, Fan Pilgrimage and the Urban Imaginary." *International Journey of Cultural Studies*, 10:4, 423–444.

Brooks, M. (Dir.). (1993). *Robin Hood: Men in Tights* [Motion picture]. United States: Brooksfilms, Gaumont.

Brooks, R. (2014). *The Knight Who Saved England: William Marshal and the French Invasion, 1217*. Oxford: Osprey.

Brown, D. (2003). *The Da Vinci Code*. New York: Doubleday.

Brown, H.J. (2014). "The Consolation of Paranoia: Conspiracy, Epistemology, and the Templars in 'Assassin's Creed,' 'Deus Ex,' and 'Dragon Age.'" In D.T. Kline (Ed.), *Digital Gaming Re-Imagines the Middle Ages* (pp. 227–239). New York: Routledge.

Brownie, B. & Graydon, D. (2016). *The Superhero Costume: Identity and Disguise in Fact and Fiction*. London: Bloomsbury Academic.

Burdett, Casey Walker. (2015). #nationaltreasure @ the national archives [Facebook]. Retrieved from https://www.facebook.com/photo.php?fbid=10104026988519571&set=pb.5004407.-2207520000.1539264074.&type=3&theater.

Burt, R. (2007). "Getting Schmedieval: Of Manuscript and Film Prologues, Paratexts, and Parodies." *Exemplaria*, 19:2, 217–242.

Bushe, J. (Dir.). (2015). *Predator: Dark Ages* [Motion picture]. United Kingdom: Big Sis Productions, Dark Age Productions, Fascination Pictures.

Butler, D. (Dir.). (1954). *King Richard and the Crusaders* [Motion picture]. United States: Warner Brothers.

Buzay, E.H. & Buzay, E. (2015). "Neomedievalism and the Epic in *Assassin's Creed*: The Hero's Quest." In H. Young (Ed.), *The Middle Ages in Popular Culture: Medievalism and Genre* (pp. 113–132). New York: Cambria Press.

Callahan, L.A. (1999). "Perceval le Gallois: Eric Rohmer's Vision of the Middle Ages." *Film & History: An Interdisciplinary Journal of Film and Television Studies*, 29, 3:4, 46–53.

Campbell, J. (2004). *The Hero with a Thousand Faces*. Princeton: Princeton University Press.

Cardwell, S. (2002). *Adaptation Revisited: Television and the Classic Novel*. Manchester: Manchester University Press.

Carter, C. (Creator). (1993–2018). *The X-Files* [Television series]. United States: Ten Thirteen Productions, 20th Century Fox Television, X-F Productions.

catherinefox9. (2015). "The Secret World Templar" [Blog post]. Retrieved from https://www.polyvore.com/secret_world_templar/set?id=120994145.

CD. (2015, November 15). "Interview with James Bushe." *Cult Film Reviews*/ Retrieved from http://cultfilmreviews.co.uk/2015/11/15/interview-with-james-bushe/.

CGR_11. (2015). "Re Harry Potter Shop at Platform 9 ¾" [Tripadvisor]. Retrieved from https://www.tripadvisor.co.uk/Attraction_Review-g186338-d3971166-Reviews-or10-Harry_Potter_Shop_at_Platform_9_3_4-London_England.html.

Chapel, Rosslyn. (2018). "#12daysofChristmas #Myths and #Legends." [Facebook] Retrieved from https://www.facebook.com/pg/RosslynChapelTrust/posts/?ref=page_internal.

Chapman, J., Glancy, M. & Harper, S. (2007). Introduction. In J. Chapman, M. Glancy & S. Harper (Eds.), *The New Film History: Sources, Methods, Approaches* (pp. 1–10). Basingstoke: Palgrave Macmillan.

Cochran, R. & Surnow, J. (Creators). (2001–2010). *24* [Television series]. United States: Imagine Entertainment, 20th Century Fox Television, Real Time Productions, Teakwood Lane Productions.

Cohen, R. (Dir.). (1996). *Dragonheart* [Motion picture]. United States: Universal Pictures.

Coote, L.A. (2012). "Remembering Dismembering: Reading the Violated Body Medievally." In C.L. Robinson & P. Clements (Eds.), *Neomedievalism in the Media: Essays on Film, Television, and Electronic Games* (pp. 15–33). New York: Edwin Mellen.

Coppa, F. (2006). "Writing Bodies in Space: Media Fan Fiction as Theatrical Performance." In K. Hellekson & K. Busse (Eds.), *Fan Fiction and Fan Communities in The Age of The Internet: New Essays* (pp. 225–244). Jefferson, NC: McFarland.

Coppa, F. (2008). "Women, *Star Trek*, and the Early Development of Fannish Vidding." *Transformative Works and Cultures, 1.* http://journal.transformativeworks.org/index.php/twc/article/view/44/.

Crawford, G. & Rutter, J. (2007). "Playing The Game: Performance in Digital Games Audiences." In J.A. Gray, C. Sandvoss & C.L. Harrington (Eds.), *Fandom: Identities and Communities in a Mediated World.* (pp. 271–281). New York: New York University Press.

Creative Assembly. (2002). *Medieval Total War* [Video game]. Santa Monica: Activision.

Curtiz, M. (Dir.). (1938). *The Adventures of Robin Hood* [Motion picture]. United States: Warner Brothers.

Daly, S. (2008, April 18). "Spielberg and Lucas: The Titans Talk!" *Entertainment Weekly.* Retrieved from https://ew.com/article/2008/04/18/spielberg-lucas-titans-talk/.

Dawtrey, A. (2010, May 7). 'Ironclad' overcomes finance obstacles. *Variety.* Retrieved from http://variety.com/2010/biz/features/ironclad-overcomes-finance-obstacles-1118018859/

Day, D.D. (2002). Monty Python and the Holy Grail: Madness with a Definite Method. In K.J. Harty (Ed.), *Cinema Arthuriana: Twenty Essays* (pp. 127–135). Jefferson, NC: McFarland.

Defon, J. (2011). "Re 'The First Templar' Trailer" [Video file]. Retrieved from https://www.youtube.com/watch?v=l1H82lij__c.

DeMille, C.B. (Dir.). (1935). *The Crusades* [Motion picture]. United States: Paramount Pictures.

de Ossorio, A. (Dir.). (1972). *Tombs of the Blind Dead/La noche del terror ciego* [Motion picture]. Spain: Interfilme, Plata Films S.A.

Dixon, T. (1970). *The Clansman: An Historical Romance of the Ku Klux Klan.* Lexington: University Press of Kentucky.

Douglas, E. (2011, July 1). "Exclusive: Ironclad Director Johnathan English." *ComingSoon.net.* Retrieved from http://www.comingsoon.net/movies/features/78522-exclusive-ironclad-director-jonathan-english.

Driver, M.W. (2004). "What's Accuracy Got to Do with It? Historicity and Authenticity in Medieval Film." In M.W. Driver & S. Ray (Eds.), *The Medieval Hero on Screen: Representations from Beowulf to Buffy* (pp. 19–22). Jefferson, NC: McFarland.

Driver, M.W. & Ray, S. (2004). "Preface: Hollywood Knights." In M.W. Driver & S. Ray (Eds.), *The Medieval Hero on Screen: Representations from Beowulf to Buffy* (pp. 5–18). Jefferson, NC: McFarland.

Duffett, M. (2013). *Understanding Fandom: An introduction to the study of media fan culture.* New York: Bloomsbury.

Echevarria, R. & Peters, S. (Creators). (2004–200 *The 4400* [Television series]. United States: Renegade 83, American Zoetrope, CBS Paramount Network Television, Paramount Network Television, Viacom Productions, 4400 Productions, Sky Television.

Edwardes, C. (2004, January 18). Ridley Scott's New Crusades Film 'Panders to Osama Bin Laden.' *The Telegraph.* Retrieved from http://www.telegraph.co.uk/news/worldnews/northamerica/usa/1452000/Ridley-Scotts-new-Crusades-film-panders-to-Osama-bin-Laden.html.

84u2c (2017). "Re Rosslyn Chapel" [Tripadvisor] Retrieved from https://www.tripadvisor.co.uk/Attraction_Review-g551764-d213666-Reviews-Rosslyn_Chapel-Roslin_Midlothian_Scotland.html

Elley, D. (1984). *The Epic Film.* London: Routledge & Kegan Paul.

Elliott, A. (2017). *Medievalism, Politics and Mass Media: Appropriating the Middle Ages in the Twenty-First Century.* Suffolk: Boydell & Brewer.

Elliott, A.B.R. (2011). *Remaking the Middle Ages: The Methods of Cinema and History in Portraying the Medieval World.* Jefferson, NC: McFarland.

English, J. (Dir.). (2011). *Ironclad* [Motion picture]. United Kingdom: Mythic International Entertainment, ContentFilm International, Film & Entertainment VIP Medienfonds 4 GmbH, KG, VIP 4 Medienfonds, Premiere Picture, Rising Star, Silver Reel, Wales Creative IP Fund, Molinare Investment, Perpetual Media Capital.

Evans, M. (1970). *Spenser's Anatomy of Heroism: A Commentary on The Faerie Queene*. London: Cambridge University Press.

Explore the Carvings. (2015). Retrieved from the Rosslyn Chapel Official website: https://www.rosslynchapel.com/visit/things-to-do/explore-the-carvings/.

Fascinationpictures. (21 April 2008). "VATICAN KNIGHTS (VK) TRAILER." Retrieved from https://www.youtube.com/watch?v=anlDWsXxnFc, accessed 10 March 2016.

Fischer, J. (2017, May 17). "National Treasure: Hollywood Film Sparks Real-Life Adventure: Philadelphia and Washington, D.C. Sites Star in Movie and Tour." *Tripsavvy*. Retrieved from https://www.tripsavvy.com/national-treasure-sparks-reallife-adventure-2669330.

Fitzgerald, M. (2016, March 24). "Indiana Jones and the Last Crusade: Learning from Stoppard." *Creative Screenwriting*. Retrieved from https://creativescreenwriting.com/indiana-jones-and-the-last-crusade-learning-from-stoppard/.

Flinth, P. (Dir.). (2007). *Arn: The Knights Templar* [Motion picture]. Sweden: AMC Pictures, Arion Communications, Dagsljus Film Equipment, Danmarks Radio (DR), Europa Film Sound Production, Film i Väst, Juonifilmi, Molinare Studio, SF Norge A/S, Sandline Production, Sheba Films, Soundchef Studios, Svensk Filmindustri (SF), TV2 Norge, TV4 Sweden, Telepool, Tju-Bang Film, Yleisradio (YLE).

Flinth, P. (Dir.). (2008). *Arn: The Kingdom at the End of the Road* [Motion picture]. Sweden: AMC Pictures, Arion Communications, Dagsljus Filmequipment, Danmarks Radio (DR), Europa Film Sound Production, Film i Väst, Juonifilmi, Molinare Studio, SF Norge A/S, Sandline Production, Sheba Films, Soundchef Studios, Svensk Filmindustri (SF), TV2 Norge, TV4 Sweden, Telepool, Tju-Bang Film, Yleisradio (YLE).

Foucault, M. (1986). "Texts/Contexts of Other Spaces." *Diacritics*, 16:1, 22–27.

Fouché, G. (2008, October 8). "Revisionism on a Grand Scale." *The Guardian*. Retrieved from http://www.theguardian.com/film/2008/oct/08/2.

Friedman, L.D. (2006). *Citizen Spielberg*. Chicago: University of Illinois Press.

Frost, W. (2006). "Braveheart-ed Ned Kelly: Historic Films, Heritage Tourism and Destination Image." *Tourism Management*. 27, 247–254.

Funcom. (2012). *The Secret World* [Video game]. California: Electronic Arts.

Fuqua, A. (Dir.). (2004). *King Arthur* [Motion picture]. United States: Touchstone Pictures, Jerry Bruckheimer Films, Green Hills Productions, World 2000 Entertainment.

GamerSpawn. (17 June 2010). "'The First Templar' –E3 2010 Trailer." Retrieved from https://www.youtube.com/watch?v=6ciS2uwyla0, accessed 10 March 2016.

Genette, G. & McIntosh, A. (1988). "The Proustian Paratexte." *SubStance*, 17:2, 63–77.

Geraghty, L. (2007). *Living with Star Trek: American Culture and The Star Trek Universe*. New York: I.B. Tauris.

Geraghty, L. (2011). "'I've A Feeling We're Not in Kansas Anymore': Examining *Smallville's* Canadian Cult Geography." In L. Geraghty (Ed.) *The Smallville Chronicles: Critical Essays on the Television Series* (pp. 129–152). Lanham, MD: Scarecrow.

Gianotti, Gary. (2018). "Re #12daysofChristmas #Myths and #Legends" [Facebook] Retrieved from https://www.facebook.com/pg/RosslynChapelTrust/posts/?ref=page_internal.

Gibson, M. (Dir.). (1995). *Braveheart* [Motion picture]. United States: Icon Entertainment.

Gibson, S.W. (2012, June 28). "The Secret World Interview with Senior Producer Ragnar Tornquist." *Gaming Illustrated*, Retrieved from http://gamingillustrated.com/the-secret-world-interview/

Gilliam, T. & Jones, T. (Dirs). *Monty Python and the Holy Grail* [Motion picture]. United Kingdom: Michael White Productions, National Film Trustee Company, Python (Monty) Pictures.

"God Wills it" [Digital image]. (n.d) Retrieved from https://memegenerator.net/instance/55214512/god-wills-it-god-wills-it.

Gordon, M. (2008). *Empire of Dreams: The Science Fiction and Fantasy Films of Steven Spielberg*. Plymouth: Rowman & Littlefield Publishers, Inc.

Grace, P. (2009). *The Religious Film*. Chichester: Wiley-Blackwell.

Gray, J. (2010). *Show Sold Separately: Promos, Spoilers, and Other Media Paratexts*. New York: New York University Press.

Gray, J. (2014, March 19). "Silly Elephants Dancing Without Meaning? On 'Paratexts Without

Texts.'" In *media res—a media commons project,'* Retrieved from http://mediacommons. futureofthebook.org/imr/2014/03/19/silly-elephants-dancing-without-meaning-paratexts-without-texts.

Gray, J. (2015). "Afterword: Studying Media with and without Paratexts." In L. Geraghty (Ed.), *Popular Media Cultures: Fans, Audiences and Paratexts.* (pp. 230–237). Basingstoke: Palgrave Macmillan.

Griffith, Jessica. (2013). "'Da Vinci Code' Tour!" [Facebook] Retrieved from https://www.facebook.com/photo.php?fbid=2518009787144&set=a.2498814907284&type=3&theater.

Griffith-Jones, R. (2006). *The Da Vinci Code and The Secrets of The Temple.* London: Canterbury.

Griffths, D. (Dir.). (1915). *Birth of a Nation* [Motion picture]. United States: David W. Griffith Corp, Epoch Producing Corporation.

Grigs27 (2014). "Re: Rosslyn Chapel." TripAdvisor. Retrieved from https://www.tripadvisor.co.uk/Attraction_Review-g551764-d213666-Reviews-Rosslyn_Chapel-Roslin_Midlothian_Scotland.html.

Grindley, C.J. (2004). "The Hagiography of Steel: The Hero's Weapon and Its Place in Pop Culture." In M.W. Driver & S. Ray (Eds.), *The Medieval Hero on Screen: Representations from Beowulf to Buffy* (pp. 151–166). Jefferson, NC: McFarland.

Guerber, H.A. (1922). *Myths and Legends of The Middle Ages: Their Origin and Influence on Literature and Art.* London: G. Harrap.

Guggenhiem, D. (Creator). (2016–2019). *Designated Survivor* [Television series]. United States: The Mark Gordon Company, Kinberg Genre, ABC Studios, Entertainment 360.

Guillou, J. (2000). *The Kingdom at the End of the Road.* Sweden: Piratförlaget.

Guillou, J. (2009). *The Road to Jerusalem.* London: Harper.

Haag, M. (2009). *The Templars: History and Myth.* London: Profile.

Haemimont Games. (2011). *The First Templar* [Video game]. Worms: Kalypso.

Handfield, D. & Rayner, R. (Creator). (2017–2019). *Knightfall* [Television series]. United States: A+E Studios, Midnight Radio, Stillking Films, The Combine.

Hannum, D. (2012). "National Treasure and American Scripture: Form, History, and the Aesthetic Politics of the Declaration of Independence." *Arizona Quarterly,* 68:2, 151–178.

"Harry Potter Tours in London." (n.d.) Retrieved from the Free Tours by Foot website: https://freetoursbyfoot.com/harry-potter-tour-london/#free.

Hartwig, Glynis. (2009). "Looking for the Da Vinci Code" [Facebook]. Retrieved from https://www.facebook.com/photo.php?fbid=76687189684&set=a.76687084684&type=3&theater.

Haydock, N. (2008). *Movie Medievalism: The Imaginary Middle Ages.* Jefferson, NC: McFarland.

Headling, E. (2008). "The Arn Franchise: Launching a Small Country Blockbuster." *Film International,* 35:6, 60–67.

Heale, E. (1999). *The Faerie Queene: A Readers Guide* (2nd ed.). Cambridge: Cambridge University Press.

Heinö, A.J. (2012). "Democracy Between Collectivism and Individualism: De-Nationalisation and Individualism in Swedish National Identity." *International Review of Sociology,* 19:2, 297–314.

Heyman, E. (2007, November 25). "Templars Occupies Avenue." *Göteborgs-Posten.* Retrieved from http://www.gp.se/nyheter/goteborg/1.113909-tempelriddare-intar-avenyn.

Hicks, C. (2015, June 17). "James Bushe & Simon Rowling Interview (Predator: Dark Ages)." *AVP Galaxy.* Retrieved from https://www.avpgalaxy.net/website/interviews/james-bushe-simon-rowling/.

Hills, M. (2002). *Fan Cultures.* London: Routledge.

Hirst, M. (Creator). (2013+). *Vikings* [Television series]. Canadian: World 2000 Entertainment, Take 5 Productions, Shaw Media, MGM Television, Screen Ireland.

Hobbs, Chris. (2018). "Re #12daysofChristmas #Myths and #Legends [Facebook]." Retrieved from https://www.facebook.com/pg/RosslynChapelTrust/posts/?ref=page_internal.

Hobsbawm, Eric. (2012). "Introduction: Inventing Traditions." In E. Hobsbawm & T. Ranger (Eds.), *The Invention of Tradition* (pp. 1–14). Cambridge: Cambridge University Press.

Hoffman, D.L. (2002). "Not Dead Yet: Monty Python and the Holy Grail in the Twenty-first Century." In K.J. Harty (Ed.), *Cinema Arthuriana: Twenty Essays* (pp. 136–148). Jefferson, NC: McFarland.

HoneyReno. (2012). "Re 'The First Templar' Trailer." [Video file]. Retrieved from https://www.youtube.com/watch?v=l1H82lij__c.

Hopper, Ashley Tucker. (2014). [Facebook]. Retrieved from https://www.facebook.com/photo.php?fbid=10204584360473782&set=pcb.10204584385794415&type=3&theater.

Howard, R. (Dir.). (2006). *The Da Vinci Code* [Motion picture]. Unites States: Columbia Pictures, Imagine Entertainment, Skylark Productions.

Hudson, S. & Brent Ritchie, J.R. (2006). "Promoting Destinations via Film Tourism: An Empirical Identification of Supporting Marketing Initiatives." *Journal of Travel Research*, 44, 387–396.

Hughes, J. (Dir.). (1985). *The Breakfast Club* [Motion picture]. United States: A&M Films, Channel Productions, Universal Pictures.

Hughes-Warrington, M. (2007). *History Goes to the Movies: Studying History on Film*. New York: Routledge.

Husemann, C. (2010, September 30). "'The First Templar' Interview." *Gaming Nexus*, Retrieved from http://www.gamingnexus.com/article/the-first-templar-interview/item2787.aspx.

An Interview with Richard Raynor (2016). *Exposition Review*, 1, 43–49.

Irvine, L. (2005, October 6). "$225 Isn't Bad, I Guess." *The Guardian*, Retrieved from http://www.theguardian.com/film/2005/oct/06/features.lindesayirvine.

Jackson, P. (Dir.). (2001). *The Lord of the Rings: The Fellowship of the Ring*. New Zealand: New Line Cinema, WingNut Films, The Saul Zaentz Company.

"Jan Guillou following series about Arn." (2007). *Dagens Nyheter*. Retrieved from http://www.dn.se/dnbok/jan-guillou-foljer-serien-om-arn/.

Jenkins, H. (2006). *Convergence Culture: Where Old and New Media Collide*. New York: New York University Press.

JewishGun. (2012). "Re 'The First Templar'—E3 2010 Trailer" [Video file]. Retrieved from https://www.youtube.com/watch?v=6ciS2uwyla0.

Johnsrud, B. (2014). "'The Da Vinci Code,' Crusade Conspiracies, and the Clash of Historiographies." In M. Butter & M. Reinkowski (Eds.), *Conspiracy Theories in the United States and the Middle East: A Comparative Approach* (pp. 100–117). Berlin: Walter de Gruyter GmbH.

Jones, D. (2012). *The Plantagenets: The Kings Who Made England*. London: William Collins.

Jones, S.E. (2008). *The Meaning of Video Games: Gaming and Textual Strategies*. New York: Routledge.

Juul, J. (2011). *Half-Real: Video Games between Real Rules and Fictional Worlds*. Cambridge: MIT Press.

Kelly, A.K. (2004, February) "Beyond Historical Accuracy: A Postmodern View of Movies and Medievalism." In *Perspicuitas*. Retrieved from https://www.unidue.de/imperia/md/content/perspicuitas/kelly_beyondhistoricalaccuracy.pdf.

Kennedy, E.D. (2009). "'Follow the Gleam': The Grail Quest in Medieval and Post-Medieval Literature." *Studies in Medieval and Renaissance Teaching*, 16, 9–29.

Kline, D.T. (2014). "Introduction: 'All Your History Are Belong to Us.'" In D.T. Kline (Ed.), *Digital Gaming Re-imagines the Middle Ages*. (pp. 1–11). New York: Routledge.

Klug, G.C. & Schell, J. (2006). "Why People Play Games: An Industry Perspective." In P. Vorderer & J. Bryant (Eds.), *Playing Video Games: Motives, Responses and Consequences*. (pp. 91–113). Mahwah, NJ: Lawrence Erlbaum.

Konieczny, P. (2013, July 6). "Movie Review: 'Ironclad.'" *Medievalist.net*. Retrieved from http://www.medievalists.net/2013/07/06/movie-review-ironclad/.

Kork, Y. (2018). "Popular Culture Tourism: Films and tourist demand." In C. Lundberg & V. Ziakas (Eds.), *The Routledge Handbook of Popular Culture and Tourism* (pp. 69–80). New York: Routledge.

Kripke, E. (Creator). (2005–2020). *Supernatural* [Television series]. United States: Kripke Enterprises, Warner Bros. Television, Wonderland Sound and Vision, Supernatural Films.

Kurtzman, A. (Dir.). (2017). *The Mummy* [Motion picture]. United States: Universal Pictures, Dark Universe, Dentsu, Perfect World Pictures (Beijing), Sean Daniel Company, Secret Hideout.

LaBerge, Camilly. (2016). Liberty Bell #nationaltreasure #whereisthenextclue [Facebook]. Retrieved from https://www.facebook.com/photo.php?fbid=10154332073985337&set=a.10 151342806700337&type=3&theater.

Lacy, N.J. (2004). "The Da Vinci Code: Dan Brown and the Grail That Never Was." *Arthuriana*, 14:3, 81–92.

Lacy, N.J. (2005). "The Round Table—Medieval McGuffins: The Arthurian Model." *Arthuriana*, 15:4, 53–64.

Laing, J. & Frost, W. (2018). "Imagining the Medieval in The Modern World: Film, Fantasy and Heritage." In C. Lundberg & V. Ziakas (Eds.) *The Routledge Handbook of Popular Culture and Tourism* (pp. 96–107). New York: Routledge.

Lamerichs, N. (2010). "Stranger Than Fiction: Fan Identity in Cosplay." *Transformative Works and Cultures*, 7. http://journal.transformativeworks.org/index.php/twc/article/view/246.

Lancaster, K. (2001). *Interacting with Babylon 5*. Austin: University of Texas Press.

Lazano, A.V. (2018). "'No Vacations from Poverty' for Philadelphia's Poor Residents." NBC Philadelphia. Retrieved from https://www.nbcphiladelphia.com/news/local/No-Vacations-from-Poverty-Pew-Report-Broke-in-Philly-Philadelphia-494413091.html.

Linden, H. & Linden, S. (2017). *Fans and Fan Cultures: Tourism, Consumerism and Social Media*. London: Palgrave Macmillan.

Lindley, A. (1998, May 28). "The Ahistoricism of Medieval Film." *Screening the Past*, 3. Retrieved from http://tlweb.latrobe.edu.au/humanities/screeningthepast/firstrelease/fir598/ALfr3a.htm.

Lopez, Fernando (2014). "The Argo Marks Mentioned in 'The Da Vinci Code' at Musée Du Louvre." [Facebook] Retrieved from https://www.facebook.com/photo.php?fbid=1020582 4890731600&set=a.10205824854450693&type=3&theater.

LordArcherdon. (2011). "Re 'The First Templar' Trailer" [Video file]. Retrieved from https://www.youtube.com/watch?v=l1H82lij__c.

Lott, E. (2008). "National Treasure, Global Value, and American Literary Studies." *American Literary History*, 20:12, 108–123.

MacNaughton, I. (Dir.). (1971). *And Now for Something Completely Different* [Motion picture]. United Kingdom: Columbia Pictures Corporation, Playboy Productions, Kettledrum Films, Python (Monty) Pictures, Kettledrum/Lownes Productions.

Madden, J. (Dir.). (2011). *The Best Exotic Marigold Hotel* [Motion picture]. United Kingdom: Blueprint Pictures.

Madsen, D.L. (1998). *American Exceptionalism*. Edinburgh: Edinburgh University Press.

Mahmoud, Zain. (2013). "Re 'The First Templar' Trailer" [Video file]. Retrieved from https://www.youtube.com/watch?v=l1H82lij__c.

Makiturha. (2012). "Re 'The First Templar' Trailer" [Video file]. Retrieved from https://www.youtube.com/watch?v=l1H82lij__c.

Mann, A. (Dir.). (1961). *El Cid* [Motion picture]. Italy: Samuel Bronston Productions, Dear Film Produzione.

Martin-Jones, D. (2014). "Film tourism as heritage tourism: Scotland, diaspora and 'The Da Vinci Code.'" (2006). *New Review of Film and Television Studies*, 12:2, 156–177.

Masters, P. (2017, December 5). "Alt-right Claims to Match in Step with Knights Templar—This is Fake History." *The Conversation*. Retrieved from https://theconversation.com/alt-right-claims-to-march-in-step-with-the-knights-templar-this-is-fake-history-88103.

Mayer, H.E. (1972). *The Crusades*. London: Oxford University Press.

Max73. (2006, October 6). "'Assassin's Creed': Interview with Jade Raymond." *Xbox Gazette*. Retrieved from http://www.xboxgazette.com/interview_assassins_creed_en.php.

McAllister, K.S. (2004). *Game Work: Language, Power, and Computer Game Culture*. Tuscaloosa: The University of Alabama Press.

Melley, T. (2000). *Empire of Conspiracy: The Culture of Paranoia in Postwar America*. Ithaca, NY: Cornell University Press.

Michaëlis, B.T. (2001). *Guillou, Jan.* Retrived from http://www.forfatterweb.dk/oversigt/guillou-jan/print_zguillou00.

Misa Pheonix. (2011). "Re 'The First Templar' Trailer" [Video file]. Retrieved from https://www.youtube.com/watch?v=l1H82lij__c.

MrsPygmyPuff20. (14 December 2010). "Arn: The Knight Templar—Only One." Retrieved from https://www.youtube.com/watch?v=VAbZo4rE4Fk&has_verified=1, accessed 10 March 2016.

Müller, U. (2002). "Blank, Syberberg, and the German Arthurian Tradition." In K.J. Harty (Ed.), *Cinema Arthuriana: Twenty Essays* (pp. 177–184). Jefferson, NC: McFarland.

Newbury, C. (Dir.). (1993). *Anchoress* [Motion picture]. United Kingdom: British Film Institute, Corsan, Upstate Films.

Newman, S. (2007). *The Real History Behind the Templars.* New York: Berkley.

North, D. (2012, August 29). "'The Secret World' sold only 200,000 copies since launch." *Destructoid.* Retrieved from https://www.destructoid.com/the-secret-world-sold-only-200-000-copies-since-launch-233970.phtml.

Okabe, D. (2012). "Cosplay, Learning, and Cultural Practice." In M. Ito, D. Okabe & I. Tsuji (Eds.), *Fandom Unbound: Otaku Culture in a Connected World* (pp. 225–248). New Haven: Yale University Press.

Oliver, J.E. & Wood, T.J. (2014). "Conspiracy Theories and the Paranoid Style (s) of Mass Opinion." *American Journal of Political Science,* 58:4, 952–966.

"One day ISIS will run into the wrong Christians." [Digital image]. (n.d) Retrieved from https://me.me/i/one-day-isis-will-run-into-the-wrong-christians-none-22000975.

Oxbrow, M. & Robertson, I. (2005). *Rosslyn and the Grail.* Edinburgh: Mainstream Publishing.

Partner, P. (1981). *The Murdered Magicians: The Templars and Their Myth.* Oxford: Oxford University Press.

Partridge, C. (2008). "The Occultural Significance of 'The Da Vinci Code.'" *Northern Lights,* 6, 107–126.

Patterson, S. (2018). "Re #12daysofChristmas #Myths and #Legends" [Facebook] Retrieved from https://www.facebook.com/pg/RosslynChapelTrust/posts/?ref=page_internal.

Petitte, O. (2013, January 12). 'The Secret World' Activity Rises 400 Percent after Dropping Subscriptions." *PC Gamer.* Retrieved from https://www.pcgamer.com/the-secret-world-activity-400-percent/.

Phillips, J. (2009). "The Call of the Crusades." In *History Today,* 59(11), 10–17.

Phillips, J. (2010). *The Second Crusade: Extending the Frontiers of Christendom.* London: Yale University Press.

Pickett, L. & Prince, C. (2006). *The Sion Revelation: The Truth about the Guardians of Christ's Sacred Bloodline.* New York: Touchstone.

Pinon, Anthony. (2016). "Re *PREDATOR: DARK AGES*" [Video file]. Retrieved from https://www.youtube.com/watch?v=YRD8jAk274I.

Praesto, A. & Sjölin, M. (n.d). In *Arn's Footsteps: Follow Jan Guillou's temple knight round Västra Götaland, Sweden.* Sweden: VästraGötlands Museum.

Pratt, R. (2003). "Theorizing Conspiracy." *Theory and Society,* 32, 255–271.

Puckett, J.L. (2017 November, 7). "John Cleese on 'Monty Python,' Facebook, bad comedy, great comedy and kids these days." *Courier Journal.* Retrieved from https://eu.courier-journal.com/story/entertainment/movies/2017/11/07/john-cleese-holy-grail-louisville/508198001/.

Ralls, K. (2007). *Knights Templar Encyclopaedia: The Essential Guide to The People, Places, Events, and Symbols of The Order of The Temple.* New Jersey: New Page.

Reggiardito. (2011). "Re 'The First Templar' Trailer" [Video file]. Retrieved from https://www.youtube.com/watch?v=l1H82lij__c.

Rehlin, G. (2007, December 27). "'Arn' charges to opening record opening." *Variety.* Retrieved from https://variety.com/2007/film/box-office/arn-charges-to-record-opening-1117978185/.

Reijnders, S. (2010). "On the Trail of 007: Media Pilgrimages into the World of James Bond." *Area,* 42:3, 369–377.

Ravenscroft, T. (1973). *The Spear of Destiny.* York Beach: Red Wheel/Weiser LLC.

Reynolds, K. (Dir.). (1991). *Robin Hood: Prince of Thieves* [Motion picture]. United States: Warner Brothers, Morgan Creek Productions.

Richards, J. (2007). "The Politics of the Swashbuckler." In In J. Chapman, M. Glancy & S. Harper (Eds.), *The New Film History: Sources, Methods, Approaches* (pp. 119–136). Basingstoke: Palgrave Macmillan.

Robbins, G. (Dir.). (2009). *C Me Dance* [Motion picture]. United States: Uplifting Entertainment.

Robinson, P. (Dir.). (1989). *Field of Dreams* [Motion picture]. United States: Gordon Company.

Rohmer, E. (Dir.) (1978). *Perceval le Gallois* [Motion picture]. France: Les Films du Losange, France 3, ARD, Société Saisse de Radiodiffusion et Télévision, RAJ Radiotelevisione Italiana, Goumont.

Roman, C. (2012). "The Use of Nature: Representing Religion in Medieval Film." In C.L. Robinson & P. Clements (Eds.), *Neomedievalism in the Media: Essays on Film, Television, and Electronic Games* (pp. 55–81). New York: Edwin Mellen.

Roxborough, S. (2017, April 5). "MIPTV: 'Knightfall' Producer Jeremy Renner on Making History's Knights Templar Epic." *The Hollywood Reporter*. Retrieved from https://www.hollywoodreporter.com/news/miptv-knightfall-producer-jeremy-renner-making-historys-knights-templar-epic-991305.

Ryan, M. (2017 December, 7). "TV Review: 'Knightfall' on History." *Variety*. Retrieved from https://variety.com/2017/tv/reviews/knightfall-history-review-tom-cullen-jeremy-renner-1202632661/.

Sandra Arévalo (2016). "Is the grail really there? #TheDaVinciCode" [Facebook] Retrieved from https://www.facebook.com/photo.php?fbid=1358444997501605&set=a.106308252715292&type=3&theater.

Sandro Del Rosario. (2012). "Re 'The First Templar'—E3 2010 Trailer" [Video file]. Retrieved from https://www.youtube.com/watch?v=6ciS2uwyla0.

Sandvoss, C. (2005). *Fans: The Mirror of Consumption*. Cambridge: Polity.

Sandvoss, C. (2014). "I ♥ IBIZA: Music, Place and Belonging." In M. Duffet (Ed.) *Popular Music Fandom: Identities, Roles and Practices* (pp.115–145). New York: Routledge.

Sandwell, I. (2018 August, 21). "'Knightfall' season 2: Release date, cast, spoilers and everything you need to know." *Digital Spy*. Retrieved from https://www.digitalspy.com/tv/ustv/a864399/knightfall-season-2-release-date-trailer-cast-spoilers/.

Sanello, F. (2005). *The Knights Templars: God's Warriors, the Devil's Bankers*. Lanham, MD: Taylor Trade.

Schall, C.E. (2014). "Multicultural Iteration: Swedish National Day as multiculturalism-in-practise." *Nations & Nationalism*, 20:2, 355–375.

Scheuring, P. (Creator). (2005–2017). *Prison Break* [Television series]. United States: Adelstein-Parouse Productions, Dawn Olmstead Productions, Adelstein Productions, Original Television, 20th Century Fox Television, Original Film, One Light Road Productions, 20th Century Fox Television, Prison Break Productions.

Schlimm, M.R. (2010). "The Necessity of Permanent Criticism: A Postcolonial Critique of Ridley Scott's 'Kingdom of Heaven.'" *Journal of Media and Religion*, 9:3, 129–149.

Score, A. (2005, February 25). "'Kingdom of Heaven' First Impressions." *Gamespot*. Retrieved from https://www.gamespot.com/articles/kingdom-of-heaven-first-impressions/1100-6119174/.

Scott, R. (2005, April 29). "When Worlds Collide." *The Guardian*. Retrieved from http://www.theguardian.com/film/2005/apr/29/1.

Scott, R. (Dir.). (2005). *Kingdom of Heaven* [Motion picture]. United States: Twentieth Century Fox Film Corporation, Scott Free Productions, BK, KOH, Reino del Cielo, Babelsberg Film, Inside Track 3, Calle Cruzada, Dune Films. International, The Ladd Company, B.H. Finance C.V., Icon Productions.

Scott, R. (Dir.). (2007). *Kingdom of Heaven: Definitive Edition* [Motion picture]. United States: Twentieth Century Fox Film Corporation, Scott Free Productions, BK, KOH, Reino del Cielo, Babelsberg Film, Inside Track 3, Calle Cruzada, Dune Films. International, The Ladd Company, B.H. Finance C.V., Icon Productions.

Scott, R. (Dir.). (2010). *Robin Hood* [Motion picture]. United States: Universal Pictures, Imagine Entertainment, Relativity Media, Scott Free Productions.

Scott, W. (1820). *Ivanhoe*. Edinburgh: A. Constable.

"'The Secret World.'" (n.d.). Retrieved from http://www.metacritic.com/game/pc/the-secret-world.

Seibert, D.J. (2014, April 21). "'Assassin's Creed' Franchise Sales Exceed $73 Million." *IGN*. Retrieved from http://uk.ign.com/articles/2014/04/21/assassins-creed-franchise-sales-exceed-73-million.

Shyamalan, M.N. (Dir.). (2004). *The Village* [Motion picture]. United States: Touchstone Pictures, Blinding Edge Pictures, Scott Rudin Productions.

Sila, D. (2010). "A Knight Templar being ordained?" [Flickr]. Retrieved from https://www.flickr.com/photos/silva_d/5360662935/in/album-72157614120927390/.

Sinclair, Scott. (2018). "Re #12daysofChristmas #Myths and #Legends" [Facebook] Retrieved from https://www.facebook.com/pg/RosslynChapelTrust/posts/?ref=page_internal.

Sora, S. (1999). *The Lost Treasure of the Knights Templar: Solving the Oak Island Mystery*. Vermont: Destiny Books.

Spellbound Entertainment. (2002). *Robin Hood: Legend of Sherwood* [Video game]. Montreal: Strategy First, Mindscape, Freeverse Software, Wanadoo, Meridian4.

Spielberg, S. (Dir.). (1981). *Indiana Jones and The Raiders of the Lost Ark* [Motion picture]. United States: Paramount Pictures, Lucasfilm.

Spielberg, S. (Dir.). (1989). *Indiana Jones and The Last Crusade* [Motion picture]. United States: Paramount Pictures, Lucasfilm.

Srebnick, W. (1999). "Re-presenting History: *Ivanhoe* on the Screen." *Film & History: An Interdisciplinary Journal of Film and Television Studies*, 29:1–2, 46–54.

Stallone, S. (Dir.). (1982). *Rocky III* [Motion picture]. United States: United Artists.

Stuart, K. (2007, May 9). "Interviews with Assassins." *The Guardian*. Retrieved from https://www.theguardian.com/technology/gamesblog/2007/may/09/interviewswith.

Stubbs, J. (2009). "Hollywood's Middle Ages: The Development of the Knights of the Round Table and 'Ivanhoe,' 1935–53." *Exemplaria*, 21:4, 398–417.

Sullivan, J.M. (2015). "A Son, His Father, Some Nazis and the Grail: Lucas and Spielberg's *Indiana Jones and the Last Crusade*." In K.J. Harty (Ed), *The Holy Grail on Film: Essays on the Cinematic Quest*. (pp. 158–172). Jefferson, NC: McFarland.

Tamahori, L. (Dir.). (2002). *Die Another Day* [Motion picture]. United Kingdom: Eon Productions, Danjaq, Metro-Goldwyn-Mayer (MGM), United Artists.

Teresatesssa. (2009, 26 February). "YouTube Eva Green—Sibylla—Blue eyes" [Video clip]. Retrieved from https://www.youtube.com/watch?v=I10fg-RYCHI, accessed 10 March 2016.

Tesich-Savage, N. (1978). "Rehearsing the Middle Ages." *Film Comment*, 14:5, 50–56.

"Text of President Bush's 2004 State of the Union Address." (2004, January 20). *The Washington Post*. Retrieved from https://www.washingtonpost.com/wp-srv/politics/transcripts/bushtext_012004.html??noredirect=on.

"This Day makes me wanna launch the 10th Crusade" [Digital image]. (n.d) Retrieved from https://memegenerator.net/instance/67497298/crusader-this-day-makes-me-wanna-launch-the-10th-crusade-deus-vult.

Thorpe, R. (Dir.). (1952). *Ivanhoe* [Motion picture]. United States: MGM.

TubeSakis. (2011). "Re The First Templar Trailer" [Video file]. Retrieved from https://www.youtube.com/watch?v=l1H82lij__c.

Tunzelmann, A.V. (2012, April 12). "'Ironclad's historical credentials are made of mulch." *The Guardian*. Retrieved from http://www.theguardian.com/film/2012/apr/12/ironclad-credentials-mulch.

Turner, V. (1974). "Liminal to Liminoid, in Play, Flow, and Ritual: An Essay in Comparative Symbology." *Rice Institute Pamphlet—Rice University Studies*, 60:3, 53–92.

Turteltaub, J. (Dir.). (2004). *National Treasure* [Motion picture]. United States: Walt Disney Pictures, Jerry Bruckheimer Films, Junction Entertainment, Saturn Films.

Ubisoft Montreal. (2007). *Assassin's Creed* [Video game]. Montreuil: Ubisoft.

Umland, R.A. & Umland, S.J. (1996). *The Use of Arthurian Legend in Hollywood Film: From Connecticut Yankees to Fisher Kings*. Westport: Greenwood.

Urry, J. & Larson, J. (2011). *The Tourist Gaze 3.0*. London: Sage.

Usama. (1969). "The Templars at Jerusalem." In F. Gabrieli (Ed.), *Arab Historians of the Crusades* (pp. 79–80). London: Routledge.

Utz, R. (2012). "Preface: A Moveable Feast: Repositionings of 'The Medieval' in Medieval Studies, Medievalism, and Neomedievalism." In C.L. Robinson & P. Clements (Eds.), *Neomedievalism in the Media: Essays on Film, Television, and Electronic Games* (pp. i-v). New York: Edwin Mellen.

Vogler, C. (2007). *The Writer's Journey: Mythic Structure for Writers*. Studio City: Michael Wiese Productions.

Wagner, R. (2015). "Just doing my best National Treasure Ben Gates climbing over a restricted rope blocking off a staircase at Independence Hall impression. 'Excuse me! Will we be going up to the roof today to see where Nicolas Cage discovered Ben Franklin's ocular device behind the brick?'" [Facebook]. Retrieved from https://www.facebook.com/photo. php?fbid=10103008499874090&set=pb.15937018.-2207520000.1539263297.&type=3&theater.

Wasser, F. (2010). *Steven Spielberg's America*. Cambridge, UK: Polity.

Wasserman, J. (2001). *The Templars and the Assassins: The Militia of Heaven*. Rochester: Inner Traditions International.

Waxman, S. (2004, August 12). "Film on Crusades Could Become Hollywood's Next Battleground." *The New York Times*. Retrieved from http://www.nytimes.com/2004/08/12/movies/film-on-crusades-could-become-hollywood-s-next-battleground.html?_r=0.

Williams, R. (2018). "Fan Tourism and Pilgrimage." In M.A. Click & S. Scott (Eds.) *The Routledge Companion to Media Fandom* (pp.98–106). New York: Routledge.

Williams, R. (2018). "Replacing Maelstrom: Theme Park Fandom, Place, and the Disney Brand." In R. Williams (ed.) *Everybody Hurts: Transitions, Endings, and Resurrections in Fan Cultures* (pp. 167–180). Iowa City: University of Iowa Press.

Windolf, J. (2008, February) "George Lucas." *Vanity Fair*. Retrieved from https://www.vanityfair.com/news/2008/02/lucas_qanda200802.

"The Wizarding World of Harry Potter." (n.d.). Retrieved from the Universal Orlando website: https://www.universalorlando.co.uk/Theme_Parks/Wizarding-World-Of-Harry-Potter.aspx.

Woods, W.F. (2004). "Authenticating Realism in Medieval Film." In M.W. Driver & S. Ray (Eds.), *The Medieval Hero on Screen: Representations from Beowulf to Buffy* (pp. 38–51). Jefferson, NC: McFarland.

Zeffirelli, F. (Dir.). (1972). *Brother Sun, Sister Moon* [Motion picture]. Italy: Euro International Film, Vic Films Productions.

Zeitgeist Game Review, "'The First Templar' Trailer." (31 August 2010). Retrieved from https://www.youtube.com/watch?v=l1H82lij__c, accessed 10 March 2016.

Zucker, J. (Dir.). (1995). *First Knight* [Motion picture]. United States: Columbia Pictures Corporation, First Knight Productions.

Index